This could be you . . .

A year ago, she was working in a dull, bureaucratic, paper-pushing job where she earned less than $15,000 a year. Today she's making twice that much and the sky is the limit!

Gonnie McClung Siegel's eye-opening guide tells you how to find your niche in the world of sales—where entry-level positions often pay as much as $25,000 a year, working schedules are flexible, and performance is measured not by sexual bias but by *results*.

SALES - THE FAST TRACK FOR WOMEN

Gonnie McClung Siegel

A JOVE BOOK

SALES—THE FAST TRACK FOR WOMEN

A Jove Book / published by arrangement with
Macmillan Publishing Co., Inc.

PRINTING HISTORY
Macmillan Publishing Company edition published 1982
Jove edition/October 1983

ISBN: 0-515-07358-X

Jove books are published by The Berkley Publishing Group,
200 Madison Avenue, New York, N.Y. 10016.
The words "A JOVE BOOK" and the "J" with sunburst
are trademarks belonging to Jove Publications, Inc.

PRINTED IN THE UNITED STATES OF AMERICA

To my husband, Bob, our son, Richard,
and
my new IBM Displaywriter
(for which I paid full list price)
They really made a difference in my productivity

Contents

Acknowledgments

SPECIAL THANKS to Richard J. Siegel, for extensive research, interview, and editorial assistance in preparing the manuscript for this book.

Thanks to my mother, Mrs. Margaret McGee McClung, for extending her visit during manuscript revisions, and to the following for their assistance: Paula Bernstein; Joy Seligsohn; Theo Steele; Lydia Prokop-Artymahyn; Larry Siegel; Dr. Jessie Shih; Barbara Graves; Warren Jackson; Leo and Laura Kornfeld; Mary Tobin; Eileen Jacobs; Vickie Mechner; Sheila Dixon; Dr. Alice Baruch; James R. Lamb, manager, public relations, of the Xerox Corporation; Nancy H. Green, assistant vice-president of The Equitable Life Assurance Society; IBM Communications; and all those mentioned in the book plus others who wished to remain anonymous.

In addition, a special thanks to my editor, Marion Wheeler, whose knowledge of the subject, suggestions, and editing skill greatly improved this book.

Introduction

A CENTURY AGO, during the great gold rush, ambitious young men were told to go west and seek their fortunes. It was the kind of call that appealed to the adventurous. The territory was big and unfamiliar. The risks were inherent and apparent. You could make it big or lose your shirt. Those brave enough to heed the call bet on themselves to win. As always when the stakes are high, there were winners and losers.

Today a new kind of gold rush is going on, only this time the call is for women. Like the earlier one, this one appeals to a special breed of people—women confident enough to move into unfamiliar territory and bet on themselves. This call is being heeded by women who accept risk-taking as a necessary part of life and are unafraid of being the "first." These women are moving into professional/industrial sales at a rapid rate.

Today, thousands of women who ten years ago might have been secretaries, lab assistants, clerical workers, teachers, librarians, nurses, researchers, dietitians, social workers, and other traditional female employees are becoming professional/industrial saleswomen. Some are earning more than they ever dreamed possible. Others are earning a comfortable living, which is more than they were doing in the pink-ghetto jobs they left behind to go into sales.

Professional/Industrial Sales

Professional/industrial salespeople sell the products and services of the country's most successful industries and corporations. These are the jobs that have always been the fast track for men, up the corporate ladder into senior management. Traditionally, outstanding salesmen move fast and far. The professional/industrial sales alumni roster reads like a *Who's Who in American Business*. An outstanding salesman has a better chance, statistically, of running the company than any employee in any other part of the business.

Professional/industrial sales, the fast track for men, has been the closed track to women—until recently. The idea of women selling steel or commodities or computers was out of the question. Selling was a man's job. There was no room for discussion and no equal-opportunity laws to challenge the assumptions. This cut women off from the number-one career path into management.

All this is changing. Thousands of professional/industrial sales jobs across the country are rapidly opening up to women. The superior performance of the first saleswomen, hired reluctantly to fulfill federal affirmative-action requirements, has convinced pragmatic sales managers that women can sell—sometimes better than men. Many a hard-nosed manager, who fought tooth and nail to keep women out of sales, is searching for more to hire. Unlike other professions where the measurement of women's success is filled with subjective value judgments, measurement in sales is simple and direct. This benefits women enormously, as many fighting discriminatory fogs in other fields can testify. In sales either you sell or you don't, and it doesn't take a committee to bring in the verdict.

Sales Pays Better

There is more good news in the pay department. These new professional/industrial sales jobs opening up to women generally pay anywhere from $25,000 to $75,000 a year. Some pay $100,000 and up, more than most women will ever earn, regardless of their credentials or abilities. According to Barbara A. Pletcher, author of *Saleswoman: A Guide to Career Success* and founder of the National Association for Professional Saleswomen, of all people who earn over $50,000 a year in this country, 65 percent are in sales. Even though millions of women have moved into the labor force in the past fifteen years, most are still clustered at the bottom of the work heap in female-typed jobs where advancement is nonexistent and pay raises seldom keep up with inflation. For example, median wage figures compiled by the Department of Commerce's March 1981 current population survey reveal the following shockingly low wages for female-type jobs:

• The median wage for clerical workers is $10,997 a year.
• The secretary-stenographer earns a median salary of $11,268 a year.
• The median salary of all teachers is $15,151 a year; $17,316 for college and university teachers.
• The median salary of health workers is $15,295, excluding doctors and dentists.

In addition, hundreds of thousands of women across the country—many in responsible jobs—earn $3.35 an hour, the minimum wage.

xiv

- On an average, a male eighth-grade dropout earns more than a female high school graduate.
- Women, on an average, earn fifty-nine cents for every dollar earned by men.

A Bright Spot

Professional/industrial sales offers a bright spot in such dismal statistics. There are saleswomen today—with and without college degrees—who earn more than male or female Ph.D.s teaching in the country's prestigious schools or working in research labs searching for a cancer cure. There are saleswomen who earn more than medical doctors, the highest per-capita earners in the country. And there are a few saleswomen who earn more money than the president of the United States.

While this may seem unfair, the same always has been true for men. The amount of money earned in a free-enterprise society depends upon supply and demand, not on humanitarian values. Rock stars frequently earn more than the president. Frank Sinatra's doo-be-doo-be-doo commands more money than the most delicate brain surgery.

Money is not the only benefit in professional/industrial sales. Many sales jobs offer flexible work schedules, a chance to be your own boss, and an end to punching a time clock. As long as you sell, you can do it at midday or midnight—it's results that count. Flexible schedules can be a lifesaver for single parents or working married women who assume most of the burdens of bringing up children. In addition to full-time careers, there are an increasing number of part-time sales jobs women can develop into full-time jobs later. Selling careers, while often demanding, may fit your life-style better than any other job. If you demonstrate the ability to sell, many sales managers will negotiate job requirements often written in stone for traditional jobs.

The Best Opportunity Today

Sales today offers the best opportunity for a woman to have an interesting and challenging career, become financially independent, and develop job skills that can be transferred to other job areas. A first-rate salesperson is always in demand; this is underscored by the fact that the business of special head hunters is to recruit top salespeople into the sales ranks of their competitors.

"I love selling," said a woman who actually went west to seek her fortune in professional/industrial sales. "Although it's frightening at first, it's exciting to realize there are no limits except what you impose on yourself," she said. "What other job offers the possibility of traveling all over the country, meeting interesting people, and doubling your salary—all in one year?"

A year ago this woman was working in a dull, bureaucratic, mid-level paper-pushing government job where she earned less than $15,000 a year. Today she's making twice that much and the sky is the limit. She expects to double her current earnings in another year. What she likes best, however, is how she feels about herself. She's on a natural high that comes from betting on herself and winning. She's survived in a competitive job where thinking on your feet becomes an acquired trait. She's learned that selling requires patience, persistence, intelligence, integrity, assertiveness, determination, and more—traits women have or can learn. And she realizes that the only currency that will buy confidence is courage. She wouldn't take back her old job for ten times the salary—not even for her name on the door and a solid gold paperweight.

Fifty CEOs by the Year 2000

So, no matter if you're in another career, in school preparing for a job, or at home thinking about getting into the labor market, think about a career in professional/industrial sales. A career in sales might fit you as perfectly as it has the women in this book. One thing is sure: There never was a better time to start looking for a job in sales.

Futurist Herman Kahn predicts that women, if they continue in the direction they're going, might be heading up fifty of the five hundred largest industrial companies in this country by the year 2000. If this prediction comes true, thousands more women will be in senior management by that time. Many of these future chief executives and senior officers—if the past continues to be an accurate guide—will begin their careers in professional/industrial sales. Why shouldn't you be one of them?

If you can't come up with a good answer in a week, start looking for a job in sales—your first stopover on the way to the chief executive's suite.

For convenience, "working" woman is used throughout this book to describe employed women who are working in order to earn money. This is not intended to imply that women at home do not work.

1

Winning

THE TIME IS MARCH 1980. The place is Miami Beach. It is the annual sales-achievement recognition meeting for the Data Processing Division of the computer giant IBM. Four top awards are being handed out.

Before each winner's name is announced, total sales figures are recited. The intensely competitive audience of IBM salespeople groan with each announcement. The figures, all in millions of dollars, are indeed impressive.

Before the awards ceremony, a brilliantly produced three-screen movie delves into one of the human traits IBM values most in its people—competitiveness. The movie focuses on competitiveness—cowboys rodeo-roping, lumberjacks competing in wood-chopping contests, giant farm tractors in pulling duels, a country music fiddler doing his stompin' best.

The movie leaves no doubt that to win—to be the best —is good. That it is the competitiveness of the human spirit that drives civilization forward into the unknown, where the meek never venture. It is clear that the competitiveness of its people has made IBM powerful, successful, and rich. The figures show how IBM, this year as in previous years, has triumphed in the marketplace.

The company's squeaky-clean image also comes through. IBM has beaten all competitors fairly and squarely. No hush money, no booze, no broads. IBM has done it the old-fashioned way: hard-driving, thorough work that cleanses the soul while trouncing the opposition. It's called the great American work ethic, the intangible ingredient that built the free-enterprise system in the first place.

As each of the first three winners is announced, men in dark pinstripe suits, brilliantly shined black shoes, and white shirts literally run from their seats in the audience to accept the recognition of their peers and management. As in the Miss America pageant, the tension builds as the moment approaches to announce number one—the best of the best.

However, unlike the Miss America show, this is no beauty contest. This is deadly serious business. The figures announced here represent hundreds of millions of dollars in revenue for the company. These are sales jobs in which several million dollars are on the line for just one sale. Selling computers is enormously complex. Winners in these contests often get rich, and the ones who consistently produce the highest sales figures may get a shot at being chief executive officer of the company twenty or thirty years down their career paths.

Finally, the big moment arrives. Salespeople throughout the audience speculate on who the winner might be. Nobody knows. They just know that Mr. IBM of 1980 is about to be unveiled.

The crowd gasps in unison as the winner's name is called out. This time not only because of the winner's impressive sales figures but also because of the petite, slim figure that emerges onto the stage—a young woman in a navy blue business suit, a light-colored blouse, and sensible shoes requiring no polish.

The division's number-one salesperson for the year is

a woman who joined the company barely five years before. She has beaten the best at a game she once wouldn't have been allowed to enter.

Adding to the drama unfolding on the stage is the fact that this woman's territory is located in the very same city where IBM's CEO and chairman of the board—the man who presents her award—began his career thirty-two years before. His career began shortly before she was born, and he would retire as CEO later that same year.

They shake hands. She greets him as Frank. He calls her Pat.

This scene could only have happened in the movies a few years ago—and a B movie at that. The plot is too perfect, too trite for anything else.

Who would believe this could happen? But it did happen. Exactly this way.

Pat Paolilli

As "input," "output," "multiprocessing," and "database" became household words, a thirty-two-year-old ex-schoolteacher with no selling experience joined IBM as a sales trainee in Los Angeles.

"Almost literally a walk-in off the streets," says Pat Paolilli.

Not only was she a woman entering a traditional male job, but at thirty-two she was also the oldest person in her group.

Like all the others in the group, Paolilli was given no assurances of anything beyond an equal chance to learn about and later compete in selling one of the most complex products ever designed and manufactured.

IBM's Data Processing Division is the part of the company that sells its most sophisticated computers—mind-boggling machines without which no man would have walked on the moon or soared into orbit aboard the space shuttle. These machines can instantly store, retrieve, compute, and analyze data, can practically program themselves and talk to each other. The product's complexity and potential application seems almost beyond human comprehension. It is a high-technology field, changing so fast that taking a long lunch break might be construed as a career risk.

For IBM salespeople, keeping up to snuff in their field means almost standing at attention. IBM's first and second generation of computers are as out of date today as the tragic stock ending of a 1940s movie starring an unrepentant career woman. Selling this product is a far cry from the sales jobs assigned women in the past. As Pat Paolilli began her training, it was enough to frighten anybody intelligent enough to understand the situation.

During the training period, she would be required to absorb mountains of technical information about computers and become an expert in the businesses of prospective clients. And as if this weren't enough, she had to combine this with learning how to sell.

"It all seemed very difficult at first," Paolilli said. "A little later, when I got more into the training program, it became less difficult. By this time I realized that everything depended on me. I could either fail or succeed, but the opportunity was there."

The Job Beyond

Paolilli was aware that when she finished her training she would step into a job in which she would be competing with what is generally considered to be the world's best sales force—IBM's crack troops of the marketplace, where no room is reserved for second-raters. A beginning IBM salesperson is faced with two seemingly harsh but inevitable choices: succeed or find another occupation outside the company. While there are exceptions to this rule, there aren't many. The team pulling IBM's $26 billion-a-year empire cannot afford to carry any dead weight.

Growing Up in Arizona

Growing up in her native Arizona, Paolilli never remotely considered a career in sales. However, she remembers vividly that during her childhood both her parents told her she could do anything in the world as long as she chose it, that the only limits on her would be self-imposed.

Regardless of this nontraditional parental advice. Paolilli chose as a first career one of the most traditional for women—teaching. The subjects she taught, however —biology and the physical sciences—were less traditional.

After several years of teaching, Paolilli left to become a research assistant in a biochemistry lab at the University of Southern California medical school. It was here that she began a process women seldom went through until the 1960s. She began to evaluate her future in terms of her own career goals instead of assuming that marriage and motherhood would replace the choice.

Realizing that biochemistry offered little upward mobility without a Ph.D. and unwilling to return to school for a third degree (she had a master's degree in English), Paolilli began another job search. She wanted something that offered more contact with people than the lab and less than being a high school teacher. She knew nothing about IBM except high recommendations from a couple of friends who worked for the company.

So, with little knowledge, but confident of her ability to learn, she walked into the IBM personnel office in Los Angeles and applied for a most untraditional job for a young woman. The rest became history in Miami Beach on a stage five years later.

Sales—Fast Track to the Top

Is it possible for Paolilli to become IBM's first female chief executive officer a quarter of a century from now? Or if not Paolilli, will some other bright, ambitious saleswoman be the one to go all the way to the top? Will it really happen for women?

Paolilli is quick—revealingly quick—to point out that she has no delusions of grandeur about such an unlikely event. Her expectations are much more modest. Yes, she would like her career to lead to management. She would enjoy helping guide the careers of others. The teacher in her is coming out. But all the way to the top? What a question!

No wonder Paolilli brushed aside the question. It's a new question for her sex, one that seems natural to ask a young man but presumptuous somehow to ask a young woman. There are generations of built-in barriers insulating Paolilli from this question. They begin at birth. They build throughout youth. They become intense during childbearing years. Both cultural and legal barriers have been necessary to keep assumptions about women and work in place. It has not been a matter of choice. It has been a sex assignment.

However, when pressed for an answer as to whether she would like to become IBM's chief executive officer, improbable as that might be, Paolilli finally replied, "Sure I would. That would be very nice."

It's doubtful if Frank Cary or his successor John Opel would have hesitated a second had they been asked the same question back when their sales careers with IBM were young. However, they didn't have to deal with a lifetime of being considered too ambitious or too aggressive. Men can't be too ambitious. Their path to success is psychologically uncluttered, a wide-open highway with no cultural speed limits imposed.

For a woman, even to hesitantly answer that question in the affirmative is an important first step. And it is a first step for more than one individual. When it finally happens somewhere down the line, to paraphrase a saying from another all-male event, it will be one small step for woman, one giant step for womankind.

CEO—Chief Executive Officer

CEO. Chief executive officer. Thousands dot the corporate landscape. Virtually all are men. Until recently, nobody asked why. Now that the question is being asked, many people are coming up with the wrong answer.

Forgetting the sex problem, how did the men who became chief executive officers get there? What was their fast track? What unique career characteristics worked for them? What wisdom and vision did they possess?

Each year *Fortune* magazine publishes a list of companies that have become known as the "Fortune 500," the five hundred largest industrial companies in the country. To become CEO of any of these companies is no small accomplishment. It is an exclusive club of men who've made it all the way to the top. In these companies, however, most of these chief executive officers made it to the top through the ranks of sales and marketing. Sales and marketing, as a category, produced the most CEOs, followed closely by finance. These men succeeded in their careers in the "money areas" of business—not research or personnel, not advertising or public relations, not science or research or dozens of other support areas.

The money areas are the jugular vein of business. Without profit there is no business. Without selling there is no profit. That the heads of companies succeed more often through sales and marketing than through any other area should surprise nobody. Sell something people need or want, sell it better than your competitors, and you'll grow in direct proportion to your marketing talents. And conversely, occupy the finest offices, gather the best research people, capture the brightest graduates, hire the most Ph.D.s, and your business will die on the vine unless your sales force *sells* the products or services of this combined talent.

Business is selling. While nobody argues against business having all the talent needed to produce competitive products, more often than not the captain of the business ship is the person who sells the business or manages the finances. Far from being unfair, this seems like a logical example of talent rewarded. It recognizes that of all the ingredients that merge in business, the most critical is selling.

A Slow Track for Women

While selling has been a fast track for men it has been the opposite for women. Until the last decade, when federal legislation opened up the marketplace, virtually all women were locked out of top selling jobs for a variety of ridiculous reasons: too little aggressiveness, too much aggressiveness; too much sexuality, too little sexuality; too many home responsibilities (married), too few home responsibilities (unmarried); too fat, too thin, too young, too old, and on into fantasy land.

Regardless of the long list of lame excuses, women were locked out of good selling jobs because they were female. There were few exceptions to this widely practiced rule, no matter how fuzzy the hindsight of many sales executives, and regardless of their attempts to blame women for the exclusion by explaining that women—back then—didn't want good selling jobs. "Back then" was not prehistoric times. Anybody past the age of puberty can remember. Women who were refused jobs remember it vividly.

Since good jobs in sales were virtually unattainable, selling became tarnished in women's minds as the kind of job you took if the bank was foreclosing and the wolf knocking at the door. Otherwise hold out for something better, like being a secretary or typing envelopes.

Of course women, traditionally, always have had access to certain selling jobs. They've sold trinkets in the five and dime, stockings in department stores, and small (noncommissioned) appliances in department stores. They have been the Avon "ladies" and other door-to-door salespeople, the telephone solicitors selling home freezer plans and magazine subscriptions. Naturally, these kinds of jobs would poison anybody's mind against selling.

Mention selling to a Vassar senior and she'll probably inform you in no uncertain terms that she has something better planned for her life. Sell? Certainly not. Women go into teaching, social work, nursing, library science, and communications—all jobs that will pay them one-tenth what they can earn in good sales jobs.

Men, unlike women, separate in their minds good selling job from bad ones. They know that hawking vacuum cleaners door to door is nothing to latch onto, while being an IBM salesman is. The difference is as great as that between the CEO and the janitor, the prince and the pauper. There are men who graduate from top medical schools yet never practice medicine a day in their lives. Instead they sell pharmaceuticals and end up running the companies they work for. There are engineers who never check a blueprint, never supervise a bridge construction. Instead they sell the bridges, the buildings, and the ideas of their profession. There are lawyers who never set foot in court. They sell oil wells, shopping centers, stocks and bonds—and often themselves, as congressmen and senators.

These ambitious men view sales as the most direct way of earning a lot of money fast and the very best way of getting a shot at running a company.

Merging Career Paths

Until recently, the career paths of men and women in sales never crossed. Men simply got all the good selling jobs while women got most of the bad ones. Under these circumstances, the attitudes both sexes developed were based on fact. Bright, ambitious young men, willing to risk their futures on the cutting edge of business, went into high-powered, high-potential sales jobs. A young woman who aspired to become a salesperson would have been neither bright nor ambitious.

Today, after more than a decade of slowly opening sales opportunities for women, the best-kept secret is that the career paths of men and women in sales are beginning to merge. Sales has emerged as the number-one sleeper in the equal-employment-opportunity struggle. Thousands of women have been quietly hired by major corporations and smaller companies into sales jobs. Tens of thousands will follow them. Women are currently being hired to sell everything from pharmaceuticals to farm machinery, from steel to commodities to computers, from airplanes to shopping centers. Virtually every area formerly closed to women is now being opened up.

The myth about women not being able to make it in the tough turf of sales is being cut down as women, like Pat Paolilli, pile up impressive sales records. Women are competing with the best, holding their own, and often winning. They are answering those annoying questions about women's biological, psychological, and sociological handicaps in competitive fields with monthly proof—a set of impressively high sales figures.

The Old and the New

"I wouldn't want to be a grubby insurance salesman," said a woman offered a job by a major insurance company. "I would rather starve than go door to door collecting crumpled dollar bills from widows with coupon books."

This woman remembered insurance as it was when she was a child and insurance salesmen did collect premiums door to door. What she didn't realize was that there are women selling insurance today who earn upward of $50,000 a year in the right company, the right territory.

This woman really needs a better-paying job. She has four children to support, two of them reaching college age within the next three years. She has an ex-husband who, like many ex-husbands, pays little child support.

He pays when he feels like it and stops when he runs short. He ran short last year because he took his new girlfriend on a European trip. He has paid nothing this year even though he has a new girlfriend. He's been in court three times, each time promising the judge faithfully to pay regularly. "If I put him in jail," the judge tells the mother, "he'll lose his job and you'll get nothing." This seesaw of domestic justice is a common problem among divorced mothers forced to be the sole support of their children. More single-parent mothers by far are supporting children than single-parent fathers. It is a simple fact of life.

However, the woman who refused the job selling insurance is working in a profession where she earns considerably less than $25,000 a year—teaching. She has two degrees, a mortgage, a backlog of bills, and little hope of keeping up with inflation. Instead of rejecting this job outright, she should have investigated further. There are still more grubby sales jobs than good ones, many of them in insurance. However, as it has been for many other women, this could have been the beginning of a sensational career for her and the end of her poverty.

Success in Sales

Women are succeeding in sales all over the country. Barriers to hiring women in sales are falling faster than there are women to fill the new jobs being created. The word is spreading that women are succeeding beyond the most optimistic expectations of their new employers, employers who in many cases were forced to hire women but ended up enthusiastic because of the results.

Regardless of the facts, many women are still unable to distinguish the new sales opportunities from the grubby selling jobs they were allowed into in the past. The word "selling" triggers a psychological turn-off in many women despite the new evidence. Many feel that selling is synonymous with dishonesty, that salespeople are forced to parrot a false line about a company's products and do anything for a sale. The years of "traveling salesman" jokes have taken their toll also. A woman hitting the road? Wouldn't any job be better? Definitely not, say thousands of women traveling around this country and beyond in good sales jobs.

Naturally, women considering sales should be on their guard. The job seeker must beware. Nothing will save the gullible from exploitation in sales or any other field. If you can be talked into a dead-end job in sales or anything else you will be doomed to repeat one bad experience after the other. Bad jobs will always be around, and badly advised people will continue to take them.

However, if you are a bright, intelligent woman who isn't afraid of hard work, likes the challenge of competition, is aggressive and proud of it, wants a good job with a bright future, and, most of all, is willing to give up other things in exchange for the chance to earn a lot of money, this book is for you. In fact, the ad for such a job might read:

Wanted:

Woman who is a winner. Quick learner. Will travel. Expects hard work. Is determined. Loves competition. Hates failure. Wants to be CEO of General Motors or reasonable facsimile and has no hang-ups about wanting to earn a lot of money.

A Xerox Saleswoman

As one woman put it, ready to move from the East Coast into America's heartland after accepting a sales job with the Xerox Corporation, "I feel like I have the world by the tail. I'm bursting with energy and I can hardly wait to get at 'em. I'm going to make the last salesman in this territory look sick. No, not sick. I'm going to make him look terminal.''

In her first full year of selling, this woman expects to earn $60,000 or more. So far, she's broken all sales records in her territory. She loves her job and is even more motivated by another woman she met on the road who works for another company. That woman is earning $100,000 a year.

Her attitude may not ensure that this woman will become the chief executive officer of Xerox somewhere down the road. Like Paolilli, she has no such expectations.

However, this kind of attitude is the magic ingredient that will someday make some woman CEO of Xerox. And also CEO of AT&T, IBM, Exxon, General Electric, General Motors, U.S. Steel, Celanese, B. F. Goodrich, Ciba-Geigy, Litton Industries, General Foods, PepsiCo, The Bank of America, and on into the telephone listing of America's biggest and smallest companies.

Call it aggressiveness, assertiveness, the will to win, the fear of losing, the American work ethic, the killer instinct, the football syndrome, the pyramid system, or whatever you like. The simple fact of life is that non-competitive people do not make it to the top of the business heap. Competitive people do.

Women or men who are uncomfortable with competition should stay out of this race. And the choice to stay out of the race should belong to everybody. However, the choice to get in should also be everybody's right. To call business "free enterprise" and bar half the human race from entering makes it—at the very least—glaringly misnamed. Male genes do not a competitive spirit make. Female genes are no guarantee against one.

So where does this leave ambitious, success-oriented women? The kind who wake up early and go to bed late in between accomplishing about four times as much as the average person. The kind who will look you in the eye and say, "Sure, I want to go all the way to the top. I'd like to be chief executive officer. Why not?"

It leaves women like this in the best position in history—on a fast track with a half-empty train. What could possibly be better? Therefore, women: If you're ready to try for the business brass ring and you can stand the heat, get out of the kitchen and into a terrific sales job. Opportunities are all around you.

2

Women in the World's Best Sales Force

AND WHAT IT TAKES TO GET THERE

OVER THE PAST FIFTEEN YEARS almost 20 percent of IBM's sales force has quietly become female. In 1980, 40 percent of IBM's sales recruits were women. There is no slowdown predicted for this hiring trend. IBM's saleswomen, with no special assistance, successfully compete in what is generally conceded to be the world's toughest sales arena. The theory is that if a salesperson manages to survive in IBM, he or she should be a star performer in most other companies.

So what does it take to become an IBM saleswoman? What special characteristics and background do you need? Is a degree in business administration required? Will you have a better chance if you have an M.B.A.? If you have studied music but now want to get into sales, are you out of luck? If IBM has such high standards, are half the new recruits washed out? Once hired, what kind of training will you get? Where will you be assigned

15

after training, and will you be able to choose the location?

Francis "Buck" Rodgers, vice-president of marketing with worldwide responsibilities for the IBM corporation, in a special interview for this book answers all these questions and more. Rodgers knows firsthand what it means to be a young sales recruit and move up through management ranks. He personally traveled the route he talks about—from a beginning IBM salesman to become the top marketing executive in the company.

In talking with Rodgers, it is easy to understand how he was a star performer in sales and why he captivates IBM salespeople when he speaks at company functions across the country. Personable, articulate, down-to-earth, humorous, trim, and handsome, Rodgers is the exact opposite of the stereotypical salesman. Like all great salespeople, he creates a special atmosphere around him. He sells himself without seeming to try.

The advice of a successful salesman who has fine-tuned his art over a lifetime of practicing what he preaches in a company with IBM's reputation is well worth heeding. IBM's success speaks for itself. Competitors may poke fun at IBM's white-shirt, button-down image, but they never minimize the marketing skills of the country's best-managed company.

My Daughter, the Saleswoman

With two daughters in IBM sales, nobody could be more enthusiastic about the company's transformation than Buck Rodgers. And the marketing vice-president's enthusiasm is conclusive proof that IBM's profit margin hasn't suffered from the integration of women into its traditionally all-male sales force.

"I wouldn't trade an IBM saleswoman for any man," said Rodgers. "IBM saleswomen have proved that they can hold their own with anybody. They are intelligent, hardworking, and if anything, more motivated than the men. Hiring women in sales has been good business, and you can be sure if it's good business IBM will continue doing it regardless of affirmative-action requirements. The door couldn't possibly be wider open to women who can meet IBM's requirements.''

The IBM Fast Track

IBM employs 341,279 people worldwide in many important career categories. Yet if IBM's future mirrors its past, tomorrow's chief executive officers will emerge from the marketing ranks, a group comprising only a fraction of the company's total population. Every CEO since IBM's founder Thomas J. Watson has followed this narrow path.

In June 1981, a *Business Week* cover story about IBM explained the philosophy behind IBM's policy of promoting sales and marketing people to high-level management positions: "Two decades ago, as the computer market began to explode, IBM elevated a band of marketing men to senior management. One of the company's methods of operation was to transform talented salesmen into managers of finance, product development, production planning and other specialties, rather than hiring outside specialists when the company needed such high-level executives as it grew."

According to the magazine, current CEO John Opel explains the company's promotion pattern. "You have to remember who pays the bills," Opel is quoted as saying. "No matter what the primary discipline—finance, manufacturing or whatever—you have to know and experience the excitement of sales. That's where you really see things happen."

The *Business Week* writer concludes that although some things are changing at IBM—like the marketing strategy that will take it from a $26.2-billion corporation to $60 billion in the next five years—the people who run the company will continue to come from marketing, the IBM fast track.

The Ideal IBM Sales Trainee

If Buck Rodgers could rub a magic lamp and have his ideal IBM sales-trainee recruit appear, he or she would have a technical degree, understand international commerce, be a whiz at finance, and be able to sell snowflakes to the Eskimos.

A lot of competitors over the years must have suspected that IBM possessed a magic recruiting lamp. The corporation is widely perceived as having put together the world's best sales force. Even those who might argue the facts acknowledge the perception. Many suggest that IBM was Japan's model for much of its postwar industrialization. "Right down to the pinstripe suits and white shirts," said one IBM executive.

So if women are doing well in the world's best sales force, are the requirements the same? Do they perform in exactly the same arena as men, or does IBM provide a safety net of special assistance for its saleswomen?

This question is one that sets every working woman's teeth on edge. It assumes that companies recruit, hire, and promote less competent females in order to fulfill federally mandated affirmative-action requirements. The message inherent in the question is clear: Women who demand equal rights cannot succeed without special concessions. This accusation sticks like flypaper, lessens the market value of all women, and demeans their individual and collective success. It sets up a no-win situation where women fail on their own but succeed only through the efforts of others.

No Safety Net

IBM's saleswomen, competing successfully and chalking up impressive sales records, may be able to put this unfair and demeaning suggestion to sleep forever. The company hires women on exactly the same standards as men and provides no special help whatsoever. IBM's saleswomen can fly as high or fall as fast as salesmen.

There is no safety net. IBM establishes identical objectives and evaluation procedures for its salesmen and saleswomen. Therefore, it is logical that women who succeed in the world's best sales force need no further proof of their ability to compete elsewhere. Their success should go a long way in convincing other companies, still fearful of hiring women in sales, that gender hiring is not justified by business objectives.

When asked if IBM saleswomen have an equal opportunity to fail, Rodgers laughed; however, not as loudly as several IBM saleswomen who were asked the same question.

"Yes, saleswomen have an equal opportunity to fail in IBM," he said. "We do to them exactly what we do to salesmen who fail. After they are given an opportunity to improve, we get rid of them."

This harsh yet evenhanded judgment goes with every IBM territory. The opportunity to succeed is coupled with the factor that makes it equal—the possibility of failure.

Therefore, using such an equal yardstick, are women failing in greater numbers than men in selling the wares of the world's biggest computer company?

"No," said Rodgers. "Women are succeeding and failing at almost the same rate as men in IBM."

How Women Got into the World's Best Sales Force

IBM has a well-deserved reputation of being number one in more than sales. Equal employment in the company began early. In 1968 the company established a corporate equal-opportunity department. IBM's EEO policy is a serious business objective on which each manager is evaluated. Each IBM division has an EEO manager and most have full-time staffs. Even without an EEO policy, IBM had one woman vice-president in 1943, and women were hired as system service personnel as early as 1935 to advise customers how to use equipment such as key punches, sorters, collators, and accounting machines.

Mary Tobin, a regional administrator of the Department of Labor's Women's Bureau—a bureau set up half a century ago to help working women—gives IBM high praise for being among the first companies, possibly the very first, to give women equal career opportunities. "Back when many other companies were awaiting the outcome of an employment discrimination class action suit filed against a major employer, IBM was establishing its EEO structure," she said. "Other companies across the country were delaying compliance with the new antidiscrimination law in hopes that the giant, by winning the case, would make compliance unnecessary." (The employer Tobin refers to is AT&T.)

Therefore, it is important that the following events about how women—in meaningful numbers—got into sales and other careers in IBM, should be viewed in the context of women's progress in the best—not the worst —of companies.

A Woman Who Made a Difference

A few years after passage of the 1964 civil rights legislation forbidding race and sex discrimination, the National Organization for Women called a nationwide women's strike. Each woman in the labor force was asked to stay away from her job and attend marches and other planned events to demonstrate the pervasive and overt discrimination against women in every facet of life in this country.

An IBM feminist had a better idea for her company. Instead of taking the day off from her job, Sally Dennis wrote to the president of the company, documenting the employment discrimination against women in IBM.

She summed up her experience of fifteen years by stating that "most of IBM's female employees were hired into traditional female-type jobs and kept there. They were at the bottom of the IBM pay pyramid, clustered into service areas, and given little opportunity for advancement into better paying jobs.

"Why," her letter asked the president, "were women ignored in a company which prided itself on the utilization of individual talent? Why did IBM management presume that women weren't interested in careers? Why did IBM systematically plan career paths for men but not for women?"

Dennis was amazed at the response her letter brought —a personal phone call from the president inviting her to his office to discuss her "interesting ideas," as he called them.

When Dennis arrived at his office a few days later, the president greeted her with, "You're right. What can we do about it?" Spread over his desk were personnel records.

Another meeting was set, including not only the president but other top executives, as well as a few additional women in the corporation.

A Strange Presentation

For the first few moments the executives must have thought this the strangest presentation ever dreamed up. Dennis began by telling a few off-color stories in which women were the butt of the joke. The point became clear when she said she wanted them to understand how it feels to live inside another person's skin. She wanted management to realize that, daily, working women face comments and attitudes from male co-workers and managers that reinforce the one-dimensional sexual concept of women. At a time before "sexual harassment" had been named, Dennis objected to this kind of treatment as totally out of place in a business atmosphere.

Among other issues, she pointed out that "management had lower expectations of its female employees, apparently assumed they would fail in nontraditional jobs, and, in effect, blocked their upward mobility regardless of individual qualifications." As an example, she mentioned an IBM job category in which males and females had done exactly the same work but were paid unequally. Systems Service Girls, as they had been called in the fifties (according to company records, the job title was Systems Service Women) did the same job as male Technical Service Representatives but were paid far less. Secretaries had no hope of advancement.

"The IBM executives seemed stunned by what they were hearing," according to Dennis. "Several were amazed by the seriousness of the women's movement and seemed particularly surprised to learn that referring to their secretaries as 'my girl' was objectionable.

"I suppose it could have been amusing had it not been so serious," she says. "However, these were the people controlling the working lives of all IBM women. As the sole support of my family, with kids in college at the time, I did not see this as a laughing matter. I was delighted with the results, however. IBM really did do something about the inequities and, as usual, did it with IBM's characteristic thoroughness."

Women in sales in IBM got their start in the early 1960s, when the former Systems Service Girls, along with male Technical Service Representatives, became Systems Engineers. By 1970, a time before most companies had hired their first woman in sales, IBM had approximately two hundred women sales representatives. In addition, at that time, the company had five hundred women managers as well as women lawyers, scientists, and programmers.

Nothing in the company's past, however, compares with the decade of the 1970s in opening up opportunities for women. By 1980, there were 2,350 women managers, 10,004 women professionals, 3,388 women technicians, 1,729 saleswomen, 634 in skilled crafts, and 5,609 in semiskilled jobs. Another figure, perhaps more dramatic, proves the IBM EEO success. By 1980, there were 12,085 males in office and clerical work as compared with 19,939 women.

A Day to Remember

"I consider that meeting the outstanding event of my entire career," says Dennis, who proved that one woman can make a difference. Now nearing retirement, Dennis is telling her story to remind not only saleswomen but all women that generations of feminists devoted their lives to opening opportunities for women. Without the women's movement, the federal reforms would never have occurred, and without the federal antidiscrimination laws, it is unlikely that even the best of companies would have initiated such sweeping changes on their own.

"Don't get me wrong," she says, "I believe that IBM is a terrific company and I have been fortunate to have had a rewarding and satisfying career here. IBM is probably the best company in the country today in providing truly equal opportunities for women. However, I'd hate for anybody to believe that all is perfect anywhere. There are still individual managers in IBM who are less than enthusiastic about women in nontraditional roles. Only the death or the retirement of some managers will remove certain kinds of subtle discrimination that affect women's careers. The discrimination is difficult to document," says Dennis, "but to paraphrase a Supreme Court justice about pornography, 'You know it when you see it.'"

Moving Past Barriers

"Women," Dennis says, "must learn to survive and move past these human barriers to their careers. They should learn the company rules on equal opportunity in advancement and use them whenever necessary. Women who wait for some managers to 'guide' their careers may not get far. Instead, women should be more aggressive in taking charge of their own lives. Make a career plan for yourself and ask your manager to help you achieve it. Management rules often lie dormant unless women insist upon enforcement. For equality to last (and there is no constitutional guarantee that it will), and for women to succeed in their careers, thorough preparation and hard work must be combined with eternal vigilance.''

Dennis joined IBM in 1956 as an applied science representative in the IBM Cleveland branch office. She is a graduate, with a degree in chemistry, of Purdue University. She also won a master's degree in physical chemistry from Case Institute of Technology—the first awarded to a woman from that once all-male school. Today a computer science professional in IBM's York-town, New York, laboratory, Dennis says she might have been interested in an IBM sales career earlier in her career had a career in sales been available to women.

In those days a sales ''girl'' was an idea whose time had not arrived; however, the revolutionary thought did cross one manager's mind back in a midwestern branch office in the early sixties. ''I'm thinking,'' he told Dennis one day, ''of turning this company on its ear. I'm considering making you IBM's first woman sales rep.''

What happened? The idea had to wait until a law passed by Congress a decade later forced it—even in a company like IBM, where morality and integrity and respect for the individual are as high or higher than in any company on earth.

Moving Up

Moving up in a sales career—especially one that leads to management—literally means moving for today's women. It means traveling from prospective customer to customer and moving your home base when new opportunities open up. It means never saying no to any move except for well-thought-out reasons.

Women have more conflicts over moving and travel-ing than men do. A man's wife, until recently, has been a movable part of his life. A woman's husband has not.

A man's wife provides mobility for him if he has children. A woman's husband, even if there are no children, inhibits her mobility. In addition, a traveling woman conjures up images of a traveling man—images that are shocking when applied to her. Whoever said life is fair was no traveling woman.

Any saleswoman who has a fear of flying will be seriously handicapped in her job unless that fear is surpassed quickly by a greater fear of failing. One of the best ways to stop your own progress in a corporation is to refuse to move up the corporate ladder when the next rung is offered. In sales, unlike other occupations, moves almost always mean better jobs, except when it's a move out of the company. People don't get kicked upstairs because they aren't making it in sales.

Buck Rodgers, during his thirty-year career, often must have thought of the industry inside joke that IBM stands for "I've been moved." The career of IBM's vice-president of marketing is a perfect example of moving up by moving on. Rodgers crisscrossed the country many times before reaching his current corporate position.

If you're interested in a sales career that leads from the base to the top of the pyramid, take a look at the twenty years of moves Rodgers made. Although IBM, along with other companies, has cut down on employee moves because of family disruption as well as cost, there's still a lot of moving on attached to moving up.

Rodger's Career Moves

Beginning in IBM's electric typewriter division in a Cleveland branch office in 1950, Rodgers moved to data processing a year later, selling punch-card accounting machines to manufacturing accounts. This job was followed by selling computers from the same home base.

In 1955, Rodgers moved from Cleveland to Youngstown, becoming a sales representative on the Westinghouse Electric Company account in Sharon, Pennsylvania, where IBM was installing a large-scale computer—one of the first-generation machines of the beginning computer age. In 1957 he was transferred to corporate headquarters in New York as administrative assistant to the executive vice-president of IBM. This was only the beginning of moving up by moving on.

Two years later, he returned to the field marketing force as a branch manager. Subsequently, he became manager of banking and finance for the Data Processing Division, then sales and marketing manager for the division's Eastern Region in New York.

In 1962, Rodgers headed for the West Coast, becoming Data Processing Division vice-president and western regional manager in Los Angeles. In 1967, he was named president of Data Processing, IBM's largest division, moving from the West Coast to the East Coast.

Three years later, Rodgers was appointed IBM director of marketing. After twenty years, he was in corporate headquarters to stay. In 1974, Rodgers was elected by the IBM board of directors vice-president of marketing with worldwide responsibilities, the job he holds today.

Relocation and Your Career

Rodgers', plus thousands of other executives' careers, establishes the unmistakable link between the willingness to relocate when new opportunities arise and success.

Saleswomen, because of the importance of mobility to their careers and the lingering feeling that women shouldn't be offered jobs that entail relocation, need to be on the alert for managers, often well-meaning ones, who can put a large dent in your career by making decisions for you. A father figure for a manager is fine until he begins to act like your father. When this occurs, you either stop acting like a child or suffer the consequences. Saleswomen—particularly those who have their eye on management—must be alert in demanding that the company commitment to equality includes moving and traveling, even when you'd rather not go. The general rule, still true to a certain extent, is that if you insist on remaining stationary, so will your career.

IBM Recruitment

If you are an enthusiastic, intelligent, hardworking college bassoon major who takes risks, thrives on competition, and prefers a bus to a limousine just to be with people, your chances of being hired into IBM's sales training program are better than those of a studious engineering or marketing major who puts a high value on security, can't handle rejection, and would rather curl up with a book than go to a party.

Not that IBM is rejecting studious, introverted science or business majors. Those students are being hired for other parts of the business.

"We don't want somebody in sales who's afraid to meet people or who can't handle rejection," Rodgers says.

IBM has been bidding for the brightest and the best potential salespeople on college campuses long enough to have fine-tuned recruitment to a degree unmatched in the industry. Recruitment has progressed to where it is more than an educated guess, if not an exact science, in a company that frowns on making the same mistake twice. IBM's recruitment is as competitive as its sales. It doesn't produce a hundred percent success, but there are far fewer failures than in most companies.

"If we need a thousand people, we recruit a thousand people," Rodgers said. "We are not interested in recruiting fifteen hundred and then getting rid of five hundred later. We expect a hundred percent success, therefore we have to be very careful in our recruitment."

Most people assume that a high-technology company would select only students in science and business to fill their never-ending pipeline of sales recruits. However, about 20 percent of IBM's new recruits each year are from the arts—music, history, language, etc. Most, however, do come from business and science. The ratio is the following:

- About 35 percent from the hard sciences such as math, physics, and engineering.
- Another 45 percent from business areas, such as finance and marketing.
- The remaining 20 percent from the arts and social sciences.

Of the total annual new recruits into sales, the educational level is the following:

- About 70 percent have undergraduate degrees.
- Around 20 percent have M.B.A.s.
- Another 10 percent have other advanced degrees.

The other human factors, difficult to define and impossible to induce, are just as critical in the selection of IBM salespeople, factors such as motivation, personality, determination, and competitiveness. The following, according to Rodgers, are qualities IBM looks for in its sales recruits:

- *Self-confidence.* Unless a salesperson has self-confidence, all the company's investment in him or her will be meaningless. A salesperson must be able to deal with customers on a one-to-one basis. Unless you can demonstrate self-confidence to a potential customer, you're a guaranteed failure.
- *Risk-taking.* Having an IBM territory is like having a business of your own with the accompanying risks. You're given a set of objectives, but you must figure out how to meet them. Except for overall company principles and pricing, you make the decisions nearest the customer. This is not the place for a person who wants a nice, safe, nine-to-five job. Decisions mean risks.
- *Extra hours.* Clock watchers who can squeeze in

eighteen holes of golf five days a week are not the kind of salespeople IBM is looking for. "We don't want workaholics," said Rodgers, "but we're looking for people who will give that extra effort whenever it's needed to get the job done." This could include long hours for weeks or months at a time in certain circumstances.

• *Integrity.* IBM wants salespeople who are trusted by customers, whose word is as good as a written contract. A company that builds its reputation on service wants follow-through on the smallest details.

"It's important to show up on time when you're meeting with a customer, answer all questions, get information back, and follow through on every detail," Rodgers says. "When you develop a habit of doing these small things each day, the customer is going to do business with you."

• *Enthusiasm.* A good salesperson must be optimistic enough to handle bad times instead of feeling overwhelmed by them.

"You've got to think that today's going to be better than yesterday when the going gets rough," says Rodgers. "A salesperson must learn that there will be days when nobody is buying what you're selling. When you get shot out of the saddle, you must retain enough enthusiasm to climb back on that horse the next day."

Salespeople must be able to take rejection as a normal part of selling. Inevitably, even the best salesperson is going to hear no more often than yes, which makes handling rejection gracefully a vital part of a salesperson's job.

• *Competition.* A noncompetitive person in sales is a fish out of water. Competing in a job and accepting the risks along with the rewards is motivating, Rodgers believes.

"The worst thing is to assume that your job is yours for life, in sales or anywhere else," he says. "Even after thirty years, I keep listening for the footsteps over my shoulder. When you don't think there are footsteps, that's when you're headed for trouble. There are a lot of people after my job—which is good. Competition is what keeps people alert and business alive.''

Training

What is the crucial difference that sets IBM's sales force apart? Is it recruitment? Management? Product knowledge? Customer service? Product development? Training? Rewards? Fear of failure? Tradition? Competition?

The answer is all of the above and more. Trying to isolate the IBM difference is like searching for the most important part of a circle. Each piece of the puzzle stands alone or fits comfortably into the overall package.

If forced, however, to choose one success ingredient that might be the most important, one would have to say training.

When asked the difference between a new sales trainee and the finished product, one IBM saleswoman replied, ''The equivalent of four years of college, two years of graduate school, and several lifetimes of experience crammed into fifteen months of intensive training.''

Her greatest fear during training was that she would contract a contagious disease and be forced to miss class. The thought of a noncommunicable illness held no fear for her. ''I would have taken it to class with me,'' she said.

No cost is spared, no detail overlooked in training the baby tigers. If they needed it for their natural habitat, Momma IBM would buy Africa and have it delivered for a practice session. There is no shortsighted, pennywise and pound-foolish philosophy going on here. The company spends as many millions as necessary to turn out the world's best sales force. If there is company belt-tightening, this blood bank that revitalizes IBM from generation to generation will not be the first in line.

IBM's training program can be as short as four

months or as long as eighteen. The time difference varies with the complexity of the product being sold. For example, it is relatively easy to understand the relationship between an electric typewriter or even a small computer and a potential customer's needs. However, understanding how complex computers fit into the needs of potential buyers is not something even the brightest student can breeze through in a few weeks.

In the Data Processing Division, the sales trainee spends the first few weeks in a branch office watching, listening, and asking questions. Trainees are taken along on customer calls. By the time the next stage of their training puts them in one of IBM's several education centers across the country, the trainees know enough to ask specific questions instead of vague, general ones.

Practical experience is interspersed with classroom theory throughout the entire training period. This combination of theory and practice produces better results than either method alone.

In the final phase of training, each person is put through many simulated sales situations to learn exactly how a territory operates, how to put together an account plan, and how to respond to customers and potential customers. Trainees are constantly put on the spot before seasoned and successful IBM salespeople. When the trainees finally get out into the marketplace, it often seems tame by comparison. Seldom do they find problems that weren't covered in training sessions. Any that do come up are included in the next year's program.

At the end of this long, intensive training period, the new recruits are ready for field assignments, a solo flight that for many will be anything but solo.

Specialization

In order to provide the kind of service that has kept IBM number one in the industry, IBM's salespeople become experts in many areas—complex areas such as insurance, manufacturing, retailing, transportation, banking, and many others. Since these areas are too large for any one person's expertise, IBM breaks them down, assigning teams of salespeople who have become experts in the sub-areas. For example, teams of up to twenty-five salespeople handle IBM's big revenue producers such as General Motors, the Bank of America, General Electric, Boeing, etc.

This kind of specialization is critical to selling IBM's products. Unless its salespeople speak each customer's language, diagnose and solve the customer's needs better than anybody else, the territories will be fair game for hungry competitors eager to move up and topple number one. In a free-enterprise society, corporations also hear the footsteps behind them. In IBM's case, the footsteps are faintly familiar. So is the label—"Made in Japan."

Selling

The intensive training is over. Territories have been assigned. Selling objectives have been set. The salespeople's abilities have been carefully matched to their assigned territories in order to ensure maximum success for each one. Saleswomen need not fear a devious plot to sabotage their success. The company investment has been too great. Management's dream is that every recruit will succeed. It has done its part. Immersion into the marketplace will be as painless as possible. There are many companies that would throw you to the wolves after a two-week training period.

However, this is the moment that separates salespeople from all others. Inevitably, the salesperson stands alone on the proving ground. You're up front. The company's support staff and huge buildings fade behind you. They can support you, but they can't sell for you. It is a heavy moment filled only by unfulfilled expectations. The bigger the company, the weaker you feel. It's a realistic feeling. That monkey on your back is the company's future.

"When you're out by yourself in a territory, driving down a lonely road, you have to open doors," says Rodgers. "IBM's name doesn't do the selling for you. You do. Talk all you want about the company's strengths—tall buildings, worldwide locations, large laboratories. What do you do when you run into somebody who doesn't give a damn about IBM? How do you respond when this customer says, 'IBM—that fat, dumb, apathetic, bureaucratic organization. I think I like this smaller outfit over here,' and the door slams in your face?"

Yes, that moment has arrived. What do you do? How do you handle the vast responsibilities ready to submerge you?

At that moment, a good salesperson does what any other good actor does. You walk out onto that stage, confident, relaxed, smiling, even though five minutes before you just threw up in the bathroom.

3

Women and the Free-Enterprise System

PAST, PRESENT, AND FUTURE

OPPORTUNITIES CURRENTLY OPENING UP for women to enter and advance in high-level sales jobs reflect dramatic economic progress for women unparalleled in American history. After centuries of sex-based job exclusion, women are breaking barriers and exploding myths about women and work. Women are proving themselves not only in sales but in new jobs from the Alaskan pipeline to the Supreme Court.

Twenty years ago, high-level sales was a closed industry to women. Sex discrimination was openly and legally practiced. Corporations didn't explain their all-male sales forces any more than police departments explained their all-male narcotics squads or fire departments their all-male truck and ladder crews. Explanations were not necessary. The answer was self-evident. Women were absent because employers refused to hire them. Sex discrimination was legal. Male and female help-wanted columns announced the workplace segregation.

Most women have a private collection of job discrimination stories. However, women past the age of forty recall the days before passage of Title VII of the 1964 Civil Rights Act, when merely questioning job discrimination was considered irrational.

Women in Sales

Twenty years ago a woman persistent enough to apply for a job in professional/industrial sales was curtly and legally informed, "We don't hire women. But how fast do you type?" With few exceptions, hiring women in high-level sales jobs was out of the question, not even a subject for discussion. This job freeze was coupled with academic discrimination which ensured that few women would enroll in college business-administration classes and graduate school M.B.A. programs. Sales training classes completed the exclusionary cycle, which seemed to have no beginning and no end. Women were blocked at every entry point.

Today, in contrast, women make up from 10 to 15 percent of professional/industrial salespeople. The distribution ranges from companies with one or two saleswomen to a few companies nearing a fifty-fifty split. The figures have increased over the past twenty years, picking up speed in the past five. The ground breaking is over, but sales jobs for women are projected to rise steadily. Opportunities are expected to increase throughout the rest of the century.

Sales Opportunities Today

Today an all-male professional/industrial sales force has become the exception, not the rule. A Bureau of Labor Statistics study shows that from 1971 to 1980 women's participation increased 224 percent in wholesale trade sales and 172 percent in manufacturing. The rapid rise of women in sales began to be noticed by the press midway into the 1970s. Magazine articles and newspaper feature stories, such as the following, began to appear:

"Women are the latest addition to many companies' sales forces in fields once covered exclusively by men," reported the *New York Times* financial pages on January 5, 1975. "The areas range from pharmaceuticals to brass products, computers to industrial chemicals."

The *Wall Street Journal*, February 5, 1981, ran this story: "Which sex does a better job of selling industrial products? Some electronics and information processing companies say female sales reps outperform their male peers. Women's commissions were 10 percent higher than men's at Exxon's Qyx typewriter division.

"Semispecialists of America, a Farmingdale, N.Y., electronic products distributor, says its average saleswoman earned $31,500 last year compared with about $25,000 for men. Qyx's top sales reps in the past three years were women. A 28-year-old saleswoman at TDX Systems, a Vienna, Va., long-distance service supplier, is making $60,000 a year after 18 months on the job."

"Salesperson" Appears

A 1979 *Business Week* story entitled "The Industrial Salesman Becomes a Salesperson" profiled women in sales across the country, explaining that "corporate sales has long been recognized as a desirable spot for an ambitious would-be manager, offering the unbeatable combination of high earnings, a chance to learn about the company by learning about its wares and their users, and a tradition of upward mobility into top management. . . . Although women predominated in retail sales, where they made up 70.4 percent of the sales force, they constituted only 7.6 percent of the 850,000 sales representatives for wholesalers and manufacturers . . . but now the picture is changing rapidly."

A 1979 *Business Week* survey found more women

becoming industrial/professional salespeople. "They are selling steel, aluminum, farm equipment, lumber, tools, heavy machinery, high-technology equipment and other traditionally men-only products, and some women are advancing into sales management. Moreover," the article stated, "some industries are pulling while the women push. A life insurance industry campaign has increased the industry's percentage of women sales recruits from 2 percent in 1971 to 12 percent in 1978. . . ."

Earnings Documented

Earnings of the saleswomen interviewed in the *Business Week* article ranged from $17,000 to $45,000. One woman, earning $30,000 had tripled her former $10,000 salary, while another had really hit the big time. She was earning half a million dollars a year selling on Wall Street.

Dun's Review in March 1978 also reported success stories of women in sales in an article entitled "Sales Jobs Open for Women." The women featured were selling everything from word processors to heavy machinery. At that time only about a hundred thousand women were employed as sales representatives in manufacturing and wholesaling, which meant that 80 percent of industrial companies had not yet hired their first saleswoman.

Nothing Succeeds Like Success

Since 1978, more and more companies have joined in the rush to hire their first saleswoman—and their second, and third and more, proving that nothing succeeds in business like success. Admittedly, pushed into hiring saleswomen because of EEO laws and federal affirmative-action regulations (a study of fourteen companies by a former marketing professor revealed that the number-one reason companies are hiring women is to meet federal EEO requirements), many of these reluctant employers have become strong defenders of equal job opportunities for women. The performance of the company's first saleswoman often destroys the myth that women can't compete in tough selling jobs—a double-edged sword that places undue pressure on the first women recruits.

A Ciba-Geigy Executive

Dr. Charles E. Ziegler, vice-president of administrative services for the Ciba-Geigy Corporation, is typical of many executives within industry and his own company who have made significant contributions to job equality for women.

Several years ago Dr. Ziegler worked with a women's employment committee which discussed discriminatory attitudes and practices that have kept women out of non-traditional jobs.

Like many well meaning and concerned executives, Dr. Ziegler's attitude about "appropriate" jobs for women changed when he realized that what is perceived as protection for women in free enterprise is actually discrimination.

Today women make up 12 percent of Ciba-Geigy's sales force. Ten years ago there were none.

"Our saleswomen have proved that they are every bit as good as men and some are better," Dr. Ziegler said. "We will continue to hire women in sales as well as throughout the company."

Interestingly, Ciba-Geigy's home base is in Switzerland, a land late in allowing women to vote but a country which recently made a giant leap ahead of the United States by passing legislation ensuring equal rights for women.

Even such traditional companies as The Aluminum Company of America and Standard Oil of California are hiring women. More than 10 percent of Alcoa's sales force is now female. Companies like International Paper, Boise Cascade, Jones and Laughlin Steel, and General Foods are hiring saleswomen. Eighteen and a half percent of Union Carbide's sales force is female, a 10 percent rise in as many years. In fact, the tide has turned so completely that companies maintaining all-male sales forces are taking a second look, especially those whose competitors have hired women.

"Show me a company whose competitors have hired women in sales and I'll show you a company that will soon be out beating the bushes for saleswomen of its own," said an employment recruiter. "In business you are pragmatic or else. You do what works or else you're out of business."

Since passage of federal antidiscrimination legislation in 1964, women have turned the tables on history. The two-paycheck family has become the typical American family, replacing the typical lone male wage earner of the past. Married women in the labor force currently contribute up to 40 percent of their family's support, and the greater a woman's education the more likely her participation in the labor force.

However, women continue to be clustered in basic female-typed jobs such as clerical work, nursing, and teaching, the result of years of segregation in the workplace. Today's percentages of women in non-traditional jobs often gives a false impression of their actual numbers. For example, when a company hires its first woman in a non-traditional area, the percentage increase is a hundred percent.

It will take many years, perhaps centuries, for women to achieve parity in the nontraditional workplace. The job advantage to 35 percent of the population is evident when the other 65 percent of the population (women and minorities) is locked out of the competition.

Ironically, work restrictions for women would have been even more severe had not our forefathers perceived a self advantage in providing limited job opportunities for spinsters in order to keep them off the public dole. Unmarried women were expected to support themselves. Many of today's female typed jobs, i.e. domestic workers, librarians, governess, developed from these early female service categories.

Part of a Vast Restructuring

Women in sales are a vital part of a vast restructuring of the marketplace which began two decades ago. During this time the most far-reaching economic revolution in the country's history has occurred. More than a million women a year have entered the labor force, swelling the ranks to more than 45 million. Periodic projections that this tide will reverse itself suggest wishful thinking, since the rate of increase has speeded up during the last seven years. According to a special "Careers" issue, published October 11, 1981, by the *New York Times*, the labor force is expected to grow by 25 million by 1995, with women accounting for two-thirds of that figure.

Such massive labor force participation by women in a wide variety of job categories is totally without precedent. Previously, women have been directed into "appropriate" areas and regulated out of the free-enterprise system, which for them has been anything but free. Job opportunities have always been limited. Half of all women who worked in early America were employed as domestic servants.

The right to choose a life's occupation and compete in the free-enterprise system should be a basic freedom for all citizens, guaranteed and protected by the Constitution alongside other basic rights. Historically, however, job discrimination has been treated as a basic right. Sex-based legislation restricted women's access to the marketplace in America from the very beginning. The same early American legislators who cried out against British abuses such as taxation without representation saw no contradiction in their own treatment of women.

A Self-Fulfilling Prophecy

Historically, the exclusion of women from sales as well as other nontraditional jobs is explained by a circular logic. Ignoring the combination of culture and legislation that actually kept women out of nontraditional jobs, the justification for their absence evolved into a self-fulfilling prophecy. For example, using this logic, the absence of women judges is proof, not of the exclusion, but that women are unfit for the profession. This justification for sex discrimination is as old as civilization itself: If women are absent from any field, their absence proves all females unfit. In professions where women are scarce, the few are cited as exceptions to this general rule. Many laws, thought to be protection for women, are based instead on women being considered unfit to serve (e.g., women and the draft).

A dramatic example of this circular logic is the familiar question "Why are all the great French chefs men?" Instead of examining women's exclusion from the French culinary schools—a prerequisite for entering the profession—those asking the question presume women are unable to perform in a job category exclusively theirs inside millions of homes.

Logically, the only fair way to determine fitness is through the free choice of individuals and open access to jobs where ability is the determining factor. Neither the individual success nor collective failure of women can be legislated. Access, however, can be. Legislation limiting women's access began centuries ago, handed down over generations and woven into the fabric of everyday life.

Regulating Women

If it were possible to add up all the hours male legislative bodies have spent regulating women's lives, it would at least prove who is overregulating whom. Government at all levels—federal, state, and local—enacted new laws on top of old laws. From state to state the maze of laws is confusing, contradictory, and ridiculous. One early state law forbade women to wear corsets and an inspector's job was created, according to a book entitled *You Can't Eat Peanuts in Church and Other Little-Known Laws*. The book, by Barbara Seuling, points out the absurdity of laws written by early Puritan legislators, whose successors continue the tradition. Ten years ago a woman in Connecticut could not legally be served alcohol if seated at a bar, while a few feet away in New York, she could not legally be served standing at a bar. It took until 1981 and thousands of hours of litigation for the Supreme Court to knock down an absurd "head and master" law in several states, giving husbands total control of all property even in community-property states.

Literally thousands of all-the-wall laws continue to clutter up the law books and the lives of women. Women, with unequal representation in legislative bodies, were (and are) a favorite target for government regulators. Long before President Reagan successfully campaigned for office on the theme of "getting the government off the backs of the people," government had staked out a permanent claim to the backs of half the people—women.

The Half-Free Enterprise System

Until very recently, the free-enterprise system in this country could be more accurately described as the half-free enterprise system, since women and other disadvantaged groups were locked out. It is clear that Adam Smith's invisible hand passed over a lot of people without touching their lives.

In his book, *Free to Choose*, extolling capitalism, it is clear by the title that economist Milton Friedman isn't writing about women. While mentioning that slaves were locked out of the free-enterprise system, he totally ignores women. Friedman's second chapter, "The

Tyranny of Controls," would have been a good spot to recognize that more than the free market has been tyrannized by controls. Instead of welcoming women's talents into the Gross National Product, they were regulated into "free" labor at home, which may have made men's lives more comfortable but did nothing to further Adam Smith's dream. In discussing nineteenth-century America, the heyday of free enterprise, Friedman writes that "everybody was free to go into any business, follow any occupation, buy any property. . . . There were no arbitrary obstacles. Performance . . . was the touchstone."

A superb teacher and debater, Friedman in the public television series based on his book welcomes opposing points of view and debates the issues, generally winning through logic. It would be interesting to hear Friedman defend the "logic" of regulating women's lives and excluding them from the free-enterprise system. Before, during, and after the nineteenth century, women could not go into any business or occupation they chose. They could not get an equal education. If single, they were permitted few choices; if married even fewer. A married woman needed her husband's permission to sign contracts or go into business, and the fruits of her labors belonged to him, not her. Her enterprises could be exploited with impunity. Adam Smith and Milton Friedman might find little incentive in this type of "free" enterprise. Women's sex, not their performance, was the touchstone that determined their lives. No arbitrary obstacles? All obstacles were arbitrary.

A century later, arbitrary obstacles remained. Women were moved in and out of the free-enterprise system like chess pieces, allowed into limited job categories but "protected" from the best jobs. Recruited into defense jobs during World War II, women who responded to the call from their country had a brief fling with free enterprise. When the war ended they were summarily fired, their jobs given to men. Nobody filed suit because no laws were broken.

Women and Work

A century after Adam Smith wrote *The Wealth of Nations*, Charlotte Perkins Gilman, an early feminist, made an observation about women and work that stirred up a hornet's nest. "The economic dependence," she said, "is the underlying ground of the helplessness of women. . . . No creature is free whose bread is in other hands than theirs."

As applied to men, this is a harmless, self-evident statement of fact. When applied to women, however, it becomes a highly subversive idea that shakes the foundations of society and threatens to bring down the family. Authors and philosophers through the ages have written eloquently about men and work. Independence through a life's pursuit has been glorified for men but denied to women.

"The crowning fortune of a man," said Ralph Waldo Emerson, "is to be born to some pursuit which finds him employment and happiness, whether it be to make baskets or broadswords, or canals or statues or songs."

Thomas Carlyle had similar views. "Blessed is he who has found his work," he said. "Let him ask no other blessedness. He has a work, a life purpose: he has found it and will follow it."

Virtually all religions counsel independence through work for men, such as the following advice in the Talmud: "Hire yourself out to work which is beneath you rather than become dependent on others."

While economic independence is praised for men, dependency is imposed on women. Instead of freely choosing a life's work, all women are assigned the same life's work regardless of their desires and abilities—to be wives and mothers and nothing else, which freed men to be husbands, fathers, and participants in the free-enterprise system. Maximum freedom for men has generally resulted in minimum freedom for women.

God's Grand Design

Nothing has surpassed the clarity of early Supreme Court decisions in justifying women's imposed position in society. An 1873 decision denying a woman the right to practice law invoked God's grand design:

> That God designed the sexes to occupy different spheres of action and that it belongs to men to make, apply and execute the laws. . . . The . . . family . . . which is founded in the divine ordinance, as well as in the nature of things, indicates the domestic sphere as that which properly belongs to . . . womanhood. . . . The harmony . . . of interests and views which belong, or should belong, to the family institution is repugnant to the idea of a woman adopting a distinct and independent career from that of her husband. . . . The paramount destiny and mission of women is to fulfill the noble and benign offices of wife and mother. This is the law of the Creator.

The Natural Order

It is understandable why economists seem not to notice the discrimination that kept women out of the free-enterprise system. Restriction of the lives of women is so universal that it seems natural. However, had this been the natural order, a network of cultural and legal restrictions would not have been necessary to keep the system in place. Legislation is not required to keep water flowing downstream. Laws forcing people to eat, sleep, and engage in sex are not necessary to continue civilization. The bobwhite willingly sits on *his* nest without federal intervention. The father seahorse carries his brood in his pouch without being forced. Egalitarian wild geese couples don't need a constitutional amendment to bring up their families in cooperation. The natural order, if forced, is a contradiction in terms. Left alone, the natural order defines itself.

To establish an elaborate cultural and legal network

excluding women, then spend centuries accumulating a body of "facts" to prove it the "natural order" requires a sales and marketing effort eclipsing any described in this book. Instead, human beings with power translated their wishes into laws, claimed divine guidance, and named what they claimed the "natural order."

Many twentieth-century decisions continue to be based on the "natural order" theme. The words change but the music remains the same. God's grand design for women threads throughout. Religion and law intertwine like a steel cable to regulate women's access to the marketplace.

Were this the choice of a higher power, it is reasonable to assume there would be no argument. Because like salmon swimming upstream, birds migrating, or squirrels hoarding nuts for winter, the Creator could have built a failsafe system into the "natural order."

Freedom and Free Enterprise

Milton Friedman makes valid correlations between free-enterprise and personal freedom where government's function is to protect basic rights. No matter how benevolent the dictator, free people don't want one. Friedman, like Adam Smith, trusts the invisible hand of the impersonal marketplace to protect the average citizen better than the government. Government, he feels, in responding to pressure gives large organized groups or influential citizens greater representation than an ordinary citizen. The market responds only to supply and demand.

Professor Friedman was kind enough to answer an inquiry for this book asking him how women, without government intervention, could have gained access to the free-enterprise system, and if he considers Title VII interference or a protection of basic rights.

His reply cited a section in an earlier book, *Capitalism and Freedom*, suggests that while discrimination is deplored, the appropriate recourse is to seek entry through persuasion. However, later, in *Free to Choose*, Friedman appears to have modified this judgment. "Equality of opportunity . . . is an essential component of liberty," he writes. "If some people are denied access to particular positions in life for which they are qualified, simply because of their ethnic color or religion, there is an interference with their rights to 'life, liberty and the pursuit of happiness.' It denies equality of opportunity and by the same token sacrifices the freedom of some for the advantage of others."

Although Friedman doesn't mention women, his description fits perfectly. Women deserve nothing more and nothing less than equal access. Friedman correctly points out that to ensure results makes business a fixed race—the same fixed race it has been for others who should have been competing fairly all along.

Affirmative Action, Early American Style

The nineteenth-century free-enterprise system was actually a pervasive social monopoly in which a conspiracy to keep women out operated much as the invisible hand of Adam Smith. All monopolists benefited by the exclusion of women. It might be called an early American affirmative-action program in that it, like current affirmative-action programs, benefited a particular group. The group who benefited, however, was white males instead of women and minorities.

Government and the free-enterprise system worked hand in glove to continue the closed shop throughout the nineteenth and twentieth centuries. Women, denied the right to compete freely in the marketplace, fitted into the cracks of the system and supplied cheap labor needed by an expanding economy. Crumbs from a banquet table, however, beat starving. Women working in sewing factories for slave wages were better off than many women totally dependent for their bread on others, particularly women with children who were (and are) dependent upon violent, drunken, or abusive husbands.

After operating for centuries as the half-free enterprise system, a strange twist of fate must have given Adam Smith a turn in his grave. The half-free enterprise system, which had fought tooth and nail to keep government off its turf, was forced by government to open up its ranks. What irony. A federal bureaucracy forcing free enterprise to live up to its name. How this happened was even more ironic.

A Joke That Backfired

During congressional debates over the 1964 Civil Rights Act, a southern legislator proposed an amendment to kill the bill. He proposed adding sex discrimination to Title VII, which forbids race discrimination. To examine race discrimination alongside sex discrimination should dramatize the foolishness of attempting to legislate personal bias. All would immediately recognize that sex discrimination is as American as apple pie, written into the Declaration of Independence, the Constitution, and our laws. The founding fathers never intended for women to have equal opportunities. The joke backfired. The bill passed.

The new joke that swept Congress was how Playboy Clubs would handle a recruitment program to fill 50 percent of their bunny jobs with men. A year later Playboy still had no male bunnies, but everybody had stopped laughing. Sex discrimination, which has never been a joke to women, stopped being a national joke.

Employment is a serious survival issue, as was proved by an avalanche of sex-discrimination complaints filed with the Equal Employment Opportunity Commission during its first year. Soon a backlog of more than one hundred thousand cases awaited action by the Equal Employment Opportunity Commission as women across the country began to use the new law to force their way into the free-enterprise system. It worked better than persuasion.

Feminism Awakens

Title VII of the Civil Rights Act of 1964 did not spring full-blown out of a legislator's bag of tricks. A decade of "persuasion" preceded it as the second wave of feminism swept the country. Dormant since suffrage, except for a band of dedicated women, the new feminism—with the wisdom of history—demanded full equality. Nothing more but nothing less. Women finally struck Charlotte Gilman's theme with an urgency heretofore unbecoming to their sex: parity in the workplace, equal pay for equal work, equal education to prepare them for a life's work. Women had discovered what the other sex always knew: that no woman (or man) is free whose bread is in the hands of others. Women would earn their bread. By 1980, almost 46 million were in the labor market. Yet more startling changes are on the horizon. According to a 1980 public-opinion poll conducted by the Connecticut Mutual Life Insurance Company, 74 percent of females surveyed between the ages of fourteen and twenty, and 72 percent of those between twenty-one and twenty-four, preferred an equal marriage of shared responsibility to the traditional marriage of the past.

The Tail Wags the Dog

Many traditional economists minimized the effects of working women on the nation's economy long past the point of rational disagreement. Even though the handwriting was on the wall in bold strokes, periodic predictions reflected the opposite of what was actually happening. The "typical" American family of father, mother, and two children continues to be used as a norm even though only 7 percent of American families fit into this mold.

Anything that became as massive as the female work force, which began building in the fifties, grew steadily in the sixties, and exploded in the seventies, is bound to affect the economy profoundly. By 1977 a few alert economists had begun to take note: Interviewed by Georgia Dullea of the *New York Times*, Columbia University economist Eli Ginzberg, who was also chairman of the National Commission for Manpower Policy (and now head of the National Commission for Employment Policy), described the work force trend as "a revolution in the roles of women . . . the single most outstanding phenomenon of this century. . . . It is a worldwide phenomenon, an integral part of a changing economy and a changing society. Its secondary and tertiary consequences are really unchartable."

In a column the same year, Eliot Janeway, nationally prominent political economist, syndicated columnist, and author, put to rest the frequent rumblings about working women playing fast and loose with the economy by taking men's jobs and thereby forcing them into the unemployment ranks. Crediting women with rescuing the economy at a time of deep trouble, Janeway wrote:

> The familiar complaint that women are stealing the jobs of male breadwinners is fading away into the mists of myth. Hard evidence is developing all over the economic landscape that women going to work—part time as well as full time—are saving jobs for men. The purchasing power they are creating can make the critical difference for thousands of businesses on the verge of going broke and laying off males with seniority. If so many women weren't making new jobs, more working men would be losing old jobs.

Janeway concluded that "the traditional nuclear family, dependent on the husband-father as its sole source of take-home pay is either wallowing hopelessly in debt or jeopardizing the life expectancy of its sole breadwinner—who is most likely exhausting himself moonlighting at a second job."

In the past twenty years whole new industries as well as old ones have become dependent upon the paychecks of working women. What the critics of working women apparently didn't notice was that history was swinging full circle. Women, long dependent on others for their bread, had turned the tables. The nation's economy had become dependent on them. The tail was wagging the dog.

An Important Milestone

At the beginning of 1980, working women reached an important milestone. For the first time in history the working woman—married, single, or divorced—had become the norm. The non-working woman was now the exception. While this had long been true for single and divorced women, it had not for married women. However, by July 1980, almost 24 million married women, living with their husbands, had joined the labor force, outnumbering dependent wives by more than 2 million. The most dramatic rise was in the more than 6 million working mothers of children under the age of six—a ninefold increase in less than a decade.

Why were all these women working? From annual family income statistics, it became obvious that an overwhelming number of women were working for the same reasons men work—to support themselves and support or help support families. The so-called pin-money jobs of the past were now survival jobs. Women were working to pay the rent and put food on the table.

Preserving the Family

"Preserving the family" has reappeared as a code for suppressing women. It is one of the oldest justifications for treating women differently under the law and the underpinnings of all sex-based legislation.

Throughout history "for the common good" and

"preserving the family" have been invoked to impose stricter rules on women than on men. Equal rights can be ignored in order to preserve the family and promote the common good. The breakdown of the family was the theme of suffrage opponents as well as opponents of birth control information—almost verbatim with language currently used by opponents of the Equal Rights Amendment. Working women today are blamed for a breakdown of the family because of the high divorce rate. Since the economic independence of working wives makes divorce more likely, working is undesirable according to this simplistic reasoning.

There's no denying that the economic independence of women is responsible for a great many divorces. Economic independence makes possible what otherwise might have to be endured. But why should't divorce be freely chosen, since, without divorce, marriage becomes a prison. Little is heard in defense of divorce, yet everybody realizes that there are "good" divorces and "bad" marriages. Handcuffing people together for life is no way to glorify marriage. Choosing to remain married when divorce is readily available *is* an endorsement.

Those who blame the economic independence of women for the breakup of the family show little faith in the family's ability to survive on its own merits. Millions of working wives and mothers show a much greater faith. In addition, marriage is not the issue, since a high percentage of people who get divorces also remarry. Using the same simplistic reasoning, it could be claimed that divorce creates more marriages and more families.

Blame the Working Mother

Without a shred of evidence, the age-old game of "blame the working mother" continues to heap abuse on society's hardest-working members. Working mothers are a convenient place to hang the collective blame for societal ills; they're accused of causing everything from an increase in violent crime to lower school test scores, teenage pregnancies and daytime burglaries. Any problem that can be linked to childhood—and what can't?—is the working mother's fault.

Not a single newspaper headline, however, pointed out that the young man who shot President Reagan came from an "unbroken" Christian home with a stay-at-home, never-divorced, longtime married mother and a traditional, full-time working father. Imagine the reaction had this young man had a working mother. Worse still, what if she had been working and divorced?

While critics of working women are quick to suggest that working mothers should stay home and care for *their* children, the underlying sentiment carefully separates which mothers should work and which should stay home. Those first to suggest that mothers stay home and take care of their own children are also the first to suggest that welfare mothers should work instead of being supported by the taxpayers. Divorced mothers are also encouraged to support their families instead of adding to the welfare rolls. What this means is that mothers with husbands who are able to support them on one paycheck should stay home—a percentage that has gone from tiny to minuscule.

Turning Back the Clock

To dramatize the absurdity of criticizing women in the work force, a woman who conducts equal-employment-opportunity seminars developed a segment she calls "Let's fire all working women." From the latest Bureau of Labor statistics, she gets the total number of working women and the total number of unemployed men. Subtracting these figures gives her the number of unfilled jobs that would result from firing all working women and giving their jobs to men. Using September 1981 statistics the following would result:

• If 45.5 million working women were fired, after giving jobs to the 4.3 million unemployed men, more than 41 million jobs would remain vacant.

• If only married women, living with their husbands, were fired, more than 21 million jobs would remain unfilled after putting every unemployed man to work.

• Even if the ax fell only on mothers of children under the age of six, more than 2 million jobs would remain vacant after giving a job to each unemployed man.

Other consequences critics of working women seldom think about would include the following:

• A disastrous skills gap, particularly in female-typed positions such as nurses, clerical workers, secretaries, and teachers.

• A dramatic drop in the Gross National Product.

• A devastating domino effect that would close down whole industries, put men out of work, and bring on a greater depression than the one that caused bank closings, investors leaping out of windows, and long lines at soup kitchens.

Some of the more humorous results this unlikely exercise could bring on, according to this woman, might be: surgeons learning to put on their own gloves, executives signing up for switchboard seminars, standing room only at Katharine Gibbs, and a huge decline in the number of "dress for success" books.

Unsung Heroines

Instead of heaping blame on the working woman for a multitude of ills she did not create, it seems logical that a politically minded, free-enterprise, work-ethic-advocating president might consider dedicating a new Labor Day to the American working woman for her unique economic rescue mission.

Justifying the exclusion of women from the free-enterprise system, in view of the economic facts, takes a mental contortionist few intelligent people would take seriously, particularly people dedicated to revitalizing the economy.

However, an off-the-wall economic theory, touted as the bible for the current administration, does just this.

Gilding the Reagan Administration

George Gilder is a writer who for years has been grinding out contorted prose about the anthropological and biological "natural order" of the sexes, hysterically trying to stem the tide of working women by warning of the dangers of "sexual suicide."

Gilder's theory—more antimale than antifemale if carefully analyzed—is that the survival of the species and balance of nature depend upon men dominating women. He claims there is anthropological proof that the only way to harness men's innately destructive tendencies is to hitch them to a GNP plow that performs two miracles simultaneously: the creation of wealth and the elimination of poverty. Married men are preferred because they work harder than single men, says Gilder. However, all men work harder than women. A woman's role in this economic structure, guaranteed to cure inflation and revitalize the sagging economy, is to give men children and remain dependent themselves. Dependents, according to Gilder, really spur men on to the creative free enterprise which increases productivity which creates wealth which produces jobs which eliminates poverty. It takes a genius to think up something so simple.

Gilder lays all this out in his latest diatribe, *Wealth and Poverty*, a love song to freedom for men through supply-side economics and domination over women. This nonsense is cranked out with footnotes in which Gilder frequently "proves" points by quoting himself or somebody equally objective about women, such as Lionel Tiger.

Gilder's theory is humorous except for the facts that the president was photographed with a copy under his arm and two members of the Reagan team have blurbs on the book's jacket. (One of these is David Stockman, the unmarried head of the Office of Management and Budget who, if he takes the book seriously, should give careful thought to remaining single because of the health hazard working any harder might present.) The theory that women work less hard at their jobs than men is carefully refuted in a 1981 four-year study by a committee of the Research Council of the National Academy of Sciences, comprised of ten men and four women. (Their findings confirm that although women work just as hard as men, often harder, they continue to earn unequal pay for equal or comparable work.)

While the book is praised for its supply-side economics, nobody in the administration has publicly rejected the accompanying barefoot-and-pregnant theories—integral parts of Gildernomics. In the book Gilder claims that women have "long horizons without their very bodies, glimpses of eternity within their wombs," and hastens to suggest they not divert their gaze. Unless men affirm their masculinity by dominating women, according to Gilder, they will turn to violence for fulfillment of basic male needs. To avoid such cataclysmic consequences, women, for the greater good of humanity, must permit the continued domination by men.

This philosophy, instead of affirming his masculinity, reveals Gilder's fear of competition. The threat that men will become violent unless women "permit" domination sounds like a child threatening his mother. His book is not much of a tribute to a mother who after the death of Gilder's father raised him in a female-headed household. Gilder finds the lack of an "authoritarian" father a prime cause of society's misfits. (In one case—his own—he could be right.) While he claims that we cannot change the "natural order" of the family, his book suggests great anxiety that what he fears most is already happening—and it is.

Political Suicide

Women have struggled too long getting into the free-enterprise system to return meekly to the sidelines. No administration can turn back the economic revolution of the past two decades. Indeed, it would seem strange that any free-enterprise administration would want to. Women's paychecks are pumped back into the economy, a capital infusion that directly stimulates growth, exactly what supply-side economists claim they want. It's obvious that a couple earning $25,000 a year can buy more goods and services than can a one-paycheck family earning $15,000. A low-income mother who works instead of being supported by the taxpayers spends her entire income on survival items—rent, groceries, transportation, children's clothes. A two-paycheck couple buys vacations they could not afford on one income. This combined purchasing power fuels the market as other people work at jobs supplying goods and services to satisfy their needs. Women have become such an integral part of the free-enterprise system we would have trouble turning the clock back ten years, much less the century Gilder suggests. In addition, stuffing a reluctant genie back into a bottle isn't easy. First you have to catch her. The attempt may cause political repercussions for those who try.

Males like Gilder, handicapped by hormones, will have to learn to control their prehistoric bodies or face their own sexual suicide. Women have gotten a look at the free-enterprise system from outside the womb. And they like what they see.

Economic Independence

It should surprise no one that economically dependent women become the country's poorest and least protected group in their later years. Encouraged from childhood into lifelong dependency and led to believe that exclusion from the workplace is protection instead of discrimination, thousands of widows and abandoned wives learn too late the fate of the economically dependent woman.

The fact that women are at last becoming economically independent through participation in the free-enterprise system should be good news to all who advocate equality. The results are dramatic when stacked up against the historical snail's-pace gains of women. In this country during the past twenty years women have made more progress toward equality than in the past 360 years of "persuasion" since the Pilgrims landed at Plymouth Rock. Earning their bread is working much better for women than baking it.

Yes, women have come a long way since Charlotte Gilman, in questioning their economic dependency, opened a can of worms. One of the things they've learned is the reason people like Milton Friedman become economists. They are rapidly learning, too, that it's not love that makes the world go round. It's economics.

Saleswomen in the Free-Enterprise System

Today's saleswomen, poised at the bottom of a long career ladder, have a unique opportunity that comes from being in the right place at the right time in history. They are among the first women through the twentieth-century free-enterprise door. How far they go and how fast they travel will depend upon many factors, some within their control, some they cannot control. Whether sales will be their rapid track to the top is unknown. A number of saleswomen have already advanced to middle management and a handful are knocking at the doors of senior management. Thousands more are preparing to follow before the turn of the century. If by that time, there are fifty female CEOs of American corporations as predicted by futurist Herman Kahn, there should also be fifty thousand female senior executives, perhaps more.

Nobody can accurately predict the obstacles women will find in their path on their way to the twenty-first century. Throughout the history of civilization, those who try to deny women equality have been both determined and devious. The current federal government, while championing free enterprise on the one hand, is pulling back on enforcement of equal-opportunity laws —an obvious obstacle to the economic progress of women. The defeat of the proposed Equal Rights Amendment extending equal legal protection, almost certain as this book goes to press, is another blow. Religious fundamentalists, like the early Puritans, are again invoking God's grand design and the "natural order" of women. They are clamoring for new laws to enforce their wishes by restricting women's freedom. And once again, legislators weighing mail and counting votes are proposing restrictive legislation dealing with the most fundamental, personal, and private rights of women.

With such black clouds looming on the horizon, yesterday's women, no matter how strong-hearted, would have little chance to overcome such grave obstacles in less than another century of hard work. However, women in the past were economically dependent. Today it's a new ball game with millions of new players.

In *The Making of the Modern Family*, Professor Edward Shorter, describing the struggles of eighteenth- and nineteenth-century women for a tiny measure of self-control, writes, "Only when wives gained direct contact with the market economy—by means of cottage industry and later by means of factory work—did they seize hold of a solid lever with which to pry themselves loose from these subordinate roles."

Today women have the leverage to pry themselves loose from centuries of restrictions. Generations of women have longed for the chance to succeed or fail on their own merits in the free-enterprise system, unchained from legal and cultural restrictions, able to enter and compete on their own ability. Women in sales today, more than in any other field, are at last getting that opportunity. Their success will help determine the future of all women.

4

What It Takes to Become a Successful Salesperson

SALESPEOPLE OFTEN SAY that no two sales are alike. The same is true for salespeople. No two fit the exact same mold. Each works out his or her own special techniques. Techniques that work for one may not work for another. The salesperson's relationship to the customer is much like the actor's relationship with an audience, a doctor's to the patient. Exactly what works and why it works is intricate human chemistry, yet the process and the results are similar. Many top salespeople can't explain how they sell. Some won't try because they are fearful of losing what they perceive as a mystical quality that makes them successful.

"I don't want to know how I sell," said one woman. "Why disturb something that works? If I couldn't sell, I'd want to know. Perhaps I just have a special gift. Instead of being able to write music or play professional tennis, I'm a natural-born salesperson. When you have a special gift, you don't look the gift horse in the mouth.''

Dr. Francis Mechner, a psychologist and learning specialist who developed a new concept in sales seminars, believes the exact opposite. He says people can learn the selling skills that lead to success. He feels that the stereotype of the "typical" salesperson—the fast-talking, glad-handing, smooth-talking movie character—is the antithesis of the real-life successful salesperson. A successful salesperson's approach to selling is much more like the approach of a physician diagnosing a patient than that of a fast-talking used-car salesman out to take some unsuspecting soul to the cleaners. Integrity is a vital part of successful selling. The effective salesperson wants to help the client. The stereotyped salesperson wants to sell the client regardless of the benefits.

The broad category of selling provides room for many types of successful salespeople, selling thousands of different products to hundreds of thousands of different clients. These professionals blend comfortably into their special business landscapes. A person selling heavy equipment, cement, or steel blends into a world different from that of an IBM or a Wall Street salesperson. Selling in the South is often different from selling in the North, and both are different from selling in the East or West. The professional salesperson diagnoses not only the patient but also the environment.

A Psychological Profile

Although "liking people" is a cliché as a reason people choose sales, it is nevertheless true. But with much greater depth. The psychology of selling is the study of human beings—why and how they react, what they need as opposed to what they say or think they need, the many tiny variables inherent in dealing with people. Salespeople are fascinated with the inner workings of people, the differences and the similarities. They see people as a vast puzzle with thousands of tiny pieces that can fit together perfectly if you invest the time and effort in putting it together, fitting the tiny pieces into their special locations.

Although professional/industrial selling has been considered a male occupation, if you put together those characteristics listed by sales experts as most desirable in the ideal salesperson, an interesting mixture emerges that is neither male nor female.

So-Called Female Traits

"Women are better at selling than men because they have been selling all their lives," said one woman who believes their disadvantaged position in society has provided women with an edge in selling.

The so-called female or nurturing traits, culturally encouraged in women, are vital in selling:

- Empathy—being able to put yourself in another's place and understanding how the other person feels
- Figuring out the needs of others
- Putting those needs ahead of your own
- Patiently listening to others
- Developing and using intuitive skills
- Paying attention to details
- Accepting criticism
- Sociability—the desire to please others
- Avoiding conflicts

Saleswomen stress the benefits of these traits. They point out how the more highly developed intuitive abilities of women are important in diagnosing the client's needs; how patience and understanding, empathy, and really wanting to help clients work to the advantage of saleswomen. Men they sell to, used to talking to women in their private lives, confide their business problems quite comfortably after they get over the initial strangeness of dealing with women in business. Also, the feeling that women are more honest than men is an advantage. The feeling of having greater trust in women also helps in selling, where trust is an important element.

So-Called Male Traits

Traits culturally encouraged in males more than females are also vital in selling:

- Competitiveness
- Aggressiveness
- Self-confidence
- Intelligence
- Persistence
- Independence
- Responsibility
- Risk-taking
- Handling rejection

Salesmen tend to stress these traits, particularly aggressiveness and competitiveness, some to the extent of failing to perceive the blend of male and female characteristics they have developed in sales careers.

Sales and Culture

Dr. Laurence Loeb, a practicing psychiatrist in Hartsdale, New York, who was also a consulting psychiatrist to West Point when the first women entered, says it should surprise nobody that effective selling combines both male and female traits. Nor does he view this revelation as a problem to either men or women interested in selling.

"Psychiatrists as far back as Freud have realized that regardless of cultural conditioning, human beings combine both male and female traits," Dr. Loeb says. "In sales as in most careers, a combination of both is a decided advantage. Most jobs require both."

Dr. Loeb says it is also reasonable to expect that certain females will have more difficulty developing some of the so-called male skills, while more males will have difficulty developing the "female" strengths. He sees this, however, as a minor problem to both sexes interested in a sales career. The capacity and the desire to develop the necessary traits for success are what counts.

"Sales, like many other careers, is self-selecting to a certain degree," Dr. Loeb says. "Women, for example, who have difficulty becoming competitive are less likely to choose sales. The same is true for men who cannot develop the sensitivity necessary for sales. They, too, choose other careers."

Growing Up Female

Sarah is the type of woman who self-selected herself out of sales long before women ever got in. Trying to cure a lifetime of serious depression, she told her new psychiatrist that she had never had a problem with rejection. "I have lots of problems," she said, "but rejection is certainly not one of them."

Two years later, still in analysis, the subject came up again. This time Sarah gasped recalling her own ignorance in asserting that rejection was not a problem. By this time she realized she was so terrified of rejection she had spent a lifetime avoiding the possibility to the extent that the hidden fear had affected her entire life.

June began going to a psychiatric social worker after her life fell apart at the age of forty. Married soon after college, she had raised three children and was happy being a housewife until her husband left her with all the children and most of the bills. She was terrified to look for a job, felt she could not get along alone in the world, and considered suicide. Ashamed to ask for help, she had lived on canned soup for weeks before finally seeking help. Even though she was in good health and could have found a job, she felt she was totally helpless.

Had both of these women been brought up males,

their subsequent problems would have been virtually impossible or, at the very least, diagnosed much earlier. Sarah would have discovered long before adulthood the problem of rejection, and June would have been forced to become self-sufficient long before her "protected" status of housewife eroded her self-confidence and rendered her totally dependent.

Males learn to accept rejection at an early age. They cannot hide from it. A boy constantly puts himself on the rejection block. Tryouts for Little League, later basketball and football teams. He is constantly rejected by older and stronger boys. His parents and teachers remind him of future responsibilities, and if he objects, they reject his objections. He is expected to be independent, take care of himself and others, and earn money. As an adolescent, a boy must make that first terrifying phone call for a date and repeat the process over and over again, leaving himself wide open to rejection.

A traditional pretty girl, like June, can marry and live happily ever after never knowing what it takes to earn a living and never experiencing rejection. Although their numbers are dramatically decreasing and the inherent risks obvious, it is still possible for a few females to live their entire lives isolated from realities males are forced to face early in life. This, however, presents other problems, as many women learn.

Self-Esteem

Bernice Malamud, assistant vice-president of The Equitable Life Assurance Society and a successful saleswoman, lived the protected life of June and Sarah for many years. She first began to question traditional female values after being forced to answer, for herself, a question many women find troubling: "Who am I?"

Each time she was asked the question, Malamud would talk about her children and her husband, never herself. Later, when she tried to answer the question for herself, she was bothered by her inability to explain her own identity. Who was she? Was she the person she wanted to be? She discovered it was very difficult to explain something you don't have, especially if you don't realize that you don't have it. No wonder it takes many women a long time to come to grips with who they are.

The Joint Commission on Mental Illness and Health twenty years ago found that a woman's self-esteem is lowered by marriage while a man's is reinforced. Marriage, however, is the vehicle, not the cause, according to the report. The cause is women's social roles.

A Woman Who "Learned" Selling Teaches Others

Carre Boyd is a Colorado woman who describes herself as "evangelical" on the subject of sales as a profession for women but admits that it wasn't always so. In fact, it would have been an insult had anybody proposed sales as a career back in her native Tennessee, where girls faded into domesticity as a life's work. She married a doctor and settled down to live out the American dream; however, life continued after "they lived happily ever after" because they didn't.

A divorce and children to support in a low-paying, dead-end, middle-management government job changed her mind about selling. She now has her own sales consulting business, Matrix Communications, and she's proud of a fistful of rave reviews from clients across the country who admit they were skeptical at first about a woman teaching men (and women) to sell. She not only teaches others how to sell, she personally sells her own services as a consultant. "When I'm not teaching sales," Boyd says, "I'm selling other clients. I eat, drink, and sleep selling, and I love it. Nothing can compare with it."

"To most women," Boyd points out, "selling is what a slick, slightly unsavory little guy does after he worms his way into our home lugging his disreputable products. With this kind of image is it any wonder that few boys, much less girls, say they want to be salespeople when they grow up? However, imagine a company without sales. Without sales there's nobody to pay salaries, no need for managers, no need for anything or anybody. Everything grinds to a halt.

"Unfortunately," Boyd continues, "there are still a lot of people who believe that salespeople are born, not made. This theory smacks of fast-talking, smooth operators dependent on force of personality and gimmicks. In conducting sales classes for many corporations, I've watched too many people develop into remarkably successful salespeople to believe in gimmicks. People develop the skills that enable them to be professional representatives, and that professionalism is the best 'gimmick' going. Effective salespeople are quickly set apart from those who give sales a bad name. Ironically, the bad press sales has had works to the advantage of the professional salesperson. And salespeople need all the advantages they can get in a world where technology makes all widgets virtually equal.

"Sales is for anybody who believes that they can learn and grow, who basically likes people, and who wants to call the shots about how much money they make and how they control their own lives," Boyd asserts. "There is *no personality type* for sales. Don't let anybody tell you there is. Some of the most successful salespeople I have known least, fit the conventional mold of what a salesperson should be. Yet when asked, most women not in sales say they could never sell. This is the intimidation of propaganda.

"If people understood that sales skills can be learned in the same way other skills are acquired, they would feel much better," Boyd concludes. "A mythology grows up around any profession that you have to turn a deaf ear to. The fact is that men or women who are successful in sales follow common guidelines whether they develop them by trial and error or they have been taught.

"If sales techniques could not be taught, why would virtually every successful company spend so much time and money training salespeople? Many things such as product knowledge are important, yet in the end it's knowing how to sell that counts more than any other single thing. The training budgets of the country's largest and most successful companies are conclusive proof that salespeople are made instead of being born."

Sales has given Boyd the challenge she needs. Looking back on her civil-service past, which she says she can barely remember because she wants to forget, she doesn't know why it took her so long to get into sales. She agrees that many women, without investigating, assume that sales is not for them because of misconceptions about sales. It took courage to go out on her own. But she decided to gamble when she took a clear look at where her government job was leading her. "I was going nowhere, but it was taking me years to get there," she laughs. "I finally figured I'd wasted enough of my life in the civil-service system, which I now call the burial ground of ambition."

Commanding a minimum fee of $600 a day with a territory stretching from Maine to California, Boyd is finally going somewhere. But she didn't begin until she discovered that for women who want to sell, there are no roadblocks except those they build themselves.

5

Advice from the Top

THE FOLLOWING chief executive officers began their
business careers in sales. From sales they were able to
rise to heights few will experience. These men have gone
all the way from the base of the business pyramid to
become chief executive officer and chairman of the
board of their companies. They have been able to fulfill
the American dream of working their way to the top.

In a personal interview with each of the four chief
executive officers, some striking similarities emerged
that might offer a clue to their success. Each

- set high goals early, and stuck to them.
- realized the value of a good general education and
thorough business preparation, although each accom-
plished this in different ways.
- stressed the value of being able to communicate
clearly and concisely, both verbally and in writing.

• saw sales as the most direct way of accomplishing his goals.

• paid his dues by learning the business step by step, succeeding first in sales, then moving up to management.

• believed that success was possible through preparation and hard work.

• was encouraged by special people who had faith in his abilities—parents, teachers, etc.

• believed in himself and was determined to succeed.

None of the four was born wealthy. In fact, the one born into the most comfortable family later became the poorest, and as a teenager supported himself and his parents.

All are enthusiastic about helping open opportunities to women and minorities and believe that women someday will be represented throughout management, that by determination, dedication, hard work, and proper preparation women will make it all the way to the top.

There Is No Battle of the Sexes

Women seeking equality have never been alone in their struggle. Throughout history, men have provided encouragement, personal support, and financial assistance to help women gain equal rights.

Unfortunately, the current controversy equality engenders seems at first glance to set up a head-to-head collision between men and women. Calling it "the battle of the sexes" reinforces the image.

Closer examination reveals that the clash is not between all men and all women but between groups from both sexes who line up on opposite sides of ideological issues. For example, as many men as women favor the proposed federal Equal Rights Amendment, while many women are against it. Celebrities like Phil Donahue and Alan Alda are feminists who actively support full equality, while women like Phyllis Schlafly campaign against equal rights. In fact, Alda and Donahue have done much to clear up the confusion over the term "feminist," which merely describes a person who believes in and works for equal rights for women.

Thousands of business executives across the country support sex equality by hiring on the basis of ability instead of sex. All saleswomen interviewed for this book described many supportive men in their lives—managers, clients, salesmen, executives, husbands, sons, and friends. Supportive executives are quick to point out that enlarging a company's talent pool by 50 percent is helpful not only to women but also to business. And hiring employees on any basis other than ability makes no business sense.

Answers to Hard Questions

The CEOs interviewed here were asked some hard questions about the future of women in sales based on how saleswomen in their organizations are currently measuring up. Are women able to compete successfully with men? Are they making it on their own or are companies providing special help in order for them to succeed? Also, if the current administration takes off the EEO compliance heat, will their companies continue to hire women? Do they believe that sales will be the same fast track for women as it has been for men? And will today's saleswomen become tomorrow's first female CEOs?

The answers to these and other questions plus the advice of the following chief executive officers supply down-to-earth, practical help for women interested in sales. Their best wishes for your success go with the advice.

*Xerox—A Company
Others Should Copy*

"I'd like to find an Equal Employment Opportunity measurement objective that Xerox could abolish, and I think the first one we could abandon would be the recruiting targets for women in our sales force."

C. Peter McColough, chief executive officer and chairman of the board of directors of the Xerox Corporation, is speaking softly, matter-of-factly, about the progress of women in sales at Xerox, a leading office-equipment manufacturing company employing 120,480 people. In front of him are charts and projections showing the measurements against the sales recruiting targets McColough personally established for the company more than a decade ago.

You might expect this electrifying announcement to appear in tomorrow morning's *New York Times*, followed immediately by angry women encircling Xerox headquarters. Is Xerox betraying its women employees? Is this a sign that women are moving in the wrong direction? Is George Gilder celebrating?

The answer is a resounding no.

"I suppose the real measure of success of an EEO target," McColough continues, "would be if we could abandon it. Because of their success, the first target we could abandon at Xerox would be women in sales. I don't think we need it anymore. Women currently make up thirty-five percent of our sales force, and I certainly expect that figure to increase to fifty percent with or without the recruiting targets."

Far from bad news, this is the kind of announcement women who seek equality in the workplace have waited years to hear. It's like being on trial for ten years and hearing the jury say you're innocent. Anytime women move into nontraditional jobs, assumptions about their biological inability to compete with men make it necessary for them to prove their worth.

Women everywhere applaud saleswomen at Xerox. McColough's announcement says that they have proved

themselves to be a financial asset rather than the
business liability skeptics predicted. It also means that
Xerox now hires women because it's good for the company, not because it's good for women, or required by
the chairman of the board, or demanded by the federal
government. It's the kind of news that squelches little
nasty rumors that women fit better on EEO forms than
into a company's sales force.

When women prove they are helping carry a company's heavy financial burdens rather than getting a
free ride because of their sex, value perceptions change
dramatically in all except a tiny minority of people
dedicated to and living in the past.

When women are good for business instead of business being good for women, it may be called good news
for women. But for business it's called the bottom line.

Xerox Opens Up Its Sales Force

Probe deeply into any company where women have
equal opportunities in nontraditional jobs and you'll
generally discover a special person at the top of the company who made it happen. Many people have the impression that a federal EEO agent is stationed outside
each executive suite counting women and minorities.
Nothing is further from the truth. Many companies are
highly successful in resisting EEO regulations and
ignoring federal laws. While the threat of federal intervention has been a motivating force in opening up jobs
for women and minorities, it is not the reason some
companies are so far ahead of others.

C. Peter McColough is the reason Xerox is ahead of
most other companies. He is the reason Xerox was one
of the first companies to open up its nontraditional
ranks to women and minorities.

More than a decade ago, McColough issued a series
of EEO executive directives. Essentially, these directives
politely suggested that Xerox managers down the line

put away the old way of doing business and give minorities and women a chance, an equal break to succeed or fail alongside white men. It was a kind of high-level soft sell. The appeal was logical, rational, and reasonable. It sounded good. The only thing wrong with it was that it didn't work.

McColough saw the handwriting on the wall. He realized that if equal opportunity at Xerox was going to succeed, it must be a business objective rather than a moral judgment by each manager. Business objectives are not optional. Managers succeed or fail in their own careers by meeting or failing to meet business objectives. This was strong stuff in those early EEO days.

When recruitment of women and minorities was written into every Xerox manager's job obligation, it leaped immediately from a low- to a high-priority status. It also got done.

For the past decade, Xerox managers have been measured on their ability to meet targeted EEO goals the same way they are measured on their ability to meet other management goals. The results are impressive. An idea that began as a failure has become a huge success, proving that in order for equal opportunity to work, commitment from the top and enforcement down the line are critical.

Xerox's EEO Philosophy

The following philosophy was developed by the company more than a decade ago and continues to be enforced by Xerox:

- There is equal opportunity in employment as well as in business transactions.
- Managers are responsible for implementing EEO policies and are held responsible for their own behavior.
- Employees may exercise their EEO rights without fear of retaliation by managers.

• A forum is provided by the company for resolving employee complaints, and management takes corrective measures whenever necessary.

Management, from top to bottom, is committed to the enforcement of a philosophy that says equal-opportunity and affirmative-action programs are two of the most significant and far-reaching business issues of the day.

It is not surprising that Xerox has made dramatic progress in increasing the proportionate representation not only of women in sales but of women and minorities throughout the company.

Xerox's CEO

During his early years in the Canadian province of Nova Scotia, C. Peter McColough hadn't the faintest idea what he wanted to be when he grew up. But he knew he wanted to be something.

Oldest of four, two boys and two girls, his world was limited by the poverty and remoteness of the area in which he grew up. His father was a Canadian government worker, and even though his family might have been considered poor by many standards, they were well off compared with the poverty surrounding them.

Encouraged and motivated early in life by a public school teacher who took a special interest in helping broaden his horizons, McColough got his goals more into focus by the time he was halfway through high school. "By that time," he said, "I realized that I needed to get a good education, work like hell, and get out of Nova Scotia."

His early blueprint for success has been fulfilled in a most ambitious way. With a law degree and a liberal arts degree from Canadian schools and an M.B.A. from Harvard Business School, he now lives in Greenwich, Connecticut, far from his native Nova Scotia. A short drive from his home brings him to a beautifully designed building in Stamford, Connecticut, headquarters of the Xerox Corporation. Here he is chief executive officer and chairman of the board of directors.

How did he reach this coveted position for which so many try but few succeed? He got out of Nova Scotia, got a good education, got into sales and marketing, and worked like hell.

A Sales and Marketing Career

During World War II, McColough served in England as an airman with the Royal Navy, then returned to Canada, where he went to Osgood Hall Law School at Toronto, Ontario, and later to Dalhousie University in Halifax. Here he received his Ll.B. degree and was admitted to the Canadian bar. However, instead of practicing law, he was interested in a business career. He entered the Harvard Graduate School of Business Administration, where he received an M.B.A. in 1949.

With this strong educational background, his rise to the top through the ranks of sales and marketing was both dramatic and direct. By the time he was forty-four, he was president and chief operating officer of Xerox.

Along the way he was vice-president of sales for the Lehigh Navigation Coal Sales Company in Philadelphia. He joined Xerox in 1954, back in the days when it was known as The Haloid Company. His first job with Xerox was general manager of the firm's first reproduction service center in Chicago.

Two years later he moved to Rochester, New York, then corporate headquarters of Xerox, as assistant to the vice-president of sales. A year later he became manager of marketing, continuing through the sales and marketing ranks to become general sales manager in 1959, and vice-president in 1960. In 1961 he became a member of the executive committee and in 1963 executive vice-president of operations.

In 1966, at the age of forty-four, just twelve years after joining the company, McColough was named president of Xerox. Two years later he was named chief executive officer, and in 1971, only seventeen years after joining the company, he was at the top of the pyramid. The long climb was over. There was no place left to go.

How did he feel about reaching the top? By the time he became chairman of the board, he felt fine. However, five years earlier, when he became president, psychologically he went through the most difficult time of his life.

Realizing it was only a matter of time before he became chairman, his satisfaction with reaching a major goal in life was coupled with a feeling of being locked into an airtight commitment to stay with the company.

"Until that time," he said, "I had never been locked into anything in my life. I had always been free to go someplace else if I wanted to. When I became president, I realized that I had made a moral commitment to stay in the company. No matter what I wanted to do, I couldn't get out of that job."

While others around him were offering congratulations for his success, little did they realize that a deep emotional reaction had set in, a reaction that often occurs when a long and difficult goal has been reached, leaving nowhere else for a competitive person to go. The race was over.

"I could make the company bigger, more successful," McColough said. "But there was no place left for me to go. I was in a deep funk for almost six months."

However, as chairman of the board and chief executive officer there are new challenges and different satisfactions. One of these for McColough has been in being in a position to ensure that women and minorities have equal opportunity at Xerox.

Perhaps there is something symbolic about closing out one race and immediately beginning another one.

Career Advice from the Top

Women interested in a sales and marketing career might do no better than follow in the footsteps of McColough. His advice resembles his own blueprint for success.

A strong believer in a liberal arts education, McColough feels that a specialization too early in a career often frustrates goals rather than helping achieve them. A good carpenter doesn't build a house until a good foundation is laid. The same is true for successful sales and marketing careers. Although McColough believes that virtually all careers would benefit by a liberal arts education, it is especially critical in sales and marketing, where verbal and writing skills are so important. Without these skills, sales and marketing careers often fail.

"I consider that my basic education was the university," McColough said. "Law school and Harvard Business School were high-level trade schools—very important, but not my basic education."

He suggests that specialized education be obtained by going to night school if a person cannot afford graduate school. However, once finished with the basic education, he strongly advises training in business subjects—accounting, economics, finance, etc.

Motivation

McColough believes that many people succeed in their careers by overcoming a handicap, be it physical, emotional, economic, racial.

"One of the best salesmen I ever knew," he said, "was a man who blinked constantly. Somebody I wouldn't have hired just by looking at him." A less determined person would have avoided a career in sales. This man, however, sought the challenge and overcame his handicap through determination and motivation to succeed.

Many successful people can recall a special person in

their lives who helped motivate them, such as Mc-Colough's teacher back in the Halifax public schools. Although he was one child in a crowded class of forty-five, this teacher sought him out, talked to him about the world outside—the League of Nations, politics, government, ideas. Great teachers are forever searching for promising students. The story in *How Green Was My Valley* is as old as civilization itself, with each generation repeating the process. It is perhaps the only real immortality.

When McColough hears young people talking about pursuing happiness as if happiness was the only thing that counts, he feels they are talking nonsense. "Happiness is a byproduct," he says. "It comes from other pursuits.

"What is important," he says, "is to do whatever you do, well; to be the best you can at whatever you choose. If you want to be a teacher, be a good one; if a priest, be a good one." Be motivated by excellence.

"Everything we have in life has come from somebody who was motivated," said McColough. "Electric lights, medicine, music—it all came from somebody who really cared." Through the pursuit of excellence people often find that elusive byproduct they never find by pursuing it alone—happiness.

Sales Success Characteristics

To succeed in sales requires a combination of characteristics. Failure requires only one. McColough believes that the prime cause of failure among salespeople is not asking for the order.

No matter how well you know your product, how good your presentation, you must overcome any hesitation or discomfort in asking for the order when the time arrives. No timid soul who hesitantly suggests that a customer might like to call later will succeed. A salesperson must be more aggressive than this.

McColough feels there are three basic success factors critical to a salesperson's career:

- Selling good products
- Knowing your products
- Asking for the order

Other, less tangible factors yet very important, include the following:

- *Liking people.* Trite as it may sound, McColough says, a salesperson must like people, want to be with them, and enjoy the selling process.
- *Confidence.* Nobody can sell to another person without first having confidence in his or her ability to sell. Confidence in yourself inspires confidence from others.
- *A good presentation.* Know your product and the needs of your customer, and how they fit together. Also, be able to communicate the benefits to your customer.
- *Intelligence.* A salesperson's job involves many factors. Product knowledge is often technical and can be quite complicated. Putting together the needs of the customer with the benefits of your product requires enough intelligence to understand reasonably complicated concepts. While you don't have to be an Einstein, alertness and intelligence are important.
- *Aggressiveness.* You must be able to assert yourself in a positive way and be aggressive enough to ask for the order.
- *Management qualities.* Executives are always on the lookout for alert, motivated, successful salespeople to promote into management. Corporations are like large families. Jobs are handed down from generation to generation, and the older members of the family devote much of their declining years to replacing themselves.

If you're looking to go all the way to the top, your

success in sales and marketing can make you a marked person—marked for success in management. The earlier you get that executive tap on your shoulder, the more likely you'll be to make it all the way to the top.

Sales Training at Xerox

When a woman is hired as a sales trainee by the Xerox Corporation, she is treated exactly the same as a male sales trainee. She takes the same courses, gets the same basic training.

The training begins at the local branch level where the new trainee will be working, followed by a more intensive training period at the Xerox training center in Leesburg, Virginia. The next step, again back at the branch level, will be actual sales calls on which the trainee is accompanied by a sales professional. Finally, the trainees become full-fledged sales representatives, out on their own.

Job measurement also is the same for men and women. All are expected to achieve the set quotas for various territories—the same quotas for women as for men.

There are successes and failures of both men and women. Although the success rate of women is not separately tracked, McColough says he has a general feeling that women, if there is any difference, have a slightly higher success rate. Often he discovers, in traveling to various branches, that half the top producers are women, even though they make up only 35 percent of the sales force.

He attributes this to the company's ability to hire from a large pool of highly qualified women—a pool, incidentally, created by their exclusion from other sales forces. Since Xerox began hiring women early, the company was able to attract better candidates. News of equal opportunity travels fast.

Success at Xerox

In 1971, several years after McColough issued those
first EEO directives, women made up only 1.4 percent
of the Xerox sales force, certainly not an impressive accomplishment. However, after the EEO objectives
became part of overall management goals, results as
shown below were dramatic. Four years later, the overall percentage had leaped to 12.9 percent, and by 1980
women made up 35.5 percent of the sales force.

Women as a percentage of Xerox
overall sales force
(not including management)

1971	1.4%
1975	12.9%
1976	19.8%
1977	22.3%
1978	29.2%
1979	32.8%
1980	35.5%

The percentage of women in sales management positions also has increased dramatically. By 1980, women
in sales management made up 16.3 percent of the 35.5
percent of women in the overall sales force. Of this 16.3
percent total, 11.1 percent are sales managers, while the
remaining 5.1 percent are in other sales management
positions.

The Future of Women at Xerox

If every federal law and EEO regulation were rescinded
by the current administration, EEO and affirmative-
action programs would continue at Xerox, McColough
says emphatically. And although Xerox could abolish
the EEO objectives for women in sales, McColough
believes the opposite is true for women in management.
  "We have not broken the back of the problem yet,"

he says. "Both women and men need to get over the feeling that women couldn't or shouldn't go all the way to the top."

Although women currently face roadblocks in becoming CEO of Xerox, he feels someday there will be a woman sitting at his desk. He wonders what will happen over the next century. Will 50 percent of the heads of companies be women? Will 12 percent be black? Nobody can answer these questions. There remain great handicaps for women to overcome. However, if you're a woman who's determined to go all the way to the top, remember the salesman with the blinking problem. When you believe that no fence can be built high enough to hold you back, none will.

Women everywhere share in the success of the saleswomen at the Xerox Corporation and congratulate its chairman, C. Peter McColough, for proving that the free-enterprise system can indeed be free.

The fight for women's equality is a very old fight with a long way to go. It would make the journey shorter if only women could find a way to "Xerox" Xerox's chief executive officer and chairman of the board.

A Man Changes His Mind

An important executive of one of the country's major corporations refused to hire saleswomen in his company and wasn't the slightest bit hesitant about making the edict public. And as if this weren't outrageous enough, he topped himself by refusing to hire salesmen whose wives were employed.

Now consider the second half of this improbable tale.

The NOW Legal Defense and Education Fund, a group that has repeatedly gone to court to establish and protect women's employment rights and part of the country's largest feminist organization—the National Organization for Women—gave the same man a special award at a star-studded banquet in New York City. Calling him "a spiritual godfather," several hundred leading feminists honored him. Among other superlatives describing him was this one: "When the history of the modern struggle for equal opportunity for women is finally written, you will be forever honored for your commitment to principle and your courage and leadership during the years when many businessmen were practicing delay, resistance, and caution."

As you might suspect, several years intervened between these two events; however, not as many as you might expect based on the historical progress of women. The time span was less than a quarter century, a mere third of the time it took for women to get the vote and less than half the time since the Equal Rights Amendment was first introduced in Congress. Contrary to the way it might seem, this man is not a slow learner. Since that day when he issued his own unequal employment policy, he has traveled full circle to become one of the best friends of women seeking equality.

Coy Eklund

Coy Eklund, chairman of the board and chief executive officer of The Equitable Life Assurance Society, is the first to tell this story about himself. He repeated it the evening he received the LDEF EEO award in order to illustrate not how far women have come, but how far one man has come in changing his perceptions about women.

"It shows interesting psychological development in a human being," Eklund said. "Luckily, we have the capacity to change." The fact that he has changed is indeed fortunate for women.

Agency Manager

Back when Eklund was an ambitious Equitable agency manager in Detroit, Michigan, eager to make a name for himself by building a first-rate sales force, the thought never entered his mind that any married woman would choose to work outside her home. Instead, he sincerely believed that any woman who worked was to be pitied. It was proof that she had erred in her choice of a mate because she obviously was married to an ineffective, unaggressive breadwinner who wasn't trying hard enough to live up to his sex-assigned role. It followed that no ambitious sales manager wanted that kind of a second-rater mixed in with the top-producing sales force Eklund was trying to build.

"I didn't want to hire any weaklings," Eklund said. "If a man's wife had to work, it was a sign the guy wasn't measuring up to his responsibilities in life."

Years later, when Eklund learned that 30 percent of all married women were in the labor force, he clung to his feelings about "proper" roles. He was shocked that so many married women were forced to work, surprised that men in such large numbers hadn't the ambition to support the women they had promised to care for.

"I thought all those women were out there helping that poor guy who couldn't make a living for them," he says, laughing now.

Perceptions Change

In the early 1960s, Eklund's perceptions about women and employment began to change. Progressing rapidly in his own career, he was now a vice-president of The Equitable. Around this time he hired a Rutgers University sociology professor to investigate developments in the country relevant to the future of the insurance business.

The professor kept talking to Eklund about women. He saw the women's movement as an enormously important sociological factor in the country's future. He tracked women's changing roles and rapid movement into the labor force.

"Women, Coy, women," the professor would say. "You're going to have to hire great numbers of women and advance them to positions of authority." The figures were there to prove the new sociological phenomenon. A million women a year were entering the labor market. A few years later those figures would increase by another half million. Periodic predictions of a slowdown didn't stem the tide. The impact on the insurance business—and all business—would be immense. The professor's words were prophetic. Nothing again would ever be the same. It was becoming evident that not all those women in the labor force had a gun to their heads. As options opened up, huge numbers were choosing to work. This fact could no longer be denied.

Changes in the Insurance Business

Before the women's movement, it was common in the insurance business for an agent to ask a woman on the other end of a telephone, "Lady, is your husband home?" That changed rapidly as a new and potentally powerful women's market began to emerge, created by so many millions of new paychecks. Other things changed in the insurance business. Coy Eklund was one of them.

"Just think of it," Eklund says, remembering his earlier feelings. "More than fifty percent of all married women and virtually all single women are now working."

Finally, Eklund's opinion of husbands improved as his perceptions of women's attitudes about employment changed. He reasoned that there couldn't be that many slothful males out there refusing to support their wives. Women must be choosing to work. And if they were choosing to work, why hadn't they done so before? Did their working have a connection to a women's movement that demanded full equality? Had women been kept at home through discrimination? Had discrimination been around for centuries?

These and other thought-provoking questions were openly debated during those early days as sex discrimination began to be clearly outlined and equality in the workplace became the main bread-and-butter issue. No single previous decade had ever produced such economic and sociological changes as the 1970s.

A Changed Man

Early in the 1970s, Coy Eklund became an active supporter of full equality for women. When Mary Jean Tully, an early NOW Legal Defense and Education Fund president who built it into an effective organization, first came to Eklund she was pleasantly surprised. "He was one of the first chief executive officers to support the fund," she said. "That really meant a lot during those early days when few executives, much less chief executive officers, wanted to talk to me. At that time, it took real courage. In the entire country, Coy was the second chief executive officer of a major American corporation to support the fund."

Nobody could be more enthusiastic about women working than Coy Eklund today. His original feelings, like those of so many men, stemmed from kind motives. Since he, as a man, had accepted the breadwinner role in life and worked hard supporting a wife and children, why couldn't other men do the same?

Eklund began to change as he realized that many women, just like men, work for more than financial security. He began to understand that the satisfaction he felt in his work is not reserved for males only. And he began to understand that ambition and aggressiveness are not exclusively male traits.

Beyond this, Eklund also began to realize that millions of women are the sole support of their families through divorce or the death of their husbands. These women are the only breadwinners standing between millions of children and hunger. In fact, more than 2 million women are the sole support of disabled husbands as well as their children. For them and many other women, there is no choice to work or not to work. The idea that all women are lovingly taken care of by men is a Victorian wish, not a fact. To need a job desperately in order to support your family and be denied one because a nonexistent man is supposed to be caring for you is a cruel hoax. In addition, for men to have the right to choose a life's work but to deny women that choice is another hoax.

Realities like these changed the mind of Coy Eklund as they have changed the minds of many other well-meaning and considerate men. However, even back in those dark days in Detroit, anybody who bothered to check out Eklund's background would have bet on him to be a man who would change his mind about women. It was in the cards.

After all, any man who grew up poor, lived in the backwoods, helped his family earn a living, sat on the lap of Chief Beargrease, was an early supporter of blacks, feels great empathy for Hispanics, and cautions you not to forget Asian-Americans, would sooner or later support equal rights for women. It just had to happen. And it did.

As Eklund says, "Equality commitment is a slippery slope. If you're for it, there's no stopping place; you've got to go all the way."

Growing Up in Minnesota

Coy Eklund is the first generation of the Eklunds to be born in this country. His Swedish grandfather came to America when Eklund's father was two years old, homesteading in northern Minnesota, where life for the early Swedish settlers was as bitter as the winters.

Eklund's father played with Indian children, teaching them Swedish and learning Chippewa in exchange. When he learned English in the first grade, it was his third language.

Like their father, Eklund and his younger brother grew up along the same riverbank in the backwoods of Minnesota. One of Eklund's classmates was Nancy

Beargrease. Eklund vividly recalls sitting on her grand-father's knee—Chief Beargrease. "I can see him right now in my mind's eye," Eklund says. "Chief Beargrease holding me on his knee on his one hundredth birthday. We were sitting in our dining room. I was only seven years old at the time."

The Eklund family was hard pressed to eke out a living in the backwoods. They were always poor. Once they lived in a tarpaper shack. "We actually lived in the woods," Eklund says. "It was not a farm. A farm would have been much more civilized."

The Eklund home had none of the modern comforts people today take for granted. A woodburning stove provided heat, but only after trees were felled and turned into firewood by human effort. A great deal of Eklund's childhood was spent chopping wood and doing other chores. In addition he learned to hunt and fish and become self-supporting. Life was hard. Parents worked. Children worked, hunted, and trapped. Survival was everybody's job.

Eklund's mother had great influence on his career. She taught him by word and deed to be considerate of others, and she constantly urged him to get an education. "Go to college, go to college," she would repeat. Once when he had carried an armful of wood into the kitchen, she told him, "Coy, I have the feeling that you're going to be very successful someday—and you're going to make a lot of money."

A Sales Career Begins

Eklund became an insurance agent for The Equitable in 1938 after counseling with an Equitable agent to whom he had sold aluminum pots and pans a few years before. The agent at that time had proposed an interesting idea. He agreed to buy the entire set of pots and pans if Eklund would buy an insurance policy in return. They struck a deal. Three years later Coy asked the same agent to help him get into The Equitable.

Except for four years in the army during World War II, Eklund has remained continuously at The Equitable. During the war he advanced to the rank of lieutenant colonel on Gen. George Patton's staff, was awarded five battle stars, and was decorated with the Croix de Guerre by Gen. Charles de Gaulle. A graduate of Michigan State University, he had taken his mother's advice and gone to college, dropping out once because his money ran out. But he went back.

Sales wasn't exactly new to him. His family, poor as they were, always ran some kind of little store. "We sold candy, pop, bananas, canned goods, anything we could get our hands on," said Eklund. Behind the counter of the tiny store, Eklund's father taught him how to wait on customers. His father was meticulous. It had to be done just right. You had to identify with the customer, know his or her needs and fulfill them. You have to have empathy and want to help the customer. Eklund never forgot.

Women in Sales

Eklund has high praise for The Equitable's women agents. They have proved that they have what it takes to sell insurance. Twenty-five percent of Equitable's new agents are women, up from 2 percent eight years ago. In addition there are now sixty women officers in the company and four women on the board of directors. Equitable is one of the few companies with a female executive vice-president in a line job next to the top.

"Women are just as aggressive, hardworking, and ambitious as men," Eklund says. "In addition, it seems that most women are able to demonstrate empathy—to sense what people are concerned about. And that's what it takes to be an effective salesperson."

Eklund's Fast Track

Back in that Detroit agency, Eklund was determined to develop a first-rate sales force. In only twelve years he built it into the second-largest agency in the company. He was elected vice-president in 1959 and then moved to agency vice-president, senior vice-president, executive vice-president, and, in 1973, president. He became chief executive officer April 1, 1975. From a tarpaper shack to an impressive private office on New York City's Avenue of the Americas is a distance few have traveled.

Convinced that women want to be in the labor force, Eklund made changes faster and farther at a time when it counted most, when the changes might have meant a financial risk. He brushes aside any suggestion of those early risks. "We are getting, not giving, in hiring women in sales and throughout the company," he says. "I have seen The Equitable enjoy a prestige and a corporate financial advantage in the marketplace because of the increasing numbers of women and minorities in management and throughout the company. I believe that a large corporation like The Equitable can be and should be helpful in the process of social improvement for the people of this country. It has been good for business."

Regardless of what happens to dilute equal-employment enforcement in Washington, says Eklund, The Equitable will aggressively continue hiring and advancing women and minorities in all parts of the company.

Would Eklund be happy if his daughter became chief executive officer of a company someday? You bet he would. He'd even go farther. He would credit her with the effort instead of blaming her husband for not living up to his provider role in life.

Will women continue their economic progress and will a woman someday become CEO of The Equitable? "Yes," says Eklund. "It's inevitable. She may not follow me directly, but it's going to happen. The day of debating that possibility is gone. Women will move to the top of everything. The force behind women in the marketplace will move on irresistibly. It is in motion.''

Women will long remember that Coy Eklund helped put it into motion.

Sales and Marketing in Television

Thirty years ago a poor but ambitious young man who came to America to escape Nazi extermination watched intently as throngs of fascinated people stood for hours staring at test patterns on strange boxlike objects in department store windows.

Ralph M. Baruch believed that he was witnessing the birth of a very large and important new American industry. He made up his mind, as he watched, to search for a way to get in on the ground floor of this emerging phenomenon. Sales and marketing became his route into an important new American industry: television.

Thirty years later, after moving up the ladder through a succession of sales and marketing positions, Baruch is now chief executive officer and chairman of the board of Viacom International, Inc. Viacom is the world's largest syndicator of television programs. A CBS spin-off a decade ago, today it is a thriving, diversified communications and entertainment company.

Viacom owns and operates cable television systems and television and radio stations, provides entertainment services for pay television, and distributes television programs and motion pictures to networks and stations worldwide, in addition to developing and producing programming for all media.

Thirty years ago, when Baruch predicted the vast potential of television, he had no idea he would be heading up an industry with even greater potential. Viacom's revenues and total assets have grown explosively in the last decade, yet the growth potential remains high in a new high-technology industry.

Baruch's rapid and fascinating rise in sales and

marketing to chief executive officer and chairman of the board is rivaled only by the drama of his personal life story—a story that could be a movie in the industry in which he has spent most of his life. Baruch's life is a testimonial to courage, motivation, determination, and survival.

It also emphasizes the advantages of selecting the sales and marketing career that made his Horatio Alger story possible.

Baruch's Early Life

Ralph Baruch was born in Germany in 1923, the second son of a prominent lawyer and his wife. Because of growing anti-Semitism, the Baruch family fled Germany in 1933, settling in Paris, where the elder Baruch continued practicing law.

The family lived a comfortable life in Paris, marred only by the accidental death of their eldest son, which left Ralph Baruch an only child. In France, Baruch attended his first year of premedical school at the Sorbonne. As an only child, he received just about anything from his parents he wanted including his own sports car. He looked forward to a comfortable life. Fate had other plans.

In 1940, Baruch's father, a member of the French intelligence service, brought home the news that the family once again must flee for their lives. France was no longer safe from the Nazi advance. Leaving behind their possessions and comfortable life, Baruch, his father, mother, and eighty-two-year-old grandmother began a four-month journey through the mountains to Spain. Baruch literally carried his grandmother most of the journey. During the long and dangerous trip, the family's survival was constantly at stake. Hunted by the Nazis, the small group was bombed from the air and machined-gunned from the ground. It was a horrendous journey, but somehow they managed to survive. Visas to America were provided by the International Rescue

Committee, an organization on whose board of directors Baruch now serves.

Although he was safe and settled in America, the comfortable life Baruch had enjoyed his first eighteen years would not be duplicated for many years. In a new land, with both his mother and father seriously ill, the financial burden of supporting the family fell to Baruch. He got a job as a shipping clerk in a shoe factory at $14 a week, not enough to provide a basic existence. He supplemented his meager earnings by working weekends as a theater usher.

His dreams of becoming a doctor vanished forever. Higher education was impossible. However, Baruch was getting a different kind of education, which would be valuable to him in later years. He learned to appreciate what it is like to work hard for a living and how it feels to be poor. As a Jew he understood discrimination. Now he understood the combination of discrimination and poverty, a lesson he would not forget when he was in a position to help those less fortunate.

Highly motivated to improve his life but not knowing what direction to take, Baruch scraped together enough hard-earned money to pay for an aptitude test, which took him a full day to complete. He longed for the test's results to reveal that he should become a great writer or producer—even an advertising director. Instead came the blunt, brief pronouncement: This young man should go into sales and marketing.

He had paid dearly for the advice. He decided to take it.

The Rise to the Top

Baruch, like most people who rise to the top through sales and marketing, held a series of different selling jobs. He sold transcription libraries to radio stations for a music licensing company. He landed a job with the Dumont Television Network, selling time to local stations at a salary of $75 a week plus 1 percent commissions. He worked for a television production distribution organization owned by the *Los Angeles Times*.

Finally, in 1954 he joined the CBS sales force. It was a partnership that would last. At CBS he rapidly moved up the sales and marketing ranks to head of a division, after which he became group president shortly before Viacom was created. Poverty behind him, Baruch was happily married and the father of four young children. Fate had been good to him, and he was grateful.

However, in a life filled with drama, tragedy struck once again. Baruch's wife died, leaving him alone with four small daughters.

He kept his family together the best he could. But it was not easy to supervise the care of his children while concentrating on a difficult and competitive career. Yet nothing had been easy for Baruch since he was eighteen years old.

His daughters, determined individuals like their father, are now grown with careers of their own. Their proud father, now remarried, lists their accomplishments: one a college teacher, one a lawyer, one a Ph.D. in anatomy, and one a graduate student studying international relations. The daughter with a Ph.D. in anatomy is also fulfilling dual ambitions, her own plus an earlier ambition of her father's. She entered Columbia University School of Medicine in the fall of 1981.

In 1971, Viacom was created with Baruch its first president and chief executive officer. In 1978 he became chairman of the board.

A Self-Taught Salesman

Baruch learned selling the hard way, through trial and error. Self-taught, he learned through his own mistakes what works and what doesn't. A keen observer, he developed his own philosophy along the way.

"You have to figure out the mentality of that person facing you across the desk," Baruch says. "The customer facing you doesn't care who you are or what you are. The customer is only interested in what you can do for him or her.''

Baruch realized early in his selling career that there is no pat sales system that will work like magic on every customer. Even though a salesperson may have a broad overall approach, the specifics must be fine-tuned for each customer, each sales call.

"I've seen salespeople who treat everybody the same," Baruch says. "But it doesn't work. You must figure out each person and change your approach to fit the customer's needs."

Baruch explains how, early in his sales career with CBS, he learned a valuable lesson when he called on a Scranton, Pennsylvania, television station in his territory. On his first customer call he discovered that his predecessor hadn't made a personal call in more than a year and had made up customer reports out of whole cloth. Baruch decided on a different approach. After receiving a great deal of personal attention, the station became one of his best accounts. Nothing can replace personal service and integrity in selling. Baruch decided his predecessor, had he been able to figure it out, was cheating himself. Baruch had no intention of following suit.

Baruch also cites an example of a Viacom salesman in a western state who embodies the qualities valuable in sales. This man, calling on the new and inexperienced owner of a television station, was asked for programming suggestions to fill a time slot requiring two programs. Instead of recommending two Viacom programs, which the station manager expected, the salesman suggested that a Viacom program be combined with a competitor's program.

"Why not two Viacom programs?" asked the new owner.

The salesman was blunt but honest. "Because I think it would be a programming disaster," he said.

Over the advice of the salesman, the new owner put in two Viacom programs. It was a disaster. Now the station owner won't make a programming move without the advice of the Viacom salesman.

The moral of the story, as Baruch points out, is that a good salesperson will recognize the difference between short-term gains and long-term goals. This Viacom salesman had the best interests of his client at heart. Instead of selling him a maximum order—which many salespeople would do—this salesman was interested in a long-term relationship. To achieve the goal, the product had to succeed. The salesman realized that the more successful his customer became, the more Viacom programs he would be able to afford to buy in the future. A good salesperson, Baruch points out, has a stake in the customer's success.

Now trusted and respected, this salesman is regularly invited to the owner's home for dinner to discuss programming. The salesman has become good friends with his customer, something that often happens in selling. It is a natural consequence in a relationship that requires the same ingredients—trust and integrity. Without trust and integrity there can be no long-term friendship; without trust and integrity there will be no long-term selling.

Unfortunately, the image of sales as a profession has been tarnished by the fast-talking huckster often portrayed as the "typical" salesperson. While there are salespeople who fit this image, their sales behavior is not professional.

"Fifty percent of the people in sales should be selling papers on the street or shining shoes. Or they should have become doctors and lawyers," says Baruch. "They may be selling, but they are not professional salespeople."

Make Your Sales Career
the First Step to Management

All too often, Baruch believes, people move up through the ranks of sales into management with little thought or preparation for it. To a greater degree than most people think, however, the direction of one's business life can be self-directed and not left to chance, Baruch believes. He suggests keeping as much control as possible.

"If you believe that sales leads to management as I do," he says, "get an education in those business areas you will need to know—business in general and business finance in particular.

"Sooner or later you're going to be faced with the problem of laying out a sale for a customer who will want to know, 'What is this going to cost and how will I recover my investment?' "

He believes that a thorough background in business management is useful in getting into sales and invaluable later as you go up the ranks into management.

"In the communications industry," Baruch says, "I see many sales executives who graduated into management through the Peter Principle—people who haven't a clue about finances, structures, responsibilities, communications, or business in general.

"If you ask the average salesperson, or even many sales executives, 'What's an ROI?' (return on investment), many won't know. Even those who know are often vague. Give them a set of numbers and ask what the ROI will be on a ten-year basis. They won't be able to figure it out. A sales executive must be able to sell on that basis. You need to know what this is all about if you have your eye on management."

Baruch believes that executives, as well as people just beginning their careers, should continue learning in their jobs. He mentions a seminar on new technology that he plans to attend the following week.

"Why would I do that?" he asks. "It's obvious that I can go further in this job."

The reason he's going to the seminar, he points out, is in order to help him do his job better. "When you've stopped learning in your job," Baruch says, "give up."

Baruch suggests that if you are interested in a sales career that leads to the top, study economics, accounting, business management, and finance. Get an M.B.A. at night if you can't afford full-time graduate studies.

Prepare yourself to take advantage of any opportunity to move up into management.

"I did it the hard way," Baruch said.

You, however, don't have to do it the hard way.

Women in Sales and Marketing

Baruch advises women interested in sales and marketing to try to get into the new and emerging technologies. He feels they are less resistant to women in nontraditional jobs than older, more established companies.

He understands the discrimination that women must battle all of their working lives, especially those who compete directly with men—the lingering feelings that women can't make it in tough, demanding jobs. He has seen firsthand how businesswomen pose a threat to many men. He believes that many men who are fearful of women in business harbor deep hostile feelings, that deep down inside they don't like women.

However, Baruch advises women to persist in sales and marketing, triumphing over the obstacles. Prove what you can do for a company, and you will eventually succeed. "Women must not feel that they are any different in pursuing sales and marketing careers than men, because they are not," Baruch cautions. "In many cases women are better and will work harder to succeed than men."

Baruch recalls the inherent discrimination in the comments of many people when his fourth child, another daughter, was born. Many friends expressed sympathy instead of congratulations over an event he did not consider a tragedy. "I never cared what sex my children were as long as they were healthy," he says. Yet people refused to believe this. They felt he was trying to make the best of a bad situation. The assumption that boys are more valuable than girls is deeply rooted in most of the world. The same friends would not have viewed a fourth son the same way.

Women at Viacom

Not long after Viacom was created, Baruch attended the first management meeting of the company's cable TV business. In a group of eighty employees, only two or three were women. "I was appalled," says Baruch, "when women make up more than fifty percent of the population."

After making known the equal-employment-opportunity objectives for the company, Baruch attended the same group's management meeting in 1981. Things had changed. More than 40 percent were women.

"Commitment in hiring women must come from the top," Baruch says. "Line management must be pushed; however, progressive new executives are emerging who recognize there is no difference in hiring women than in hiring men. The only important question is, 'Can the person do the job?'"

Baruch feels that hiring women in Viacom has been good business. It will continue regardless of current federal policies to relax enforcement. Women are in sales and marketing jobs throughout the company—they are selling radio and television time, programs, and services in all areas of Viacom. Women are also moving up in management, although not as fast.

"I would love to see a woman become divisional president and be in line for my job," says Baruch. "And it will happen."

Asked if he would be pleased if one of his daughters became chief executive officer of a company, he is quick to reply. Reflecting the soundness of his advice about women looking toward the new technologies for the best opportunities and the least resistance from men, particularly men at the top, he answers, "Certainly. Why wouldn't I be pleased?"

Early in the women's movement, feminists began to realize that a man who is the father of intelligent, ambitious daughters is quicker to understand discrimination against all women and, if in a position to do so, is more likely to give other women equal opportunities.

Ralph Baruch, chief executive officer and chairman of the board of a new, emerging-technology company in television, does little to disprove this point. In fact, he seems about four times as aware as most executives of the subtle and overt discrimination that women face in their careers. And he seems about four times as determined to do something about it in his company.

A Salesman
Grows in Brooklyn

Earl Graves, publisher of *Black Enterprise* magazine, came up through sales and marketing, but he did it the way the founders of the Industrial Revolution did it: outside a corporation. First he got the experience, then he created a corporation. Today Graves heads six corporations, thanks to the remarkable ability, dynamic personality, and determination that have characterized his life. There have been times when he was down, but Earl Graves has never been out.

Earl Graves is a black man whose success is an inspiration to everyone, no matter what sex, color, or race. He is a man who bet on himself and won when the odds were against him.

It is a simple fact of life that to be born black in America loads the odds against you. To be black and poor, like Graves, increases the odds. If you happen to be black and poor and female, the odds against your success increase proportionately. Black women are at the very bottom of the economic pyramid.

Earl Graves's route to success can provide some special insights to black women. While understanding fully the hostile world around him, Graves kept control of his life every step of the way. He set goals and stuck to them. He didn't wait around for others to make things happen for him. He made them happen for himself.

Each individual has the potential to turn his or her life around. A determined person like Graves—black or white, male or female—is very difficult to stop. Success creates success if you have a goal and don't allow yourself to be distracted. In accomplishing his goals, Graves never allowed his anger with the white establishment to trip him up. He used his anger in the most constructive way it can be used—as fuel to propel him up and into a better life where he had a fighting chance of helping eliminate the prejudice that has held blacks back for centuries.

Black women, combatting both sex and race discrimination, have had the toughest tasks in overcoming obstacles to success. Nothing has ever been easy for black women. In addition to surviving emotionally and economically in a hostile world, black women have provided enormous support for others. Throughout generations of unique hardships, black women have been strong individuals. Yet instead of being praised for such a desirable quality, their strength has frequently been compared unfavorably to the culturally induced dependency of white females.

An Early Starter

It's small wonder that Earl Graves is the consummate salesperson. He started early and never slowed down. Back in Brooklyn, when he was five years old, he sold seventy-five boxes of Christmas cards at a dollar a box. His territory, however, posed a confining handicap for the young salesman to overcome. His mother wouldn't let him cross the street. He made up for this disadvantage by selling harder to the people he was able to reach on his block.

Graves has crossed many streets since that time, but he's still selling harder to those he is able to reach. With his magazine, *Black Enterprise*, he is able to reach much farther than he ever dreamed possible, to more than a million readers.

Other things have happened to him since he sold his way to success back in Brooklyn, in college, and beyond. For example, he was named one of the ten most outstanding businessmen in the country. The president of the United States presented him with the National Award of Excellence in 1972. His name is listed in *Who's Who in America*, and *Time* magazine named him one of the two hundred future leaders of the country.

He now heads six corporations, including one in broadcasting, all spinoffs of Earl G. Graves, Ltd. His life-style has also changed dramatically. From his two floors of offices on Madison Avenue in New York City, he travels to his large home on five acres in one of the most expensive suburbs in Westchester County, New York. He serves on boards of directors of major corporations, and his phone calls are answered by the powerful people in this country.

Graves's success, however, hasn't gone to his head. Just because he's successful, he hasn't forgotten where he came from or where his people still are. He uses his magazine to sell social progress and to sell other blacks on the idea of becoming successful entrepreneurs like himself. Although he doesn't take credit for it, there are now four times as many black entrepreneurs in this country as when Graves began publishing his magazine. The magazine constantly features successful blacks and how they made it. Special issues are devoted each year to "Careers and Opportunities," "Money Management," and "Be 100," the one hundred most successful black businesses in the country. The difference between fighting for blacks now and twenty years ago is that today Graves is more effective. People listen to him.

His advice to his eldest son, a Yale University student, is good advice for all black youths. "When you're black in America," he says, "you don't have time for the frivolous things white kids can afford to spend their time doing."

Getting a good education and getting into sales has been the way out of poverty for Graves. It can do the same for others, both black and white.

Delivering Two Messages in One Telegram

As he was growing up, Graves worked at anything he could get. He was always on the lookout for a new job. As a teenager, he delivered telegrams. It didn't take him long to figure out that a pleasant attitude and a big smile brought a bigger tip than an impersonal approach. If he rang an apartment in one of New York's tall buildings and a voice said, "I'll come down," Graves would reply, "No, I'll come up." In addition, he made sure he always had a pen ready in case the person needed to sign. He suggested he hoped the telegram wouldn't bring bad news. His attitude said he cared. People responded.

Without being too obvious, Graves didn't allow anybody to lose sight of what was important to him—his tips. When absentminded people forgot his tip, he found ways to remind them. If nothing subtle worked, he jingled some change in his pocket. "That was my hard sell," Graves laughs.

Graves grew up in a poor household, the eldest of four children. Although his father earned little money, he always had a job and a roof over his head. The family never went hungry, but neither were there any luxuries. In poor families children are expected to contribute. When Graves worked, he always gave part of his earnings to the family. When he decided he wanted to go to Morgan State University in Baltimore, Maryland, he knew he would have to pay his own way. In addition, however, while he worked to save money for college, he still contributed part of his earnings to help support the family.

Selling His Way through College

When Graves left for Morgan State, he had only enough money to pay for one semester's tuition, with enough left over for train fare. Traveling through segregated Delaware, where blacks at that time couldn't even stop and buy a cup of coffee, he wondered how he would earn the rest of his tuition for three and a half years. How large the world must have looked. How small he must have felt. Somehow, though, he would make it all happen. He had faith in himself.

He made it happen through his ability to sell. He offered to become the campus sales representative for two florists eager for college business. One florist was at first reluctant to sign on. When he asked Graves how he could tell which customers were from Graves, the reply was, "If they're black, they're mine." The florist balked. Graves took his sales rep idea down the street to a competing florist. The first one signed up quickly after watching his competitor's business flourish.

In the flower business, Graves suffered his first business reversal. With thousands of dollars at stake in expected orders for flowers for a homecoming football game, the college kids got militant and boycotted the game. The florists and their sales rep lost their shirts. Graves, however, learned a valuable lesson: The constant business companion of an entrepreneur is risk.

Down but not out, Graves looked for new opportunities. He noticed the neat brick row of houses near the college campus and noted the green grass, particularly the lawns that needed cutting. The fact that he was black and the people in the row of houses were white didn't stop him. He made up a flyer advertising his newly thought-up lawn-cutting business, personally distributing two hundred throughout the neighborhood. Expecting, at the most, three or four jobs, he signed up almost fifty customers—so many that he had to hire friends to help him fulfill his contracts.

Soon the white homeowners began asking him questions about various gardening problems. He saw another sales opportunity and went into the gardening consulting business. Whatever they wanted to know, he would go back to the college, find out the information, and sell it to the customers.

"Actually, the whole thing showed the racism of

white America," Graves says. "The whites saw a black guy and assumed that I knew everything about gardening. They probably thought I'd been picking cotton. They didn't know I was from Brooklyn. If I'd seen cotton I'd probably have thought it was snow."

Regardless of his private thoughts, he didn't allow the opinions of his customers to interfere with his sales venture. He learned that in order to do business with people, they don't have to look like you, think like you, or even like you. It would have helped neither his poverty nor their attitude had he told them off. He later would be in a much better position to do that from a much better vantage point—as the publisher of a magazine reaching a million readers.

Commitment to Sales

By the time he was a sophomore in college, Graves knew that he wanted to go into sales. He wanted an occupation that would not limit him twenty years into the future. Attending a lecture on marketing and compensation given by a real estate broker, he came away fascinated with the amount of money it was possible to make selling real estate. The broker suggested that most good salespeople would be able to sell two houses a month. Graves figured if most could sell two houses, he could sell three. With a 5 percent commission on a $20,000 house, that would be $3,000 a month, a very impressive figure to him at that time.

When he graduated from college, however, opportunities for blacks—in sale as well as everything else— were few and far between. No sales recruiters from corporations canvassed his campus. He had few options, and he needed a job immediately. His choices, as he saw them, were to become a teacher earning about $6,000 a year, work for the Social Security Administration earning $5,000 a year, or enlist in the army. He chose the last, volunteering for the toughest assignments. He became a first lieutenant, getting valuable leadership experience. But when his hitch was over, he did not reenlist.

Recalling that real estate lecture back in college, Graves began selling real estate in Brooklyn but left to become a narcotics agent for the Justice Department, where he first met Sen. Robert Kennedy. After working for the government a year, however, Graves went back to real estate, where he became manager of the firm's Bedford-Stuyvesant office earning $15,000 a year.

Graves had begun to be active in local Brooklyn politics when he was asked to organize one of five Christmas parties for Robert Kennedy to be held in New York City's five boroughs. The Brooklyn party was a huge success, while the other four were near disasters. Kennedy discovered why the Brooklyn party was a success. It was Graves. Four months later Graves was working for Robert Kennedy as a political organizer. He remained with the senator and was with him at the time of his assassination in Los Angeles.

Deeply affected by Kennedy's assassination, Graves took some time out before accepting another job offer. He was searching for something that would enable him to earn money while also giving him the opportunity to help his people. During this time the Ford Foundation offered him a grant to study black-owned businesses in the Caribbean countries, an offer he accepted. This was the spark that ignited the idea for his own magazine.

Starting a magazine, however, is an idea that occurs to many people, most of whom pour money into a losing venture before admitting failure. Friends discouraged him from the attempt. Two banks turned him down cold when he asked for loans. Finally, Chase Manhattan Bank agreed to take a chance on his idea. They loaned him $150,000 and put up an additional $25,000 for a 25 percent interest in the business.

With only himself and one assistant, Graves was off and running. He personally sold 90 percent of the ads for his magazine's first issue—seventeen golden pages out of sixty-four, the magazine's total pages. He went through some frustrating times trying to sell enough advertising to stay in business. Once, standing before a mirror shaving, wondering where his next advertiser would come from, he packed up the shaving can with its remaining contents and mailed it off to the president of the company that manufactured it. His message was short but persuasive. Why should blacks use products that advertise exclusively in white publications? *Black Enterprise* got another advertiser.

Frequently during those early days a company he called on to sell advertising would ask him to see its community affairs director rather than the advertising director. Graves quickly let them know that he wasn't there for a handout. He was there to sell something they needed, if they'd only give him a chance to explain why they needed it. His magazine reached a new market for their products. He had all the facts and figures. He was hard to turn down.

To this day, Graves says, he or his salespeople generally spend one third of a forty-five-minute meeting explaining to a potential advertiser that blacks drive cars, buy furniture, take vacations, and own houses. It is frustrating to go through repeatedly, but Graves keeps a keen eye on what is important to the success of the magazine—the bottom line, not the satisfaction of telling somebody off.

By watching the bottom line, Graves was able to pay back his loan in record time and also buy back the bank's equity share. The magazine earned money after its tenth issue, a rarity in the publishing industry. Advertising revenues have grown to more than $5 million annually, and advertising has increased 10 to 15 percent each year. This, along with his spinoff businesses, has fulfilled Grave's fondest ambitions. Twenty-five years out of college, he is still not limited by the choices for his life he made back in Morgan State. The sky is the limit—just the way he planned it.

Success Factors in Sales

Now maintaining a staff of salespeople, Graves says he can size up a promising candidate in about five minutes if it's a slow day. Nobody can fool him. He's a tough but understanding taskmaster. He sets quotas for his salespeople and gets rid of the ones who don't make it. To minimize the worst part of any business—firing people—he chooses salespeople carefully based on the following criteria in addition to their educational background:

- *Determination.* "When the customer says no," says Graves, "that's when the sale begins."
- *Ability to listen.* A good salesperson knows when to talk and when to listen. Graves says he's been with beginning salespeople who continue their pitch after the customer has said yes. That's not the time to ramble on, Graves says. You risk the yes turning to no.
- *Ability to assess the customer's needs*. No matter what it is—shoes, real estate, cosmetics, or advertising —you can't sell it until you understand the customer's needs. You certainly can't sell advertising in a black publication at $9,000 a page unless it buys something for the customer.
- *Communication.* The most important thing, says Graves. People who cannot communicate both verbally and in writing, "won't be worth a hill of beans." Graves's sales reps are required to write a follow-up letter to each client immediately following the sale. Knowing how to write is a must. Spelling? That's a problem a dictionary can cure. But the inability to write clearly is a problem too severe to cure by on-the-job training.
- *Hunger.* Graves feels people are motivated by their own needs. He likes to find people who, like him, came up the hard way. Struggle brings its own rewards. It tests endurance, toughens fiber, and builds character. "I like to find hungry people and put them where they belong," says Graves. "Up front."

Sex Differences in Selling

Graves's sales staff is split about fifty-fifty, half men and half women. He didn't try for this percentage. It just worked out that way. "What we look for is the best person regardless of other factors," he said. Women get no special treatment in sales. They either measure up to their set quotas or ship out. If he has noticed any difference, Graves says, it's that when a woman is good she's likely to be a little more motivated than a man. Possibly a little hungrier.

In management, also, women have an equal opportunity in Graves's businesses. Half of all vice-presidents at *Black Enterprise* are women.

Graves has one problem that could be considered a compliment if it weren't so expensive. His staff is constantly being raided by other publications seeking an easy way to meet their EEO requirements. In the past few months he's lost two top people to the staffs of well-known national magazines.

A black man who has lived with race discrimination all his life, Graves finds it easy to understand sex discrimination. He feels that black women, combining race and sex, have experienced the worst discrimination of all. Because he expects more understanding from those who have also known discrimination, he is angered when he finds a white female advertising director who exhibits all the bigotry of some of her white brothers. His anger is similar to that of women upon discovering a black man who rails against racism but defends sex discrimination. Both happen. It's a touchy subject.

A September 1980 article in *Black Enterprise* entitled "Struggle for the Executive Suite—Blacks vs. White Women" discusses deep ambivalence over competition between white women and blacks. Graves, like many other blacks, believes that white men are more comfortable promoting white women, rather than blacks, to executive positions. Many white women, however, believe that white men tend to promote and surround themselves with other males, black and white. In either case, it is black women who lose most often.

Blacks and white women both should not overlook the fact, in this controversy, that neither blacks nor white women do the hiring and therefore should not be blamed for the actions of others. Divide and conquer is a very old game. "An alliance of women and blacks," Graves points out, "would be a potent political force."

This will not occur, however, unless both blacks and white women understand that certain individuals among both groups will continue to cling to deep prejudices and behave accordingly. To expect all blacks or all white women to behave in an exemplary fashion is itself a prejudice. A better title for the article might have been "Blacks and White Women vs. Racism and Sexism in Business."

Deeply committed to equality for all, Graves is a member of a National Businessmen's Council working for passage of the Equal Rights Amendment. "Ability, not sex, race, or anything else, should be the determining factor in employment," Graves says. "We're a long way from this goal," he admits.

Sales has been good to Graves. He is enthusiastic about sales as a career choice for young people. With less subjective value judgment operating in sales than in other career choices, it is a good field for blacks. Blacks across the country are proving themselves in sales.

When asked whether he would be pleased if his three sons chose sales as their choice of a life's career, Graves replies, "Pleased? Barbara [his wife] and I are counting on it. If they don't we won't be able to retire."

By the time his sons take over the business, their father hopes he will be turning over the reins of a $75-million annual business. Who knows? It might be more. There's a lot of selling time left before Earl Graves hangs up his dreams. He's got a big edge now. His mother lets him work both sides of the street.

6

Learning How to Sell

SEMINARS teaching sales techniques have spread across the country during the past ten to twenty years with varying degrees of success. Some are sold to the public; many are sold directly to business and industry for the exclusive benefit of their sales forces. The logic used in selling the seminars is that the return on the investment will be eclipsed by increased sales.

Dr. Francis Mechner, a soft-spoken Vienna-born American psychologist, designed in a single weekend a program that has become the best-known sales seminar in the country today—PSS, Professional Selling Skills. The seminar is sold nationally by Xerox Learning Systems, a subsidiary of the Xerox Corporation.

The eventful weekend, which forever changed sales seminars, took place in a ski lodge when Dr. Mechner was forced to remain inside rather than spend two days on the ski slopes as he planned. In a fall the first day, he dislocated his shoulder; therefore, he decided to work on a new project for a client.

He developed two programs for a pharmaceutical company, one a "listening" program that would teach salespeople how to listen more effectively, the other a "selling" program to teach them how to sell, the first of its kind and a totally new learning concept. By audio tape the program simulates actual selling situations in which participants exhibit the same behavior as in real-life selling situations. Previous techniques relied on paper-and-pencil, question-and-answer methods to teach selling skills.

The Basic Psychology of Selling

Today the XLS Professional Selling Skills seminars teach the techniques of successful selling, increasing the productivity of a fair number of motivated salespeople. The graduates, by applying what they learn, often do return far more than the company's investment in the seminars, depending upon a number of variables.

While nothing works perfectly for everybody, the seminars work for enough people to keep them selling briskly around the country. It is by far the largest-selling and most widely used sales-training system of all time. Xerox's management is delighted that the company plunked down $13 million of Xerox stock back in 1965 to buy Dr. Mechner's company, which owned the program. The company, now Xerox Learning Systems, continues to grow. It grosses around $50 million annually, with PSS accounting for a major portion of the business.

Why and how PSS seminars turn some people into supersalespeople and fail to make a dent in the selling behavior of others is another one of those complex learning problems that fascinates Dr. Mechner. He doesn't have the answer, nor does he believe that anybody does, even though predicting success through aptitude testing has become big business. "The only reliable predictor of a salesperson's success," Mechner says "is his or her sales record."

A Professor Becomes a Salesman

Francis Mechner was born in Vienna, Austria, the son of a physician who moved his family to New York City when Mechner was twelve years old. Although expected to continue the family medical tradition, Francis Mechner chose instead to study psychology, specializing in learning theory. Immediately after receiving his Ph.D. from Columbia University, he joined the faculty, teaching experimental psychology and continuing his research. He is fascinated by how organisms learn, how skills are acquired, retained, and forgotten.

In 1960, Mechner gave up teaching and began selling. He set up his own company, Basic Systems, Inc. Combining his special knowledge of learning with an entrepreneurial spirit, he began designing learning systems and selling them to business and industry.

In business he survived a difficult dual process—creating ideas, then personally selling them. With no track record, no satisfied clients to point to, and no guarantees that his ideas would work, Dr. Mechner learned firsthand the complexities and difficulties of selling. Two years later, his company had a hundred employees, including its own sales staff.

"Nobody except me could have sold the programs when I first began," Dr. Mechner says. "I was the only one who understood them. I'm sure that my sales techniques could have been improved, but I did the best I could. I would design a program, then modify it as I got feedback from the marketplace."

An Interesting Challenge

In 1961, a pharmaceutical company hired Dr. Mechner to design a more efficient system to teach the company's salesmen (there were no women) technical medical information important in calling on physician clients. After doing this successfully for a year, the sales manager confided a more pressing problem. What his salesmen really needed, he said, was to learn how to sell. Regardless of their technical back-up information, no matter how much product knowledge they had accumulated, regardless of their motivation to sell, the greatest single problem he had with his salesmen was that they didn't know how to sell and he didn't know how to teach them.

Could Dr. Mechner do anything about this? Was it possible to design a program that would teach people how to sell? Never one to turn down interesting learning challenges, Dr. Mechner said he would investigate the idea.

Watching Salesmen Sell

Mechner began accompanying pharmaceutical salesmen on calls to physician's offices. Watching intently, he listened to dozens of presentations by salesmen who had complete mastery of technical product knowledge. Many had been selling for years. After a few weeks a pattern emerged.

Each time a doctor interrupted a salesman to express a doubt, reveal a problem, or explain a perception about the product, the typical salesman would listen politely, brush aside the doctor's comment, and continue the sales presentation.

"The salesmen generally made no attempt to understand the doctor's needs or explore the possible solutions," Mechner says. "In fact, when the doctor spoke, the salesman would get over that little hump in the conversation and proceed as though the interruption had never occurred. This happened over and over again.''

Dr. Mechner's report to the sales manager was short and blunt. To dramatize his point, he told the sales manager that assuming a doctor would take the time to play it, an audio tape mailed to his office could sell the company's products as well as many of his salesmen.

Dr. Mechner initially diagnosed this problem as the ''inability to listen.'' He saw effective listening as one of the keys to the problem, but only half the solution. Effective selling must be combined with effective listening. Together they work. Separately, they don't.

In retrospect, how simple the idea seems. How logical and reasonable that listening and selling should be combined. New ideas that are simple—and work—keep business exciting. Dr. Mechner was onto one of those exciting ideas.

Although the original program designed by Dr. Mechner has been improved and modified in minor ways by both Mechner and Xerox Learning Systems, the principles of successful selling and the basic structure and design of the program designed that weekend remain the same. Also, many other similar sales seminars have sprung up across the country.

The selling principles in sales seminars may seem simplistic; however, putting the ideas into practice requires intelligence, concentration, and the ability to understand complicated concepts. It also takes practice perfecting sales performance.

A Unique Vantage Point

Johanna Peter, now a salesperson with Xerox Learning Systems, is able to evaluate the sales seminars from two unique vantage points. First as a teacher and now as a salesperson. As an administrator of XLS seminars she became interested in sales. Although most of her time now is devoted to selling, she continues to conduct sales-training seminars.

''The longer I taught sales techniques, the more interested I became in the profession of sales," Peter says. "Naturally, the most logical entry into sales for me was with XLS, since I knew the product. I had seen the concepts presented work for others, so I had no difficulty believing in my product. I knew it worked."

The selling concepts are simple, yet they require practice and dedication to apply properly. Nobody performs perfectly right away. It usually takes a few months of practice to become skilled. To improve, a salesperson must analyse old habits and practice developing new skills. It's hard work, but it pays off handsomely. When taught by a skilled trainer, and practiced by salespeople who are willing to work hard to improve, the skills are effective.

"Many terrific salespeople, when asked how they sell, can't tell you. They say things like, 'I'm good with people,' or 'I'm Irish,' or 'I'm a born salesperson.' Their difficulty is understandable. It's difficult to observe yourself objectively. The seminars, we have discovered, are just as valuable for veteran salespeople as for beginners because they provide them with new skills plus a system for using their old skills more effectively.

"The training programs offer the basis for self-improvement," Peter continues. "Even though I've been out in the field selling for almost two years, I continue to assess my progress, analyze my use of skills, and work constantly on improving my performance. Some days I give myself a terrific rating and other days I'm pretty hard on myself, but the important thing is that I continue to improve."

Validation studies by Xerox Learning Systems have documented the effectiveness of the skills taught in the seminars. In addition to providing seminars on Professional Selling Skills, the company has developed other skill-based programs in advanced sales, management, and communications.

When asked if selling seminars that teach selling skills puts extra performance pressure on the XLS salespeople, Peter says yes. "Certainly, prospective clients observe us closely in our sales presentations," she says.

"And we'd better be good. However, this kind of pressure is beneficial. It keeps us on our toes. More than other salespeople, we see the direct link between these specific, well-defined sales skills and success."

The Basic Steps of Professional Selling

In designing the Professional Selling Skills program, Dr. Mechner defined a set of basic steps to maximize selling success. Nothing will clinch a sale every time. Rejection is a fact of every salesperson's life and must be dealt with realistically. However, success factors can be maximized.

Dr. Mechner had seen that the pharmaceutical salesmen were so intent on their own performances that they failed to listen to the doctors' needs—the first critical mistake in selling.

Aside from this, the pharmaceutical salesmen in their selling attempts began at the end—and ended at the beginning. They were so eager to explain their product's features that they didn't realize the seller and the buyer were like ships in the night—silently passing each other.

In designing his Professional Selling Skills program, Dr. Mechner separated selling into several parts, providing simple steps for the salespeople to follow. Those parts are the following:

- Diagnosing the customer's needs
- Getting the customer to reveal his or her needs
- Presenting the features of the product or service as benefits
- Eliciting the customer's objections to the product
- Overcoming the customer's objections
- Closing the sale

Diagnosing the Customer's Needs

To maximize success, a salesperson must begin, not with his or her product, but with what the product will do for the customer. The first basic step is diagnosing the customer's needs. Finding out the customer's needs is the building block of sales, the foundation. Until you diagnose the customer's needs, any attempt at selling will be like shooting blind into a dark alley. If you hit your target and the sale is made, it will be an accident. It will not be selling.

Most customers who bother to talk to you at all are generally eager to explain their needs. They are looking for solutions. However, successful selling involves skillfully and smoothly leading a customer through a series of steps that clarify his or her needs.

In this respect, selling can be compared to the work of a skillful television newscaster who, in addition to reading the news, must be aware of timing, commercial breaks, difficult pronunciation, various camera angles, lights, and other elements that are an inherent part of the performance. The more professional the newscaster, the less the audience is aware of these details. The less professional the performance, the more the audience sees beyond the camera and into the production problems. In sales, as in television or stage productions, a professional salesperson's performance is so smooth that the client never becomes aware of the production problems.

Getting the Customer to Reveal Needs

If the prospective customer, early on, is resistant to discussing his or her needs, diagnosing the unspoken needs becomes a more complex task, says Dr. Mechner. For example, often a customer's objections are based on price, yet he or she may be reluctant to reveal this fact. It becomes critical for the salesperson to figure out a correct diagnosis, piecing together all the parts of the puzzle. The salesperson must successfully get to the bottom of the sales resistance before going farther in the selling process. Often this is a back-and-forth process, since the customer may leap ahead, ask questions. Selling is not a scripted performance in which a salesperson and customer play rehearsed parts. Only the salesperson's part is rehearsed, a fact that not only makes the process more difficult, but sometimes adds surprise endings. Salespeople say this is what keeps sales fresh and exciting. "Imagine how dull selling would be if you could keep total control?" says a saleswoman. "The element of surprise is always with you in every sale. No matter how often I think I have every detail figured out in advance, it never happens. Anybody interested in psychology has a built-in laboratory."

In getting the customer to open up and reveal his or her needs, never ask questions that can be answered by a simple yes or no, unless that's the response you want. Keep control of the conversation and skillfully lead it to where you want it to go. Generally, you have human nature on your side, since people love to talk about themselves and their needs once you get them started.

Presenting Benefits

Customers don't buy products or services. They buy benefits, direct benefits or indirect benefits. The customers buying IBM and Xerox machines are buying benefits just the same as a person buying an electric toaster. The companies buying Professional Selling Skills are buying benefits. The people who buy this book are buying benefits. Sometimes, interestingly enough, buying itself is the benefit, Dr. Mechner says.

Ask a Rolls-Royce salesperson why people buy the most expensive cars on earth. There will be as many answers as there are customers. The benefit of owning a Rolls-Royce for one person may be quite different from that for another.

Salespeople love to swap stories about how a sale was

made, how they figured out what would clinch the deal. "Sometimes figuring out what will get me over that final hurdle in selling to a client reminds me of trying to figure out the ending to a mystery story," says a saleswoman selling expensive medical equipment. "You've got to use the kind of logic the client uses, put yourself in his or her place, then go with your gut feelings. It is a fascinating combination of logic and emotion that blends in selling."

Back when the Xerox Corporation was young and copying machines a new and exciting product, Xerox salesmen lost many sales because they concentrated on the complex machinery that made up the new machines. They were eager to explain the inner workings of the new business phenomenon.

However, the salesmen discovered that no matter how interested a customer might be in the new product, discussing the complex machinery made some customers contract-shy. Carried away with the newness of the product, the salesmen failed to present the product in terms of benefits to the customers. The customers translated the flashing lights, gadgets, and complex machinery in terms of their own needs and fears. Many felt that anything so complex would break down frequently. When high-speed copiers first came on the market, many customers felt they had no need for such efficiency. They didn't need a hundred copies a minute and didn't want to pay for what they didn't need. It was logical to the customers that the faster a machine produced copies, the higher the cost.

Once the salespeople became aware they were scaring away customers, they changed their sales presentation. They toned down the gadgets and flashing lights and played up the benefits to the consumers. It worked much better.

Elicit Objections

Never ignore even the slightest objection to your product. Meet the customer's objections head on in a positive, helpful, convincing way. It's much better to get all the objections out on the table than to leave them lurking in the customer's mind, where they will interfere with your sale. For example, had the Xerox salespeople first elicited objections to their new machines, they would have found it more productive to concentrate on less complex features—durability, service, cost savings, etc.

Eliciting objections, says Dr. Mechner, is often a step-by-step process done simultaneously with eliciting needs. Once you discover a need you may also uncover an objection. Stringing together these objections also becomes a factor in diagnosing needs.

In listening effectively to the customer, the salesperson hears many things beyond the words. He or she figures out the possible roadblocks—is it price, production, service, competitive products, distrust, inability to make a decision, fear of making a mistake? The effective salesperson, like a psychologist, can often diagnose the general problem in a short time. Pinpointing the specifics takes longer.

A computer saleswoman, selling in a new job with a firmly established company, couldn't quite figure out the sales resistance in several loyal and trusted customers of the company. Her company had just come out with a new product, and she was sure her most fertile sales ground would be former customers who also were familiar with her new company. Instead, she kept getting rather strange responses—not quite a turndown, but not quite a sale either. Finally, she made a call on a client who filled in the blank spaces for her. Her company's chief competitor had circulated the rumor that her company was going out of business. They cited a major stockholder as the source. No wonder the customers hadn't wanted to buy a new product with a service contract that might not be worth the paper it was written on.

Overcoming Objections

A successful salesperson works painstakingly to overcome all the customer's objections to his or her service or product. The salesperson must be ever mindful of the customer's needs, highlighting the needs while overcoming the objections. Only after this successful step comes the magic moment—closing the sale.

After ferreting out the objections one by one, direct or indirect, real or perceived, the salesperson's job is to overcome each one, bringing the customer closer and closer to closing the transaction. Don't feel bad if it takes a while to learn the process. People who have spent their lives in sales are still perfecting their performances.

In selling expensive and complicated products such as computers or medical equipment, overcoming objections occurs over a period of months. It's a process that involves many highly technical people. Often, even with less expensive products, customers are pleased when salespeople devote time to solving their needs. They feel they are getting more for their money. However, don't spend needless time without some assurance of getting the order. As a saleswoman explained to her manager why she cut short a conversation with a prospective client, she called him a "tire kicker," a term used to describe somebody who will talk your ear off but won't buy. It's your job to guess correctly about who's serious and who's wasting your time.

Closing the Sale

Much has been written and said about closing a sale. Each salesperson develops his or her own closing expertise. A few people put great stock in intricate signs such as body language, eye movements, rapid breathing, toe tapping, white knuckles, and a host of other details that are supposed to alert the seasoned salesperson of the perfect closing moment.

You'd think from all the fuss that there are fleeting seconds when prospective customers become order-signing zombies, willing to hand over the family farm and put the kids up for collateral. Some legislators apparently agree with this, since laws in several states give customers a cooling-off period in which to change their minds about purchases, bought in presumably weak moments from high-pressure salespeople.

Dr. Mechner believes these arcane "signs for the closing" are irrelevant even if they exist. "Even if these things were true," he says, "they would still be peripheral. Because the moment the salesperson should close the sale is when all the customer's objections have been overcome. It is just that logical and simple."

Dr. Mechner feels that inexperienced salespeople are often reluctant to try to close the sale. Salespeople, like other human beings, fear rejection and constantly avoid its possibility instead of learning to be comfortable in handling it. "A salesperson may have a fifty-fifty chance of rejection." This often causes the less experienced salesperson to avoid asking for the order, a fatal mistake. In doing this, the reluctant salesperson conveys the wrong message to the customer, thereby creating the response he or she is trying to avoid.

Rejection

Each beginning salesperson must deal with rejection. Dr. Mechner feels that the best way to do this is to maximize your possibilities for success. He feels a salesperson should improve those things possible to change rather than worrying about changing the impossible.

He suggests concentrating on developing selling skills by practicing your performance, which in turn will increase your confidence, which will enable you to deal more effectively with rejection. Once having chosen sales as a career, you've automatically chosen rejection as a lifelong companion. Although rejection looms large in the life of a beginning salesperson, a little time cuts it down to size. Rejection is probably discussed less by salespeople than any other part of their business. This saleswoman is a prime example.

When Alexandra Hatcher first began in a career in sales for a publishing company, like all beginning salespeople she had difficulty facing the inherent rejection. She cured it by forcing herself to sell by phone for several weeks, cold-calling new prospects. After a few days the fear totally disappeared. Hatcher explains that a customer's rejection is not personal rejection of a salesperson. "Forcing yourself to sell regardless of how difficult it seems will build confidence. And in order to sell, you must have confidence."

This "ice plunge" idea, although difficult, certainly worked for Hatcher. Now head of the Alexandria Hatcher Agency in Manhattan, she gives sales classes and business seminars. Her business activities include a literary agency, corporate communications, group programs, and assistance in the development of small businesses.

Generally, it takes a beginning salesperson only a few weeks to understand, emotionally, that a rejection is not personal. Even a person who slams down the phone or bangs a door in somebody's face is rejecting the intrusion, not the person. Within a short time, salespeople separate out the type of rejection, which allows them to deal with it rationally. Besides, if examined closely, it's rejection that makes selling a creative and exciting profession. Without rejection, sales would be little more than taking orders over the phone or behind a counter.

To maximize the possibility for success, Dr. Mechner suggests that instead of asking a buyer *if* he or she wants to make purchase, ask how many, how much, what color, when the client wants to take delivery—anything that will elicit a favorable response. Some companies allow their salespeople to throw in closing incentives—a special time-limited savings, additional features free of charge, etc. Other companies refuse to do this, feeling that it adds a gimmicky element and, in the long run, does nothing to enhance the product.

After you have overcome all objections, the reasonable response to expect is an affirmative one. Don't expect rejection. Why else would a customer spend valuable time talking to you? Assume that time is as valuable to the customer as it is to the salesperson.

Overcoming New Objections

Frequently, when a seller thinks he or she has overcome all objections and asks for the order, the buyer will bring up new objections. When this occurs, Dr. Mechner suggests systematically and patiently going back and clearing up each objection as it arises—back and forth until there literally are no more objections. This process may be repeated several times. However, each time you get to the point where all the objections have been overcome, again ask for the order. Perseverance and the ability to separate real objections from stated objections are critical at this stage of the sale.

Perhaps the customer has been burned by bad service, and yours is a product requiring service. Reassurance about this aspect may get you over that last objection. Early delivery may be another way to clear objections. Once a customer makes up his or her mind to buy, most would like instant delivery. Perhaps your competitor can't deliver the goods as fast as you can. Whatever the advantage is—and you should make it your business to know—use it as positive reinforcement. Customers are always fearful that a product will not live up to the expectations created by your presentation.

Nothing is more convincing than a list of satisfied customers, particularly if somebody the client knows is on the list. You might suggest a phone call to one, or supply a name and an address to contact. Be creative. Put yourself in the customer's place and find something that will make the sale.

Then, once again when all objections are overcome, ask for the order. "At this critical moment," says a former IBM saleswoman, "*shut up!* If you think of sales in terms of winning or losing, the next person to speak is the one who loses." She suggests outsilencing the client. "The next thing you hear," she says, "should be the sound of a pen scratching on the order blank."

Selling after the Sale

The time to reinforce your position with the customer is after the sale is signed, the deal closed. This is the moment when a mysterious self-selling process takes over, reinforcing all your efforts unless you interfere. After buying, customers want to believe. They are ready to be your back-up sales force if you treat them with respect and live up to every single promise you make, large or small.

Dr. Mechner believes the biggest myth about selling is that a good salesperson is somebody who can sell you something you don't need. He believes the reverse is true. A good salesperson often has assessed the client's needs more thoroughly than the client. He or she has cared enough to blend the product and the customer's needs and has made sure the customer was not misled in any way—no tricky contract, small print, or explanations after the fact. Salespeople who oversell build future failure instead of success. Nothing makes a more lasting impression on a client than a salesperson who lives up to his or her word and takes care of seemingly insignificant details: a phone call to see how the product is working out, stopping by the sales literature, making sure delivery occurs on the date promised, just letting the client know the salesperson is still around. Dozens of small details determine repeat business.

Nobody wants to be fleeced by a fast-talking salesperson out to make a buck and disappear. There will always be enough of this kind of character around to poison the well for reputable salespeople. Therefore, the prime time for a salesperson to make points with the customer is after a sale. When a company's name becomes synonymous with trust, integrity, and service, the percentage of repeat sales goes up and word-of-mouth testimonials are a free addition to your advertising department.

IBM is a company whose name became identified with service early in the company's life. There are IBM customers today who wouldn't accept a competitor's products for free because of IBM's service. Customers whose business depends on fast, dependable service know that a dead computer, with their valuable records locked inside, is nothing to attack with a home service kit. They are at the mercy of the seller's advice. The high quality of IBM's service has been a difficult sales obstacle for competitors to overcome.

Dr. Mechner's philosophy is that the easiest customer to sell to is a satisfied customer. The only way you can build a solid reputation that will make all future sales easier is to promise only what you can deliver and deliver everything you promise. One salesman describes selling as a perfect boomerang: "Whatever you throw out will come back to help you or haunt you."

Innate Differences Between Men and Women in Sales

Are there innate differences between men and women that interfere or enhance their ability to sell? Should women pattern their sales success after successful salesmen, or should they develop different techniques of their own? What similarities and differences in selling behavior does a psychologist who is a learning specialist see in males and females?

"I don't know if there are innate differences in males and females that relate to selling," Dr. Mechner says.

"But if there are, they are totally irrelevant."

Irrelevant? After years of assumptions that women can't withstand the rigors of selling? After this so-called innate inability kept them out of good selling jobs for so many years? Since it seems so relevant to women, why isn't it relevant to him?

"Because you cannot change what is innate," Dr. Mechner quietly explains. "Therefore why spend time worrying about things you can do absolutely nothing about? That's not a very intelligent use of time." In his own experience and observation however, he adds, some of the most effective salespeople he has ever known are women.

Besides, regardless of what is innate, the *learning process* is exactly the same for women as it is for men. In the ability to learn, there is no known difference.

It isn't often you come across an idea so simple and logical that it warrants being labeled profound. However, Dr. Mechner's suggestion that women not waste time over real or imagined selling differences is profoundly helpful advice.

Just remember. Those who doubt you on this score will never be convinced by your words. But they cannot deny your results. So do as thousands of saleswomen are doing. Don't waste time discussing the world's oldest and most useless argument. Let your sales record speak eloquently for you.

7

The Hidden Success
Factor in Sales

WOMEN IN IMPRESSIVE NUMBERS are succeeding in
sales. In a remarkably short time they have proved their
competence, disproving long-standing "innate" theories used to justify sex-typing jobs. Interestingly,
women are succeeding in sales at a greater rate than in
many other areas where it might appear that sex should
matter less than in sales.

When examined closely, the structure of sales and the
requirements for success reveal some hidden benefits for
women that are absent from other nontraditional job
areas. First, women are succeeding in sales because
many are being hired into first-rate companies that provide the training and support necessary to maximize
success. In these instances, women are competing successfully and making the most of their new opportunities. Second, sales to a certain extent is self-selecting,
attracting women who are most success-oriented.

However, there is a deeper psychological reason for

131

the success of women in sales, which is a factor increasingly recognized as critical in the working lives of all women. This very old phenomenon, quite recently discovered, is subjective value judgment. And whether women know it or not, subjective value judgment can sometimes detail or wreck an otherwise promising career.

Subjective Value Judgment

Success in most jobs and careers is determined by an evaluation process, which is a management function. How well you are doing can be accurately and simply measured in some jobs but not in others. For example, if you're working on a manufacturing assembly line packing widgets into boxes, it isn't difficult to measure whether or not you're keeping up with the demands of the job. Either you do it or you fall behind. It's clearcut. Suppose, however, that you were being considered for a job as supervisor of widget packing. The fact that you knew the job would be one plus factor among many intangible factors that might be considered in promoting you up the line. It's in these other factors, few of which are clear-cut, where the subjective value judgment of the person or persons deciding your working fate becomes important. Often it is the critical factor. This is an area of hidden discrimination against women which has only recently begun to be explored. It has always been an integral part of the workplace. It continues to be detrimental to the careers of many women.

Sales Success Criteria

The success of women in sales is measured for the most part on simple, objective, impersonal criteria. It's like widget packing. A saleswoman sells or she doesn't. She is measured on a set of sales figures. Regardless of the personal feelings of her management, her production is the proof that determines her success. Subjective value judgment may play its part in keeping her out of the job. And it can keep her from being promoted up the line to management. However, once a woman lands a job in sales, she is measured in that job the same as the salesmen.

"Sales is the last true meritocracy, virtually the only job area left where you win or lose on a set of figures uncolored by your manager's personal opinion of you," says Bernice Malamud, assistant vice-president of The Equitable Life Assurance Society and a former insurance saleswoman. "It has nothing to do with the 'old boy' network. The sole criterion is whether you achieve the job objective. It's one of the things I hated most to give up. In management, subjective value judgment plays a large role. You are no longer in control of your own fate as you are in sales."

C. Peter McColough, chief executive officer of the Xerox Corporation, recognizes the subjective value judgment factor operating against promoting women into Xerox management.

"We could eliminate the EEO targets for women in sales. Women will continue to do well in sales without them," McColough said. "However, we couldn't eliminate the targets for women to move into management. There is still too much resistance to women there." The resistance he is talking about is the value judgment of male managers who quite often don't understand their own subjective value judgment. they firmly believe they are being totally objective when, in fact, they are measuring a woman subjectively.

The prejudice that has kept women in low-level, low-paying, female-typed jobs has not disappeared from the marketplace regardless of the remarkable progress made in certain areas in the past twenty years. Thousands of years of deeply ingrained discrimination takes much longer to eradicate. No woman living today will see the end of job discrimination in her lifetime unless science comes up with a fast cure for aging.

Successful Women

Many people, employers among them, continue to believe that a successful woman is the exception, instead of the exceptional. The success of a woman still sets her apart from her group, while a man's failure does the same for him. Women, particularly in nontraditional jobs, need to be aware of the unconscious as well as the conscious discrimination that flows from the belief in the inherent inferiority of women. It is alive and well and determining the working lives of many women each day. And while conscious discrimination is hard to deal with, unconscious discrimination is hardest of all to prove. It's like fighting an invisible fog. You know it's there, but try proving it.

A good example of the hidden prejudice you'll run into is a banking industry senior vice-president attending a management awareness seminar. He admits that he feels women are less intelligent than men, too emotional to handle tough business decisions and should be attractive in order to get ahead in business. Yet in the next breath, this same banker protests that he hires women for his bank strictly on the basis of performance. "I am objective," he says. "Whether it is a woman or a man makes absolutely no difference to me."

This is the kind of discrimination that drives women up the wall. This man is being totally honest. He really believes that he is objective in hiring and promoting, that his feelings in no way influence his business judgment. He continues to justify his "objective" actions even when forced to admit that he has no women in management jobs in his bank.

"I haven't found any who measure up," is his response. Again he believes his actions were based on logic, not emotions. He cannot come to grips with the fact that the emotions of men influence their decisions and have a powerful effect on the career progress of women.

Far-Reaching Effects

The success of women in sales should have far-reaching effects for women in other fields who are struggling year after year and getting nowhere, those women who discover how easy it is to get equal work but how difficult it is to get equal pay, equal recognition, and equal promotions. Women in the workplace constantly fight the hidden subjective value judgment that keeps them from fulfilling their potential. Those with downright hostile managers are better off than the ones whose managers, like the banker, keep their heads in the sand and continue to believe in their own objectivity, never recognizing that pure objectivity doesn't exist.

"At least I know where I stand, with my manager," says a saleswoman who is now in management. "I don't like his attitude, and I hope to be able to help change it, but I prefer people who are up-front about their prejudices. He doesn't think women can manage as effectively as men and he's honest about it. There are lots of other managers who feel the same way but refuse to admit it, not even to themselves. When I was in sales, I didn't like my manager, but it didn't matter as much. As long as I sold, he couldn't touch me. Now it's different. Unless I get a fair shake in management, I'm planning on going back to sales."

The Harvard Business Review
and Sex Stereotyping

In 1974 Benson Rosen and Thomas Jerdee, two professors of business administration at the Graduate School of Business Administration of the University of North Carolina, dramatically revealed the hidden psychological discrimination that holds women back in their careers and jobs. They conducted a survey of fifteen hundred *Harvard Business Review* subscribers in a questionnaire designed to sample executive judgment in a variety of common areas. The results of the survey were published in the March-April 1974 edition of *The Harvard Business Review*. Sex was the only different factor in two versions of the questionnaire. Half the subscribers were asked to react to situations dealing with males; the other half got the exact same situations, except they were asked to react to females. A hypothetical organization was described, and participants were asked to assume the role of vice-president in the company.

In one of eleven hypothetical situations, a forty-six-year-old female employee of the company who was only a high school graduate, competed with a twenty-six-year-old man with a college degree, who had been with the company for only three years. The winner would be chosen to represent the company at an important conference. In half the questionnaires, the forty-six-year-old woman changed places and became the twenty-six-year-old man. The "man" won out over the "woman" in both instances. The forty-six-year-old man won because of his greater experience and loyalty to the company; the twenty-six-year-old man won out over the woman because of his greater potential to the company.

In another role-playing situation, an employee's wife (husband on half the questionnaires) had been offered a job by a company in another city. The employee had a bright future in the company. What, if anything, should management do to keep the employee? Almost twice as many respondents wanted to try to convince the "man" to stay with the company as compared with those wanting to keep the "woman," revealing that greater efforts are made to retain valuable male employees than females.

In another situation, a young aspiring female executive was married to a free-lance writer. She and her husband disagreed over whether the husband should attend a cocktail party at the home of an important executive of her company. The woman was interested in going to the party because she hoped to talk to the executive about a new sales campaign. He had been too busy in the office to see her, and she was anxious to present her ideas instead of waiting for an appointment. The husband had tickets to a play and insisted on going there instead, saying he didn't want to talk to a bunch of creeps at a dully party.

In half the questionnaires the man became the aspiring young executive and the wife became the free-lance writer who didn't want to attend the party.

Alternatives presented the respondents were that (1) the reluctant spouse should go to the party and stop making such a big issue out of it; (2) the junior executive should attend the party alone; or (3) the aspiring executive should not attend the party.

Almost 70 percent of the respondents felt the wife should attend the party with the husband and stop making a big deal out of the obligation, while slightly more than 40 percent said the husband should go with the wife and stop making the issue into a big deal. Almost 40 percent who chose the number-two alternative, that the spouse go alone, felt the wife should go alone, but fewer than half of that percentage said the husband should go alone. The fewest respondents chose the alternative that the junior executive shouldn't attend the party, but of those who did, more felt the woman executive shouldn't attend the party at all than those who decided that the man executive shouldn't. Said the authors:

> The conclusion we draw is quite clear: managers consider that women are obliged to participate in the social activities associated with their husband's careers; much less is expected from the husbands of working women. The difference in expectations could make it easier for men to combine their professional and social lives and thus give the appearance of complete dedication to their work. Career women might find it more difficult to combine their work and social lives, and, therefore, might be seen as less dedicated to their work, even though they spend just as much time and energy on the job.

Another interesting situation favored the woman in a problem of taking leave from her job to take care of three young children. When Ruth Brown, the accountant, became Ralph Brown, the percentage of executives approving the appropriateness of his request for a leave of absence dropped dramatically. And of those who would grant the leave without pay, more granted it for the woman than for the man.

This doesn't tell working mothers much they didn't already know. They understand all too well which working parent is *supposed* to take care of the children no matter what the individual circumstances. In fact, a man who takes time off to care for his children is considered somebody who, at the very least, has made a monumentally bad matrimonial choice.

Survey Findings

Among other findings, the survey showed that in business, milder disciplinary action is applied to males in petty rule-breaking than to women in similar situations; sexual misconduct is tolerated to a greater extent in male employees than females; women are expected to help their husbands succeed in their careers while the reverse is not true for men, and family demands are perceived as far less disturbing to the business for male employees than for females.

These attitudes in business create an upward-mobility blockage for all women, regardless of individual circumstances. It is a hidebound presumption based upon the imposed sex roles of the past.

However, a ray of light shows through this dense psychological jungle in careers like sales, where the criterion for success is cut and dried and clear: production.

"When the job requirements are exact and the applicant does not match them, respondents reject both a male and a female for the position," according to the authors. "This suggests that it may be relatively easy to make unbiased decisions in situations where a candidate's qualifications are clearly unacceptable or clearly acceptable.''

There is no similar good news for women in management or in thousands of other jobs where subjective value judgment will continue to play an important role. The authors write about these areas:

"On the other hand, in situations where available information is ambiguous or contradictory, decision makers may fall back on preconceived attitudes—sex role stereotypes in this instance—to arrive at their ultimate decision. In a sense, respondents may be providing more information for themselves by filling their own prejudices or some widely held societal expectations.

"When the results [of this survey] are extrapolated," the authors conclude, "to the entire population of American managers, even a small bias against women could represent a great many unintentional discriminatory acts, which potentially affect thousands of career women. The end result of these various forms of bias might be great personal damage for individuals and costly underutilization of human resources. . . .

"Social and psychological barriers to women interested in a management or professional career still exist despite recent changes in policies on the employment of women.''

Women in Sales

Although women in sales are not totally free from bias by their management, they are far less affected by the subjective value judgment of others than women in other careers. Some examples:

• A young woman selling word-processing equipment for a large corporation was having difficulty with her manager. She felt he constantly disapproved of her life-style and her direct approach in the office. She was divorced from her husband and living with another man. Her manager openly disapproved of this relationship, discussing his disapproval with others in the office. He was harsh, curt, and constantly critical in his treatment of this woman. Although hurt and angry because of such treatment from a manager who was supposed to provide sales support, this woman became determined to get out from under the oppressive situation through her selling achievements. Her territory covered a large area; therefore, she spent about half of her time on the road. When she asked her manager about changing territories, he turned her down cold, saying instead that there were many attractive things about her "large" territory. "An absolute lie that only a fool would believe. I have one of the worst territories in the company," she said.

Undaunted, this young woman continued to spend as little time in her office and as much time out in the field selling as possible. She knew she was on the right track when her manger's manager informed her she was the number-one saleswoman in her group, a "detail" her own manager failed to mention. Upon the advice of another woman in the company, this saleswoman began to communicate with her manager in writing. She drew up her own long-range goals—consistent with company policy—and found out more about her manager's job, what he was supposed to do in managing her. Before accumulating this information, this saleswoman was at a distinct disadvantage. She had only a vague idea of company policy; therefore she had no idea whether her manager's behavior toward her was appropriate. She discovered that it wasn't.

She confronted her manager directly with a request for a salary increase, long overdue. She mentioned, not in a threatening way but as information, that she understood company policy. She forced herself into these confrontations even though they were uncomfortable. She behaved in as businesslike a way as possible no matter what her manager did to provoke her. Over a six-month period she assessed the results of her actions and chalked up the following accomplishments:

• Her territory was changed. She is driving about half as much as previously, which leaves her more selling time.

• She got her long overdue pay increase.

• There are no more remarks about her personal life, at least not to her.

• She is less fearful of her manager. Previously, she felt as if she was being scolded by her father each time her manager criticized her. She worked on decreasing her fear of authority.

• She feels much less in need of her manager's support, realizing that while a sales manager's support is nice, it is not critical.

• She isn't out from under her manager yet, but she's working to get a transfer to another area. In the meantime, she's selling more than ever. She expects that her earnings will be close to $50,000 this year, not bad for a woman who's been selling five years and is still under thirty.

Control over Your Working Life

Because this young woman was in sales, her manager had much less control over her working life. The fact that she was the top-producing salesperson in her group was great protection, although she didn't fully understand this fact. Her manager should have been proud of her record; however, he reacted emotionally. He revealed his discomfort in dealing with businesswomen. Turned around, this manager probably wouldn't have cared a whit about a young salesman's private life, except to admire it. He certainly would have felt no obligation to comment on it unless it affected business.

This saleswoman learned that her manager was behaving in direct opposition to company policy. Her personal life is her own business as long as it doesn't affect business. Many managers react emotionally to similar situations that offend their ideas of "proper" behavior for women. To protect against such presumptuous managers, every saleswoman needs to be familiar with management policy. Unless you know what your manager is supposed to do, you won't know whether his or her actions come with the blessings of the company. Most employees, never bothering to learn the rules, exaggerate the power of their managers, automatically believing they adhere strictly to company policy. This is frequently not true. In this case, the head of the company's sales force would have been horrified by her treatment. But in a large company with layers of management between the top and the bottom, there is little chance of his finding out.

Just remember, the person responsible for company-wide sales is much more interested in motivating salespeople to produce rather than in how, or if, they reproduce.

• A saleswoman in a branch office of another large corporation told a similar story about her manager, a man who reluctantly hired women into sales only after he was forced to because of company policy. She first had been interviewed at the home office and practically forced on the unhappy manager, who made no bones about his displeasure, and the reason for it.

"Women can't sell no matter what the goddamn federal government thinks," he said flatly. "Four thousand years of history can't be wiped out with dumb regulations. Broads are broads. They ought to do what they do best—which isn't selling," he'd add, winking so nobody could miss his sexual message.

For the first six weeks, he seemed determined to prove himself right. He made this woman's life as miserable as he could. He seemed to sense that no matter what he did to her, she would never complain to the home office. He was right. She wouldn't.

There were some positive results from the manager's abuse of this woman. Other men in the office, embarrassed over his behavior, became protective. "They fell all over themselves to be helpful," she said. "I couldn't have made it, except for their support."

In addition, the women in the office went out of their way to help her. They provided a cheering section for her when hard work and determination paid off and she became one of the top salespeople in the office.

The manager, although still defending his attitudes, has modified his "all women can't sell" to "most can't sell." With this woman around, it's clear that at least one can sell, even if he chooses to point her out as an exception. Although she was the first saleswoman to be hired in that office, there are two more now, each hired with much less harassment by the manager.

Realizing that this man isn't likely to change, she is looking forward to the day he is replaced. Since he is near retirement age she will get her wish within another year. In the meantime, she ignores him. She can do this as long as her sales figures remain high. However, she points out, except for providing a nicer atmosphere and being a better teacher, the same would be true of the best sales manager. He or she would have to get rid of any saleswoman who failed to make her sales quotas. In many other occupations, job security may be high, but so is the flak that comes with the job security.

A Word of Caution

Although subjective value judgment is a fact of life in the marketplace and can be easily identified by most women, there is a danger that some will see it where it doesn't exist in order to avoid facing up to their own shortcomings. It can be easy to assume a paranoid view, blaming everything on the subjective value judgment of others. Complicating the situation, subjective value judgment doesn't necessarily operate alone. Often it is half the equation, combined with performance that is legitimately questionable. In recognizing that you may be held back by the subjective value judgment of your management, also take an honest look at yourself. When you've done everything possible to improve your performance and you're still convinced subjective value judgment is the only thing holding you back, it's time to look for alternatives in the free-enterprise system. However, make sure you aren't exchanging one set of problems for another, which is what you'll be doing if you blame others for your own mistakes.

Betting on Yourself

These women in sales, along with many others, prefer to risk their careers on the cutting edge of competition and performance rather than trust the personal quirks of managers who have little understanding of powerful human emotions and the part they play in women's career success. Entrusting your career to such hidden feelings is often far more risky than betting on yourself in sales.

"It's a great feeling to be in control of your own destiny," says one saleswoman, "even if it's frightening at first."

Women from birth are conditioned to have somebody other than themselves in control. Being in control, for many, seems frightening at first. Many find it difficult to break out of the old male/female patterns. The marketplace, until recently, has been an extension of the family, patterned on women performing in lower-level jobs under the direction of men. Changing these patterns requires swimming up a cultural stream. Often it takes enormous motivation to overcome cultural handicaps. However, women in sales have learned, like the salmon, that swimming upstream is not impossible. There is a powerful instinct helping women along—the instinct to create something of their own and control their own destiny.

8

Your Own Empire:
A Sales Territory

HOW GOOD ARE YOU at managing yourself? Can you set your own deadlines? Can you get yourself up and moving each morning? Are you a whiz at organizing your life and your family? Are you able to take rejection without falling apart? Do you work best when the odds are against you? Are you aggressive and proud of it? Do you want to earn a lot of money? Would you rather paint a sunset than sit and stare at one?

If you have a positive reaction to all these questions, the line of work that might be right up your alley is a sales territory where you are queen of your own empire. Before you race to the phone in anticipation, however, there's one tiny fly in the ointment you should know about. In order to become queen of your own empire, you'll have to build it. No beginning salesperson steps into a ready-made gold mine. More often, it's a rock pile abandoned by other prospective empire builders who didn't make the grade.

Aside from the obvious reasons—like failing to get out of bed each morning—nobody can accurately pinpoint all the factors that cause one person to fail in a territory while another succeeds. It is a fascinating combination of mixing and matching intangibles. Seasoned sales managers often shake their heads in amazement when a person they have tagged a loser ends up a big winner. It happens. Nobody totally understands the deep resources some people are able to call into play in competition. Competition brings out the best in some people, while others can't stand the strain.

Therefore, nobody can predict your success any more accurately than you. Perhaps not as well. Reacting to the competitive aspects of a territory is a little like reacting to other unknown situations. How would you behave in a medical emergency or in a rescue attempt? What would you do if you awoke in a hotel room and smelled smoke? How would you react on a battlefield? What would you do if a mugger demanded your money or your life?

You probably think you know the answers to these questions, but until faced with the situation you cannot actually know your own reaction. You can only imagine how you would react. The same is true in sales. Until you have been tested under the competitive pressures of a sales territory, determining how you will measure up is at best an educated guess. Often in a sales territory it is the overly confident person who will fail rather than the more realistic one. While fear can be an inhibiting force, the fear of failure can be a powerful motivating force. In competition, running scared gets you out front and helps keep you there.

What Is a Sales Territory?

A sales territory is your own special hunting ground. The boundaries are staked out by the company as the best place to look for customers who can buy whatever you happen to be selling. A territory can be as small as a city block or even one city building in unusual cases. It can also cover several counties or states. It can be national or international. It might be assigned exclusively to you or you may share it with a partner or a team of partners. The size, terms, and boundaries of your territory are determined by your company. Your overall responsibilities and the methods by which your success is measured in relation to your territory also are decided by your company.

Just because you usually have little or nothing to say about the structure of your territory doesn't mean it shouldn't concern you. How territories are put together is crucial information, often the critical determining factor in whether you want to sell for one company or look for another with greener territories.

In large corporations these questions generally are less important because territories are not assigned until after salespeople complete a training period, often a lengthy one. Here your assignment will depend upon a number of conclusions the company's management reaches about placing you in a location where your chances of success are maximized. In well-managed companies, every effort is made to maximize the possibilities for your success. Careful selection of your territory is an important factor. After a costly training period, have no fears that your company wants you to fail. Management wants you to win. Sabotaging your success would be sabotaging the company's investment.

Other Territories

If you take a sales job with a company that invests little or nothing in training, the selection of a territory becomes more negotiable; therefore, you'll need to learn more about it before you make up your mind. Talk to the last two or three people in the territory, if possible. Unless the current sales manager was the last sales rep, there's little incentive to make a sow's ear into a silk purse. No matter how fantastic the job may seem at first glance, never leap before you've assessed your own possibilities for success in the territory. Find out the following:

- the annual revenue for the past five years; percentage of increase
- how many sales reps preceded you; average length of time each spent in the territory and why they left
- the lines of the territory; if they've frequently been redrawn, why they have
- your quota; if it's realistic—high or low
- all of the above in relation to your financial arrangements—salary and commission percentages

Remember, far more things are negotiable than most people realize, and all of these are if the company wants you badly enough. So just because you've been told the terms are unchangeable, don't believe it until you've tested it. If you are a beginner, most things aren't negotiable. If you have a good sales record and the new company needs you more than you need a job, practically everything is.

Often a territory with the greatest potential might not be the biggest revenue producer. There are territories the star salesperson of the century couldn't spin into gold, while potential diamond mines lie dormant awaiting an alert salesperson.

While no company wants its salespeople to fail since their success means the company's success, keep in mind that companies whose risk is higher because of their investment in you will do more to maximize your success than others. Recovering an investment is self-interest. Unless you sell, the company chalks up all your training time as a sizable lost investment. A company with no investment need only replace you. The greater the investment, the greater your job security because the company works harder to help you achieve their (and your) goals.

How Territories Are Assigned

Territories, like people, have personalities. The word gets around which territories are the best and which ones should be avoided like the plague. Beginners are generally assigned to the least desirable territories, which may seem unfair until you are no longer a beginner.

Naturally, everybody would like a top-producing territory located in or near his or her favorite city. But somebody has to get shipped to all those hundreds of places considered less than the garden spots of the world. Beginners who do well in Siberia-type locations often sell their way out. Getting noticed by management counts; therefore, a bad location can be a motivating factor. Many companies feel it is better for business to change salespeople in territories occasionally. Familiarity and motivation do not always remain compatible. On the other hand, there are companies who keep the same salespeople stationary as long as productivity remains high and the salespeople want to stay. However, often when a salesperson takes over a new territory and applies fresh entrepreneurial ideas for beating the last salesperson's record, both the company and the new salesperson benefit.

But you don't have to keep moving around in order to find good sales jobs in first-rate territories. There are sales jobs where you can stay put until the company gives you a retirement party and a gold watch. If you are not interested in moving, make sure you discuss transfer policies with the company before signing on. These may not be the kinds of jobs that lead to top management, but you may not care. Just be sure that you have a clear mutual understanding with the company before you accept the job. Assume nothing. More than one person, thinking he or she was set for life, has been shocked by an unexpected territory switch.

Before accepting a sales job, it's a good idea to investigate the location of the territory in relation to the product you'll be selling. Unless you have access to

customers who will buy your products, you'll set yourself up for failure no matter how motivated you are.
Many factors affect sales, such as the economy of the area, population characteristics, the work force and its makeup, whether companies are moving in or out, government policies—even the weather. These factors are especially important if you take a job with a company where your risk is greater than theirs. Keep in mind that any potential territory figure, tossed out to challenge you, promises your efforts. It sounds good when a prospective employer says you can earn $50,000 a year. However, if you end up making $5,000, the employer won't make up the missing $45,000. Make sure your efforts aren't overpromised, or you'll get a treadmill instead of a territory.

The Benefits of Having Your Own Territory

Entrepreneurial types who don't require a boss and a time clock to keep them in harness flourish in their own territories. They cherish the freedom to regulate their own lives, make their own business decisions, and put into practice their own unique ideas for building business in their territories. The sense of accomplishment is the same as succeeding in your own business.

For others, who cannot set and meet goals or discipline themselves without the aid of outside motivational factors, being on their own can be a disaster. Put certain people in a car on a lonely road in search of new customers and they'll stop and count the daisies. An entrepreneur will open a flower shop and sell them.

"The first day in my territory was so overwhelming I stayed in bed the whole day and ate an entire box of chocolates," says one saleswoman. "I reacted like a kid playing hooky. A few days later I got a short, curt note from my ex-husband informing me that he was discontinuing child-support payments and leaving the country, but not to worry about the children's college educations."

This saleswoman never discovered the reason for reacting so strangely to being on her own; however, it ceased to matter. The shock of being the sole support of her family superseded all other concerns and galvanized her into action. There's a long, expensive stretch between small children and college. She turned out to be a first-rate entrepreneur who loves the freedom of her sales territory. Her children now are almost college age and she's working harder than ever to save money to pay for their education. The father, still living in another country, writes pleasant postcards, but he hasn't repeated his original offer.

Structuring Your Own Time

The rigid time schedules of the workplace were established during a more simple working era. They make some basic assumptions about the way people live and work that are no longer valid. They assume that no worker must feed a baby at noontime or meet a school psychologist at 10:00 A.M. After all, what nineteenth-century man had to do such things?

"Instead of rigid work schedules failing to consider women," a saleswoman with three small children says, "they consider women very much. They assume women will stay home and free men to meet the rigid work schedules."

This is certainly true for today's nine-to-five work crowd. No employer frets over how a father will manage to balance his home responsibilities with his work life, yet the same employer is very much concerned about how a woman will juggle hers. The reason for this is that employers assume men have women to take care of their children but women have difficulty finding anybody except themselves to take care of theirs. Unfortunately, this is often a true assumption and a self-fulfilling prophecy."

However, while the rest of the world struggles with new approaches to solving the work scheduling through flex-time or part time or adjustable time, thousands of saleswomen have solved their own problem. Their jobs have been operating on flex-time for years. In no other job area are so many job options left up to the job holder.

"My boss doesn't care if I work fifteen hours or fifteen minutes each day. She is only impressed with numbers—how much I sell," says a saleswoman who sells mainly during evenings and weekends. "In fact, as long as I keep up my production no questions are asked about the time I spend. It's not even a subject for conversation. I love sales because there's no such thing as being early or late to work. After years of punching a time clock, this is sheer luxury."

Saleswomen all over the country say that one of the greatest advantages in sales is the feeling of being in charge of their own time. If a saleswoman needs to see her child's teacher or stay home with a sick baby, she doesn't answer to anybody except herself. The following are examples of saleswomen who are successfully mixing, matching, and meshing their jobs with their lives.

A Mother and a Saleswoman

Joan B. is the mother of four children, one still in kindergarten. She sells a line of gift items to specialty stores. Her suburban territory includes the county in which she lives, plus two counties in an adjacent state. It has a concentrated population near a major metropolitan center with several large shopping centers, where she calls on the owners of gift shops and specialty stores carrying her products.

Since part of Joan's job involves phoning prospects and record-keeping, she structures her work day so that this is done during the time she needs to be home with her children. Three days a week she makes calls in her own county, beginning after she drops off her youngest at kindergarten and ending four hours later when she picks her up. Two days a week a neighbor picks up the child and keeps her until Joan's older children get home from school. At that time they take over babysitting until their mother gets home. This enables Joan to devote two full days plus three partial days to selling. Her total selling time added to her phone work and record keeping is a full forty-hour week, often more. As with most working mothers, Joan does almost nothing else except work and care for the children. She seldom entertains and cannot spare the time to be involved in community activities. Keeping a spic-and-span house is not a high priority either, although Joan says the house is as clean as it ever was before she started working. She has become highly organized and has discovered it is actually easier to be organized than not to be.

For example, she buys groceries in bulk, utilizes a large freezer, and has a great many convenience appliances, including a microwave oven, a timed-bake oven, and a bottled-gas grill that she loves—no cleanup. Her children and husband help with the housework as long as she tells them what to do, which she doesn't like, but it beats nothing. The house is clearly her responsibility, not theirs. They remain "helpers," but at the moment she's grateful for the help. Later she says she will try to get them to take more responsibility. She longs for the day when she achieves helper status.

Next year her youngest child will be in school a full day and Joan plans to add to her territory. Although her earnings are less than $15,000 a year for the first two years, she feels she will be able to earn twice that much, perhaps more, by building up the territory and selling more efficiently. She is proud of the fact that she hasn't lost a single client since she began selling.

Although overworked, Joan feels that she would not have been able to work at all had it not been for the flexibility of her sales job. She also feels that she wouldn't have been able to afford to work at a job with inflexible hours because of the attached expenses. So many mothers who would like to work can't afford to take the kind of jobs they can get because childcare and other costs cancel out their earnings.

A Beginner Gets a Big Break

Ellen J. works for a commercial real estate company, selling and leasing commercial property. She and her husband, a small-business owner, have three children, two in private schools and one grown daughter who is working. Ellen had a little early experience selling real estate. For a short time fifteen years before, she successfully sold real estate, but quit because she felt guilty at not being a full-time mother.

"When I first quit working I couldn't wait to get back to work," Ellen says. "However, the longer I waited, the more reluctant I was to go back. I kept using every excuse possible. I was bored and fat and I have always hated housework, but still I found excuses for not looking for a job."

Ellen stayed out of the job market so long she had a great deal of fear about going back. She kept blaming her children and her husband for keeping her home, when she was the one keeping herself home.

Finally, her husband and children bluntly suggested she find something to do besides staying home and blaming them. They were paying a price for her unhappiness. Stop driving them crazy. With no excuses left, she put together a good one-page résumé with something that interested the first employer who read it: her prior sales figures and the rate of increase he achieved for the real estate firm. She was offered a job and she had no more excuses to turn it down.

As luck would have it, the first week on her new job, one of the children became ill. It was no problem. She stayed home and made phone calls to potential clients.

On straight commission, Ellen was afraid she wouldn't earn enough money to pay her commuting expenses. Her first day, she called a friend to explain what a "mistake" she had made. The next time the friend heard from her she had a different story to report. On the job only six weeks, she had initiated a $3-million deal for an industrial site. Her old confidence has returned. She's selling the way she used to sell—very aggressively. If this and other deals are successful, she could end up earning six figures in her first year. She's lost weight and is delighted to get out of the house each morning. "It's all coming back to me," she says. "I remember how much I enjoyed selling fifteen years ago. It isn't just the money, although earning money is important. I feel more alive, more a part of the rest of the world. It beats playing tennis, which I've given up. I'm too tired to play when I get home from work."

Single Heads of Households

The previous two women are married with husbands and children living at home. Sales has been a good answer to their problems. However, sales is an even better solution for another group of mothers—those single heads of households who must shoulder all or the largest part of the financial burden of supporting their children and themselves. Theirs is by far the hardest task of all. The critical advantage sales offers them is the opportunity to earn a decent living. In addition, it offers flexible hours that single mothers need even more than those living with husbands. These women constantly compare what they earn in sales with what they would be able to earn in other fields. The comparison brings into sharp focus the new battle cry of working women—equal pay for comparable work, not merely equal pay for equal work, which professional saleswomen have achieved.

Women in their own sales territories are earning twice and three times as much as they were able to earn in many professions requiring an undergraduate and often advanced college degrees. For example, many former teachers and nurses have transferred their skills into selling. Theirs are professions requiring many of the attributes necessary for success in sales, and they have made the switch because sales offered more money plus flexible time.

"Supporting a family of four on a teacher's salary," says a Xerox saleswoman, "is fine if you like permanent poverty. I couldn't make enough money to pay all the bills, much less have anything left over for my kids' college. Perhaps some people have the luxury of not worrying about money and therefore continue to teach, but I just couldn't make it financially. I'm earning three times what I earned as a teacher, and I have only been selling for two years."

"I used to work the hospital night shift just for the time differential in pay," says a nurse turned saleswoman bringing up four children alone. "In sales I'm away from the children a few days at a time occasionally, but by and large I have more time to be with them than I ever had in nursing, unless you count my sleeping body as spending time with them."

These women had been earning less than $20,000 a year. They both had graduate degrees and one had been working on a Ph.D. in education. They wouldn't take back their old teaching jobs on a bet. Both were concerned not only about earning a living day to day, but how they would be able to afford to send their children to college.

When asked why their ex-husbands aren't helping support the children, both give the sad but truthful answer so many divorced women discover. They don't have the time or the money it would take to track down ex-husbands and force them to help support their children. Says one, "The judicial system may sound good, but just try to collect child support from a man who is unwilling to pay. I found out that its virtually impossible. Lawyers don't work for free, and if they did I couldn't afford the time it would take. Therefore, it's easier to concentrate on earning more money rather than chasing my ex-husband. One works and the other, at best, is a high risk."

Her Children Come First

Geraldine S., a Chicago single head of household, solved her financial problems when she began selling insurance five years ago for The Equitable Life Assurance Company. Her children were nine and eleven years old. Even though she works out of an Equitable office, there is a vast difference in how she is able to arrange her hours in comparison to a regular nine-to-five job. If she needs to stay home with a child, she merely switches her base of operations from her office to her home. She is always on call to her children in case of an emergency and can leave her job at any time. Accountable only to herself for her time, she wouldn't give up the freedom.

"My priorities have remained the same since I went to work," she says, "and my children come first. Next on my priority list are my work and social commitments. Last on the list is cleaning the house. My mother told me early in life that if you keep looking straight ahead and don't look down, you won't see the dirt. It's good advice."

Geraldine also has solved her financial problems. She sells estate planning to corporate executives and has been extremely successful. She is well able to support her children in a comfortable life-style. She wouldn't trade the independence of her sales job for any other. Her independence is important to her, and her production is important to her company. They appreciate her, and she appreciates the life-style her work allows her. So far, it's been a perfect marriage for a single parent with double responsibilities.

Women in the Insurance Business

There are thousands of saleswomen across the country with similar stories. Women and insurance companies are discovering each other. Both are learning that selling insurance offers single-parent women great opportunities, and it offers companies an ever-growing talent pool of highly motivated women. The insurance industry is vast. There are thousands of jobs in territories stretching from Maine to California. But let the job seeker beware. Not all offer happy experiences or high-paying jobs. As with all other sales positions, it's important to investigate the job, the company, the policies affecting women, and the territory.

Traditionally, selling insurance has been a man's job. It has been the kind of sales job in which an energetic, intelligent young man through skill and hard work could rise to the top of his company. It is also the kind of industry in which highly successful salesmen choose to remain in sales because they often have to take a pay cut when they give up selling and go into management.

Insurance agents build a base of clients over many years, allowing some to earn six-figure incomes. Often in a highly successful company, not doing well in the insurance business means doing very well indeed in many other fields. It is the kind of sales job that can offer rich rewards if you choose the right company, get a good territory, and learn how to sell. Like almost all other good sales jobs, insurance virtually excluded women until the past ten to fifteen years, when thousands of insurance jobs began to open up. Even though there was much resistance to women selling insurance—and some remains—women as a whole are doing well regardless of statistics showing they are selling 20 percent less than men. That figure doesn't account for the difference in the length of time women and men have been selling, which is exceedingly important. Comparing male sales agents on the same basis would produce the same if not a greater disparity.

Currently, there are more jobs in insurance than there are women to fill them. And most companies require that sales managers recruit women agents. However, progress is not all downhill. It is still possible to join the best insurance company and discover a nineteenth-century boss whose feelings about women selling insurance makes the job very difficult. Some branch offices still plaster their walls with their top producers, who all turn out to be men. That should tell you something right away. If a district manager hasn't been able to recruit one top-producing saleswoman in fifteen years, he can't be trying very hard, no matter what the slick recruitment brochures from the home office would have you believe.

Choose carefully if you're interested in selling insurance. It's possible to find an exciting and lucrative career with a first-rate company—and it's possible to find the exact opposite. Whether or not the insurance company is really committed to giving women equal employment opportunities is critical. Ask the following questions if you're considering taking a job selling insurance:

- What is the company's EEO policy? Ask for a copy.
- How many women
  - agents?
  - managers?
  - executives?
  - members of the board of directors?
  Find out
  - what kind of support management provides for its women agents, such as training for its male managers in dealing with women agents
  - average earnings of women agents compared with men's averages for same length of service in company
  - if the EEO policy is voluntary or part of management's overall financial objectives

In addition, talk to saleswomen in the company, particularly the successful ones (companies are generally delighted to give you names of successful women agents). Even if you have to make a phone call across the country, it will be money well spent. Ask the following questions:

- What accounts for her success?
- What kind of sales manager does she have?
- Is the support provided by the company for women helpful or merely window dressing?
- What are the pitfalls to avoid in this company?
- Is top management really committed to hiring women?
- What are her goals? Have women gone from sales into management?
- If she could choose any company, would it be the one she's in or a competitor?

Before you ask these questions, make sure the saleswoman understands you will never reveal her name or her answers. Except in unusual circumstances, saleswomen are your best information sources. They are anxious for more women to succeed in sales and are delighted to be helpful. Gain their trust and you'll be able to get valuable inside information that often can make a large difference in your own failure or success. But make sure you keep your part of the bargain. Never reveal confidential information, even if you're tied to the stake and somebody is lighting the match. When a saleswoman puts her job on the line to help you, repay the favor with lifelong silence. Of course, if she's said only good things about the company—things you later learn are true—talking may be good for her career. If so, reveal all.

Inspiration

If you think all those women succeeding in sales are different from you, that somehow you are an exception and could never be a success in sales, read on. In the next chapter you'll meet a housewife who thought that anything beyond washing the kitchen floor and neatly folding the laundry was not for her. But now she's an executive.

9

A Housewife
Becomes an Executive

FOR GOOD REASONS, nobody is a greater booster of insurance saleswomen than Bernice Malamud, a former housewife who might never have left her cozy kitchen had not fate and the insurance industry intervened.

Today she is a director of The Equitable Life Assurance Society and assistant vice-president of Selected Resource Development. In this capacity, she serves as a bridge between Equitable's women agents across the country and insurance men trying to resolve their inner conflicts with the company's strong EEO recruitment policy. Insurance salesmen and male managers, with some remarkable exceptions, have been lukewarm—to put it mildly—about bringing women in any numbers into their ranks. Some can't shake their feelings that women should type instead of sell; therefore, conflict is built into Malamud's job. Without hostility, she brings to this delicate task understanding that comes from living on both sides of the fence.

Malamud's job requires a great deal of travel, public speaking, and counseling. Neat and trim in a crisp business suit, a touch of gray at her temples, she sits in her tidy office at The Equitable's New York City corporate offices minimizing her accomplishments.

"If I could do it, anybody can do it," she insists. "I was the kind of person who was determined to be a lifelong mother whether my children needed it or not—because I needed it. You realize, I am only a high school graduate.

"At one time I was afraid—actually afraid—to go out alone in public. I became panic-stricken once when I went to a department store. I suddenly realized that my husband and children didn't know where I was and wouldn't be able to find me if I needed to be found. I was terrified. I got out of the store by following what looked to me like a strong woman. I followed her out of the store, into the subway, and home. And I never went back."

It's hard to imagine that Malamud could ever have been the woman she is describing. She is just the opposite now. "When I tell this story in public," she says, "women all over so identify. I can't tell you how many come up to me later and say they have had similar experiences."

During her "happy housewife" days, Malamud constantly tried to figure out why any woman with a nice husband and healthy children would want anything more. She felt she had everything any woman should want.

"I remember not being able to understand why a woman who didn't have to would choose to work. I was content in my small world, taking care of my husband and children. Ring around the collar and the Tidy Bowl television commercials were made just for me. I spent hours waxing my kitchen floor. I was your homemaker of homemakers. I was dragged from my kitchen kicking and screaming."

Malamud is being humorous, but she is dead serious.

No wonder she understands the feelings of sales managers who are also being dragged into another world. She has real empathy for their kicking and screaming. The path of changing from that housewife of not so long ago to her current life is a dramatic story of inner conflict thousands of women will understand.

A "Happy" Housewife

Bernice Malamud was engaged at seventeen, married at eighteen, and the mother of two sons a few years later, "I was 'happy, happy, happy,' " she says. "I had it all —my husband, my children, and my small apartment where I could cook and clean and stay home and be protected." When it began, Malamud felt threatened by the women's movement and kept wondering what was wrong with "those women." She used to ask a neighbor, a woman who worked, Freud's famous question, "What, oh what, do women want?" The woman's answer—that she liked her job more than she liked keeping house—made Malamud vaguely uneasy. She didn't know why.

Malamud's life as a happy homemaker came to a crashing halt when the family's small apartment over a candy store was sold. They would have to move. She and her husband, wanting to provide a better life for their children, decided to buy a small home in the suburbs. But there was one hitch. They had no money, and her husband's salary couldn't possibly stretch that far. Malamud would have to go to work. There was no other way to afford to move out of the city and into a $19,000 home on Long Island. Already deeply in debt as a result of borrowing the $9,000 down payment from relatives—a thousand from one, two thousand from another—they were financially strapped.

Malamud's total working experience had been as a "gal Friday" in an office for a short time before her marriage. Through a relative, she landed a job as a file clerk in a small insurance office near the new home. Frightened by the thought of working and miserable over being forced to leave her comfortable home life, she felt constantly torn. "I used to go into the children's rooms and hold their pillows. They didn't even know I was gone," she says. "I was so miserable being away from home. I wanted to stay forever in my own little kitchen."

She performed so badly in her job that the company considered firing her. She had been hired to rebuild a filing system after a fire. "When I finished," she says, "the files were in worse shape than they were from the fire."

In addition to hating her job, Malamud was frightened of authority. She was afraid of talking to the men at work. Her hands would shake when she handed one of them a paper. "Any man in a three-piece suit frightened me," she says. "I think it was the vest. Any man in a vest seemed so sophisticated. Even the teeny-boppers snapping their gum were sophisticated compared with me."

The company decided to move her to the switchboard instead of firing her. Maybe she would work out better there. It looked like a very tough job to Malamud. For one thing, she would have to learn to talk to men in vests.

The Turning Point

The turning point in Malamud's life occurred when she raced home one day by cab to search for what she thought was a "missing child"—her youngest son. Leaving her switchboard uncovered, panic-stricken because her son hadn't answered his daily after-school phone call from her, Malamud was convinced something dreadful had happened. And whatever it was, she would be at fault for not being home where she belonged. Instead of a disaster, Malamud found the child safe and sound. He had taken a little longer to walk home from school because a spring rain had formed fascinating mud puddles and he had lingered, watching the swirling leaves in the water. Something clicked in Malamud's head when her son began to apologize for his delay.

"Take all the time you want from now on," she told him. "By all means, take time to watch the swirling leaves in mud puddles." She wanted him to feel comfortable doing all those wonderful, harmless things little boys love to do, instead of sharing in her anxiety.

On the cab ride back to her office she made up her mind to stop driving herself and her family crazy. Instead she would put that energy into her job. If fate had forced her into a role she didn't want, she would make the best of it. She made a commitment to succeed. Arriving back at the office, she asked an important question that every working woman committed to success eventually asks: How do I move up in this organization? At her level, there was only one way to go. Up.

A Long Climb Begins

Success didn't come overnight. It came step by step over a long period of time in which Malamud conquered many problems, in both her personal and working life. It is a road many women have traveled.

Having lived a sheltered, childlike life, Malamud began to assert herself. For example, over her husband's objections she learned to drive. Her husband, protective with the best of intentions, felt the highways were too dangerous for her to drive. "The highways are much more dangerous now that I am driving," she says, laughing. There were other problems with her husband. Upsetting a comfortable balance of power never occurs without resistance.

Now determined to succeed, Malamud began where she was. She became the best switchboard operator the company ever had. She learned to type. She conquered her fear of men in vests. She helped the insurance salesmen with their reports. She studied the insurance business. She changed jobs, going with another insurance company, where she finally got into sales after threatening to leave otherwise. Her boss, also with the best of intentions, told her all the reasons women shouldn't sell insurance. But he finally sponsored her for her insurance license when she remained determined.

This confrontation was a milestone for Malamud. It meant standing up to a boss who wanted to keep her where she was, not because it benefited her but because it benefited him. It was a great victory. Her boss was wearing a vest. It had taken years to get into sales, but at last she was ready to begin.

As a saleswoman, Malamud made calls at night, constantly learned more and more about her business, and worked to improve her sales skills. It paid off. She began to earn a very nice income and was able to replace the old battered car she had bought for $65. She enjoyed her job even though it was hard work. She looked forward to going to work. She began to feel differently about herself. In addition to being a wife and mother, she was becoming a person in her own right. Having been forced kicking and screaming through the process, she was grateful for the push into full adulthood.

Trouble at Home

By this time Malamud was earning more money, and her paycheck was as important as her husband's in supporting the family. She was working hard. By example, she became a different kind of parent to her children. Once, when her young son asked her for a ten-speed bicycle, she told him that in order to buy the bike she would have to make three additional sales that month. Then she asked him how much money he was willing to put to it. Each evening, before she reached the goal, her son would ask her why she was home instead of out trying to make the sales.

She made the three sales, but she felt she was teaching a more important lesson: that her son's contribution was important, no matter how small, and that it takes hard work to reach your goals. She was also teaching him what millions of children know: that mothers support families in a world that has never been any other way for thousands of women.

During all those years of dependency, things went smoothly on the home front. When Malamud was forced to work at a job she didn't want, her husband and children were sympathetic. But when her job became a fulfilling career, she discovered that her relationship with her husband and children began to change. "My voice changed," Malamud said. "One day I realized it when my son said to me, 'You're using your business voice on us,' and it was clear that nobody liked my business voice." Previously, when talking to her family, she had had sounded like a woman in a television commercial who just discovered a new kitchen floor wax—breathless, infantile, and happy.

Malamud explained to her family that her voice had changed because she had grown up. She compared it to the process her own sons had gone through when their voices changed, signifying an end to childhood and the beginning of manhood. She was not a child bride and child mother anymore. She too was an adult, and happy about the change. Even if they liked her old voice better, she liked the new one. The children quickly adjusted. Her marriage did not.

In the painful process of becoming a total person, Malamud felt that needing to earn money was literally her salvation. If she had never needed to earn money to help support her family, she might still be putting a shine on her kitchen floor and asking the age-old question "What, oh what, do women want?"

Moving to The Equitable

After a successful career selling insurance for an agency, Malamud set up her own insurance company. A few years later, she moved from her own agency to her current job as a vice-president with The Equitable Life Assurance Society, one of the country's major corporations. Her experience fitted perfectly with plans of The Equitable's chief executive officer to bring women into full participation in every area of the company. With a thorough background in insurance, a successful career as an agent, and a personal understanding of those deep conflicts separating men and women, Malamud was made to order for her new job.

Often, in talking to groups of insurance managers, she role-plays many conflicts they experience in hiring and advancing women. She can play any part with success. She's been there.

"The scab is still there," she says. "All I have to do is scratch it. It is a part of my past that I feel deeply. It isn't difficult for me to go back to all those conflicts."

Once, in a simulated job situation, a manager got so angry that he shouted, "You're fired." "I felt the shock and the pain of being fired. It was make-believe, but the feelings were real," she says.

With great skill, she breaks through the hostility of males and females in working situations, striving for a middle ground that will make them more productive. When female agents confide in her about discriminatory managers, she explains to them that their situation is not unlike that of an older man holding back a younger one. It doesn't only happen in male/female situations. She counsels them to go beyond the roadblock and create their own success. They are in an entrepreneurial business, where a self-starter can produce her way out of all her business problems.

"Learn all you can from your manager," she advises women. "How nice if love and understanding and affection are also provided by your manager. However, I don't believe in the tooth fairy. So try to get your warm fuzzies elsewhere and settle for what your manager can teach you.''

This tells women to succeed no matter what obstacles they find and not to waste energy on the wrong things. Change what you can change—your productivity—and don't worry about things you can't change—your manager's behavior toward women.

Malamud has discovered that male managers frequently tend to be *too* understanding of female agents, which can hurt their careers more than hostility. They try too hard to solve problems no manager can solve. When a manager symbolically becomes a parent, a lover, or a husband to a female, he sabotages her success. As one manager confessed to Malamud, "I love my women agents right out of the business.''

The Kind of Manager Women Need

Malamud also found a different kind of manager in a role-playing situation, the kind she hopes to help develop at The Equitable. This man cut right through the complicated personal problems that were being presented and came up with precisely the right answer.

"I cannot solve your personal problems," he said, "but I can help you become more successful in your business life, which might be a factor in helping you solve your personal problems.''

Managers need to identify, Malamud believes, the fine line that separates personal problems from business problems and "manage only to the business of business.'' Until managers emotionally understand this separation, they will frustrate themselves, the women they are trying to help, and the company as well. They will serve nobody well. There are complicated, tragic, personal problems a manager can do nothing about except make worse if he oversteps his managerial responsibilities.

This seemingly simple rule, so difficult to practice, trips up many managers. Unfortunately, the person who is hurt most is the women who is "helped" when she should be left with the decisions for her own life. No matter what her decision, the right decision for the manager is to steer clear.

In helping both men and women become better managers at The Equitable, Malamud gives them a list of management steps that come right out of effective parenting. "I tell them to use this list in the office and then take it home to use on their children. It works well either place."

- Identify and define the conflict.
- Generate possible alternative solutions.
- Evaluate the alternative solutions.
- Decide on the best acceptable solution.
- Work out ways to implement the solution.
- Follow up and evaluate how the solution has worked out.

In addition, she gives Equitable managers a final step that is often valuable. It is: Delay your response.

Often, if a manager listens, providing nothing more than understanding and sympathy, it gives employees time to come up with their own solutions. People with problems sometimes want nothing more than a sounding board. They don't expect answers. Most people, even those whose behavior suggests the opposite, realize that in the end each individual, male or female, must come to grips with his or her own problems. As Malamud says, "There is no tooth fairy."

Men, however, due to their traditionally dominant role in society, often feel great pressure to provide solutions, especially to women. Women managers in this respect have an edge over men. Women, traditionally warm and understanding to men's problems, have never been expected to provide solutions. They are expected only to listen. Many managers and husbands would benefit by doing the same instead of attempting to solve the problems.

She's Still Selling

Even though Malamud is now an executive, she's still selling harder than ever. She is selling a philosophy more difficult to explain than a client's insurance needs, even though both are intangible products. At times she is greeted with enormous hostility, and it takes great skill to overcome her clients' objections to her product —tolerance in the workplace.

For example, many men at The Equitable, both agents and managers, are often eager to confess that they are "male chauvinists" and proud of it. It may take a few deep breaths to repress an unchivalrous response to such an announcement. Malamud could easily do this, since she's quick on her feet and has a good sense of humor. Instead of reacting with anger or hostile humor to the inherent hostility of the situation, she suggests that being a male chauvinist is not a permanent condition. "It is what you are at the moment," she tells them. "Unlike your height, sex, or color, this is a condition that can change."

Right before her eyes, a change is occurring in the insurance business. She finds enthusiastic managers across the country delighted with the progress of their women agents. There are some new faces among those walls and walls of top insurance agents whose photographs are displayed in branch offices and newspaper ads. And these days, nobody is prouder than the manager of the district where it is happening. Most recognize that the vitality of the business depends upon the vitality of the agents out on the selling line. Women are becoming a vital part of the insurance industry. At The Equitable women are also beginning to appear in the ranks of the top earners, in a company where more than one hundred agents currently earn more than $100,000 a year and more than one thousand earn more than $45,000 a year.

Malamud confesses that occasionally she misses the old days when she was out selling enough insurance to make her a top producer. She took a pay cut when she became part of management, as frequently occurs in the insurance business. What does she miss most? "The ability to give myself a raise," she replies. "Also, in management you're not really so clearly in control of your own destiny. Your success to a much greater extent depends on others. In selling, you control your own destiny. It's hard to give up."

A New Question at The Equitable

Women in the insurance business have risen so rapidly that before some managers become comfortable hiring women agents others are already asking a very different kind of question. Rather than questioning *whether* women can sell, they are asking, "Why do some women outproduce men?"

Much credit for the answer to this question goes to those agency managers who, like true entrepreneurs everywhere, saw the same possibilities for success in women agents as in men. These managers have supported women enthusiastically because they were interested in the prosperity of their companies. They gave women a chance to sell and measured them on the results. Unfortunately, these men have been in the minority, but it's fortunate for women that a few always existed.

One example of this kind of manager is Marvin R. Rotter, an agency manager for The Equitable in St. Louis. Reprinted here, with his permission, is a letter he wrote to another manager who asked the new question "Why do some women outproduce their male counterparts?" His letter speaks for many managers in many companies who hire and promote people on the basis of ability. They are the kind of managers who make an enormous difference for women.

Mr. Paul Fanning
Agency Manager
Portland, Oregon
Dear Paul,

You asked me, "Why do some women outproduce their male counterparts?" I cannot answer that question in all cases, but I will try to give you some of my views on why this happens and not so infrequently.

Up until three years ago, this agency had very little luck in the recruitment, let alone success of women. The biggest reason was a disbelief by managers that women could succeed in our business. Most of the managers had either a macho-type attitude (only the strong survive, or keep them barefoot and in the kitchen) or a patronizing attitude, (Oh, how pretty you look today, or don't worry about not being Club, you are doing fine for a gal). All the sermonizing and all of our discussions in regard to the recruitment of women seemed to end up with a district manager saying to me, "All right, Mr. Agency Manager, I will do it because you are telling me to do it, but I won't like it." Obviously, that didn't work. What they needed to observe was a woman being successful in our work. That is also what the prospective women agents needed to see.

We were going no place. On one hand, the district managers didn't believe women could be successful. On the other hand, women looking at our business didn't believe women could be successful. They had no role model—they were fulfilling a prophecy. The district managers were bringing in women halfheartedly, and women were picking up on that.

Three years ago I decided to visit with several successful women in the St. Louis area. Finally, I got lucky. Michele Fischback was recommended to me. I interviewed her twice and found that she had the same goals, the same needs, and the same desires to succeed as any other good prospective agent. I then contacted my newest district manager, Steve Pieper. I selected Steve knowing that he would have the most time to spend with Michele; and in this case, it worked. They got along well. She got off to a quick start, was National Leaders Corp for her first full year and again last year. District Manager Pieper credits Michele for helping him build his district to NCA status. Michele was recently promoted to district manager and has hired four people, two of them men.

This, I believe, opened the managers' eyes quicker than my preaching or statistics or moral obligation lectures. They saw that they could be missing a market. Soon each district had some women; soon the agency had fifteen women. In 1979, a woman by the name of Marion Yaap was #1 DSF agent in the agency and #2 overall in the region. In 1980, Martha Horrell was #2 DSF agent in the agency and #3 in the region.

I think that the reason women will at times outproduce their male counterparts is partially coincidental. There are successful women in the agency who are competing with the male agents for production honors. They are not competing among themselves—they don't need to. They can observe other women producing at high levels; they observe other women outproducing the men. They have confidence they can do the same. In addition to this intangible, there are certain traits I have observed in successful women that may differ from the average producer but not any different from a successful male producer.

- Women will use the phone more frequently and more efficiently.
- Women will stick to a goal plan.
- If women feel you have their interest at heart, they will learn rapidly and take direction enthusiastically.
- Successful women agents call on businessmen as frequently as they call on women.
- Women will be good prospectors and will bring a good market to our business.

One of their top priorities will be to act, dress, and present themselves in a thoroughly professional manner. In a very short time, they will not only appreciate our business, they will love it. It will be the first time in their lives that no one has told them when to come in or check out or take a coffee break or go to lunch. They will work awfully hard to hold onto that freedom.

Really Paul, these traits are no different than the traits that most successful agents display. An added bonus is that many of our successful women take a great deal of pride in considering themselves pioneers of the industry.

They are terribly enthusiastic about visiting with any prospective agent about our business. They are believers —we gave them an opportunity and they made the most of it.

I have found that successful women agents have the respect of their male counterparts because anyone who knows our business knows what you go through to be called a success!

Sincerely,

Marvin R. Rotter, Agency Manager St. Louis, Missouri

10

Technique, Motivation, and Guilt

"SALES IS A VERY PERSONAL ACT. It is a one-on-one relationship," says Athley Gamber, who sells airplanes internationally. Gamber is right on target. Sales techniques that work for one person may bomb for another. People who are fascinated by intricate human chemistry are more likely to be successful salespeople than those who don't care what makes people tick.

Salespeople often have difficulty explaining how to sell to others because they can't figure out exactly how they, themselves, sell. They develop their own style by trial and error and instinct, keeping those techniques that work and discarding the ones that don't. For those who last in a sales career, this sorting out develops into a personal selling style after a few years.

Interestingly, there are extremely successful salespeople who seem to defy every selling rule, while others who go by the book couldn't sell five-dollar bills for two dollars each. "One of the reasons sales is so interesting," one saleswoman says, "is that there are so many ways to do it right and just as many ways to do it wrong."

Motivation

"Most successful people overcame some handicap—physical, racial, or economic," says C. Peter McColough, CEO of Xerox. McColough feels he was motivated to succeed by growing up in the isolation and poverty of Nova Scotia.

Successful salespeople are motivated by money and success. They have high aspirations. They aren't satisfied with a nine-to-five job with incremental raises. They want the chance to be very successful and earn a lot of money. They know this takes more effort, but they are willing to work harder. Salespeople are the first to admit that success, although not everything, is important. And they are the last to put down people for earning money. Salespeople are direct and honest about the human needs money supplies. Unlike some people in other professions, salespeople seldom couch motivation in idealism, although they too enjoy the gratification that comes from helping others.

"I've never met a doctor who'll publicly state he went into medicine for the money," says a salesman who became president of his own company. "However, I know quite a few doctors who'll admit it privately. Conversely, salesmen freely admit they're in sales for the money, yet they'll talk your ear off about the kick they get from helping people."

Here's an example of a successful and motivated salesman whose style is most distinctive and who is open and honest about his motivation. While this man's style will not work for everybody, it works for him, which is what counts in the long run.

A Nonconformist

George Smith is a man who grew up extremely poor in a family of nine children and a widowed mother but made his first million buying and selling by the time he was forty. Secure at last from the poverty that had afflicted his life since birth, Smith decided to retire and lead a carefree existence. Instead, he became aware of a factor he never dreamed possible back in his youth when he was working hard just to survive. He discovered that although the absence of money can make life miserable, having money—no matter how much—does not necessarily make you happy.

Without a goal, Smith felt worthless. Without work, there was little purpose in his life. Therefore, he gave up the so-called good life when his risk-free living brought on his first and last bout of depression. He also created his own need to continue working.

"I got myself in hock with a few business deals and I've been fine ever since," he says. "I'm the kind of guy who'd rather put together a plan to make some money than go jogging down some road."

Smith personally continues to do most of the selling for his primary business, a general contracting firm that began as a chemical cleaning and sandblasting company in Buffalo, New York. Thirty years ago Smith chose the name, Ajax Smith, Inc., in order to be listed among the first in the phone directory. "I think I had the name before the sink cleaner," he says. Since that time, Smith has branched into a number of side businesses for which he is the number-one salesman.

One of these sidelines is buying and selling property in the Florida Keys, where he began years ago when ocean frontage was plentiful and cheap. He buys and sells everything from land, restaurants, and condominiums to boats and supplies. He's the kind of salesman another salesperson instantly likes because when he's not selling, he buying. He likes the bartering process and he can't resist a good deal.

Back in Buffalo, Smith once went to an auction to buy bricks for one of his companies. He bought a few things, then had a few drinks with the auctioneer. After repeating this process until well past midnight, he bought the building. "I had to," Smith said. "I couldn't afford to move all the things I had bought."

Impulse

Unlike salespeople who study their customers and practice their techniques, Smith sells the way he buys—on impulse. He's a gambler at heart who says he's had more winners than losers. He's motivated by money, stemming from his early poverty, which he recalls as fortuitous. "If I had been born with a silver spoon," he said, "I probably would have been a playboy."

A nonconformist who insists his clients go to lunch where he can get a drink ("food mixes better with a little alcohol"), Smith's most memorable sale was based on the candor for which he's famous. He arrived home one Friday only to learn that an official of a Christian Science Church had requested that he make a sales presentation that same evening, at the church. Smith's wife, observing that lunch must have lasted longer than usual, suggested he phone his regrets, but to no avail.

At the church Smith began his sales presentation with total honesty: Yes, he had had a few drinks, and his wife thought it injudicious of him to appear in his condition before a church group, particularly a church whose members don't drink alcohol. However, Smith explained that as a hardworking Catholic who had had a very difficult week, he was celebrating surviving it with a few beers—quite a few, since he'd lost count. He was sorry, but he'd do the best he could. He got the $150,000 order.

A Selling Style Develops

Smith says he doesn't know how he sells, but he has developed a philosophy that works for him. Integrity is paramount. His word is as good as a contract. He offers fair prices and fulfills his promises. If he bids too low on a deal—which he doesn't often do—the quality of his work doesn't suffer. However, if anybody questions his integrity, they have just ended the discussion. He walks out. He has a low boiling point, never wears a tie, doesn't carry a briefcase, and generally borrows a pen from the client to sign the contract.

Smith doesn't know the source of his motivation—why he'd go right on buying and selling for free rather than live a life of leisure he could well afford. He has no plans to retire, ever. He points to his family of nine brothers and sisters, all achievers, as a possible clue to the mystery.

"They're all hustlers, just like me," he says with a smile. "I have a brother who is a Jesuit priest, yet he's essentially doing the same thing I'm doing. He keeps trying to sell me on the evils of materialism. So you see, he's selling his ideas, just like me."

From Saleswoman to Publisher

Although it's still more difficult for women to be honest about pursuing success, many have dropped the self-effacing attitudes of the past. Gone are the days when it was chic for a women to claim that money and success meant nothing to her. Many, like Constance Sayre, freely discuss their ambitions. And many, like her, credit a sales career with helping them develop the self-confidence so necessary in management. However, few did it as early as Sayre. You get the feeling immediately upon meeting her that had Sayre been born in Victorian times she might have had a little difficulty getting the hang of demurely dropping her handkerchief.

Back when Sayre began her publishing career selling

subsidiary rights, virtually no women in the industry were in sales. Despite this, Sayre harbored high aspirations. If she feared anything, it was failure, not success. Ambitious, confident, and outspoken, Sayre has moved from subsidiary rights into management. She is director of marketing for Viking Press, and she has no difficulty charting a career course that will take her to the top of the ladder.

A Line Responsibility

Sayre is in the vanguard of former subsidiary rights saleswomen who have successfully transferred their sales skills to marketing management. In directing marketing for Viking Press, Sayre has a line responsibility that makes her accountable for the company's bottom line.

If anybody worried about a woman taking over an important money area three years ago, he's resting easier now. During Sayre's first year, the company's sales tripled.

Sayre, who developed her own style, feels that selling taught her the kinds of things women need to know to be successful in management. "Being in subsidiary rights make a difference," she says. "It teaches you to fight for yourself and become a better negotiator."

It is apparent that Sayre, a no-nonsense person with a good sense of humor, is a fast learner. Gone are the days when she was eager to work twice as hard for half the pay just to be in the glamorous publishing industry. She still loves the industry. "The idea of selling books rather than salt and pepper shakers is very appealing to me," she says. "It is a very special kind of selling."

Baby Books and Cookbooks

Sayre recalls the industry back in the mid-1960s when she began her career with Simon and Schuster, Inc. A year after starting her low-level entry job; she began selling subsidiary rights, which was a minor part of publishing at that time. "Subsidiary rights used to be handled by the editor-in-chief's secretary out of her back pocket. Nobody cared about it. Since it was unimportant, woman came in and cornered the market," Sayre says.

After a series of publishing jobs over the next several years, including one in London ("Back then the only way to get a raise was to change jobs.") Sayre became director of subsidiary rights at Holt, Rinehart & Winston, leaving four years later to move into her current position. During the early days in publishing, Sayre says, women were virtually excluded from sales, and woman editors, the last to make it in publishing, edited cookbooks and baby books.

Today women have better jobs throughout the industry. Some of these jobs are in sales. Many women are now publisher's reps. They sell exclusively for specific publishers, while others have become independent reps, selling several publishers' lines.

A Valuable Lesson

Sayre credits her experience in selling with helping her get rid of the handicaps so many women face, the cultural trappings that make competition seem pushy for a woman but courageous for a man. "Learning to stand up for yourself is a long and difficult process," Sayre says. "But when you're out there pushing and shoving, having to justify your books over somebody else's, saying buy mine and not theirs, it gives you the courage of your convictions. In sales, standing up and making a lot of noise becomes second nature."

That's the kind of valuable experience that can help clear your vision and motivate you toward goals traditional women never think about in their wildest dreams (like the dream of becoming a publisher). Of

course, nobody ever accused Constance Sayre of being a
traditional woman.

A Fast Track and Mixed Emotions

Unique problems complicate the lives of career women,
not an unexpected result of the vast twenty-year re-
shuffling of traditional roles. In addition to those
caused by the different socialization of females, one
problem facing ambitious and motivated career women
is truly innate. It can be neither unlearned nor changed.

At an age when many women are struggling to
develop a style and a technique that will help move them
into management, thirty-one-year-old Sarah Levinson is
the director of marketing for Group W Satellite Communications of the Westinghouse Broadcasting Co.,
Inc. With a bachelor's degree from Cornell University
and an M.B.A. from Columbia, she's been on a fast
track since she completed her M.B.A. and landed a job
in an advertising agency. From this job she moved to
Viacom, becoming national marketing director then to
her current job.

With a great job and years of potential stretching out
in front of her, the world should be her oyster, and in
many ways it is. Although delighted with her job and
ambitious to move up the corporate ladder, Levinson
shares a problem with many women. After the age of
thirty, women must come to grips with a biological decision—whether, when, or if they ever will have children.
The span of years in their lives when the greatest career
advancement occurs—between thirty and forty—is also
the time their biological clock is running down.

A Nagging Worry

Levinson is concerned about the problem. It's the kind
of nagging worry that comes when she's unable to sleep.

She would like children but can't see how it would be possible in a job as demanding as hers. It's a thought unique to women. Many deal with it as Levinson does. She brushes it aside. After all, she has several years left on the clock before the decision becomes critical. Besides, there's the new campaign, and the budget, and so many exciting new marketing ideas she'd like to try out.

She's got branch locations all over the country to worry about. Perhaps in five or ten years she'll have her career well enough under control to take some time out and succeed in being one of those women who has it all—a home, husband, children, and a career.

At least Levinson has thought far enough ahead to plan one important detail many women neglect until it's too late. When the time comes for this modern-day, efficient career woman to have it all, Levinson is not the slightest bit interested in joining the new species of superwomen who, in addition to having it all, do it all. When that day arrives, Levinson says firmly, what she plans on having is lots of *help*.

Guilt

Perhaps Levinson is characteristic of the new career women who understands the demands of parenthood before experiencing them. However, get two saleswomen together who are mothers, and in less time than it takes others to comment on the weather, they will be talking about the number-one subject among working mothers: guilt and how to deal with it, followed by the number-two subject: the overwhelming workload and how to do it.

Guilt for the working mother is a wellspring that never runs dry. "If I didn't feel guilty about working," says one saleswoman, "I'm sure I'd feel guilt over not feeling guilty."

For the working mother, guilt needs no justification. It just is. It is ever-present, ever-nagging, fading away as the children grow older. The younger the children, the greater the mother's guilt. Women, the world's nurturers, feel totally responsible for children and totally guilty whenever they fail to live up to the impossible expectations placed on mothers. Even those mothers who intellectually disagree with the idea that child care is their exclusive responsibility emotionally feel that it is. This may be more understandable for divorced or widowed mothers; but it is usually just as true for working wives who feel their outside jobs should not interfere with their inside duties.

"I chose to work," says a mother of three children, including a set of twins. "Therefore, I accepted the responsibility for both jobs. My husband didn't have my choice, so why should he suffer?" This woman, now retired, has kept her bargain throughout a thirty-year teaching career. But younger women are renegotiating the terms of the marriage contract. Nine out of ten college seniors surveyed by Market Opinion Research for the International Women's Year Commission in 1975 said they expected to combine a career with homemaking, a fact not in itself so surprising. However, they also said they expected their husbands to do exactly the same thing, certainly a different kettle of fish from the way it used to be and the way it still is for thousands of women.

Sharing the Responsibility

Although husbands are "helping out" more in the home, that's one of the problems. Whenever a husband helps his wife, it implies that he's a good guy who's lending a helping hand with *her job.* If he gives his kids a bath, he's doing her a favor. If he puts a frozen casserole in the oven, he's pinch-hitting for her. If he washes his own shirts or takes his clothes to the cleaner, he's fulfilling her obligation.

The home with all its responsibilities sticks to women like fresh tar on a shoe. No matter who does the work, women keep the responsibility. "I can't get over the feeling that I should be doing the same things around the house that I did before I went to work," says a saleswoman working for a short time. "It isn't a matter of how my husband feels. *I* feel it's my responsibility. I don't think it, but I feel it. How can I change others when I'm having such difficulty changing myself?"

It's a good question. However, once you believe intellectually that housework should be shared, it's only a matter of time before feelings follow. The old idea that behavior follows attitudes works just as well, if not better, in the reverse. So try it.

"What working wives need are husbands who stop helping and start dividing up the household responsibilities," says another saleswoman. "One of the problems is that since housework has never been counted as 'real work' it's supposed to be effortless. It's little wonder working wives are supposed to be able to hold down two jobs—one real and the other make-believe."

What Every Saleswoman Needs

Saleswomen have identified an overwhelming need and a fundamental contradiction. Virtually all agree they need a wife. However, none wants a husband who would be a "wife." It is interesting that virtually no woman wants a man who—if one could be found, which is debatable—would play the helpmate role sanctioned by society for women. All favor an egalitarian marriage in which husband and wife share the household chores and the financial burdens. But none wants a man who would accept the role that just under half of all married women still fulfill.

A divorced mother of two who sells machinery in North Dakota confirms this sentiment. "When I was a housewife, my husband used to bring clients home two or three nights a week. Even though we had two small children who were difficult to care for, I never refused to make dinner whenever he called. I hated it, but I did it anyway. Now that I'm entertaining clients myself, I wouldn't think of suggesting that another person do this for me. I wouldn't ask a man any more than I would ask a woman to perform the chores I felt were part of my obligation as a wife. However, if some computer company wants a lead on a hot seller, let them come out with a mechanical wife. I'll be the first in line, and I won't ask the price."

This woman ended up getting a divorce after being so unhappy with her life that she considered suicide. To make matters worse, she went to a psychiatrist who blamed the inability to accept her role as a woman for her problems. After a short time working days and going to a non-Freudian psychiatrist evenings, she had ended up deciding for herself what she likes and what she doesn't. And she doesn't like housework. The most elaborate meal she'll make is a peanut-butter-and-jelly sandwich with a cup of canned soup on the side. Her husband ended up living alone and taking clients out to dinner. No matter how impressed they might be with a home-cooked dinner, he doesn't do it.

Children Help

Many saleswomen, none of whom wanted to be identified, say they get more cooperation with housework from their children than from their husbands. All agree that their lives are burdened by a thousand details wives perform. All wished for a "wife" to take over the trivia of their lives—to pick up their cleaning, shop for groceries, cook a candlelight dinner, clean up the mess, and pack their bags for a business trip—not necessarily in the same evening. They are willing to settle for much less than husbands expect.

"Listen," says a Washington saleswoman, packing for a trip out of town, "I have a terrific husband. He's supportive. He's good with the kids when I'm traveling and he doesn't complain about a job his mother thinks he should have grounds to divorce me on. But he's not wife material. If I asked him to pack my bags and phone my secretary—things I used to do for him regularly—he'd head for the nearest bar. And I wouldn't blame him. I wouldn't expect him to do what I used to do routinely. There's something insane about this.''

Emotional Support

Although important, the housekeeping services of a wife aren't the only thing these saleswomen talk about. They also mention the emotional support wives give husbands who work long hours pursuing difficult careers. Husbands, although there are remarkable exceptions, have less tolerance when placed in a supportive role. Instead of being sympathetic, their solution often is to suggest that their wives find ways of working more efficiently or cutting down on the work at the office. When wives work long hours, husbands tend to consider it personal neglect.

"You'd think my job was another man the way my husband carries on," says a newly married saleswoman whose husband is already urging her to stop working so hard. "If I'm not home on time, he calls the office. If I make evening calls, he asks a lot of questions. And when I get home he lets me know, in a thousand unspoken ways, that he's not happy. However, when he works late, it's a different story. He behaves as though I should welcome home the conquering hero. He has reminded me several times that his job is primary even though we currently earn about the same money. Unless he changes—and I hope he does—I'm going to split.''

Children, even though they are more cooperative about doing household chores than husbands are, make larger demands upon their mothers than on their fathers. They too expect more from mothers than fathers. One saleswoman tells how her twelve-year-old son revealed his different expectations of mothers and fathers. One evening when the child stayed late at school and needed a parent to pick him up, he called his mother at her office even though his father's office was more convenient to the school. When asked why he had chosen to ask his mother to pick him up instead of his father, the child answered, "I didn't want to bother Dad. He's working."

A Pleasant Surprise

One saleswoman has a pleasant "guilt" story to tell. She had moved from the East to the Midwest in a sales job for which she traveled in several adjoining states. Before she settled into her job routine, school registration arrived. The day her three children registered in their new school, she decided that motherhood had to supersede her new job.

"There was no way I was going to let the kids register alone," she says, "even though they are capable. It was a feeling that's hard to explain. But I just had to be there with them. There are times when my guilt overwhelms everything else. This was one of those times."

Stopping at a phone booth after registration, this woman called her new boss to let him know she was on her way to the office. She had no intentions of explaining the reason for her absence. Caught between the demands of motherhood and the responsibility of her job, she was particularly sensitive to any hint that she might be letting down on the job.

The secretary who answered the phone told her that her boss wasn't in the office yet. "He's registering his child for school," the secretary said. "I suppose you're doing the same thing?"

This saleswoman was delighted to learn that her boss is a single father who understands her problems. He is divorced and has custody of his young son. However, even though he would understand why she wanted to be with her children the first day of school, it is doubtful that he would be perceptive enough to understand the reason she didn't want him to know what she was doing. Divorced mothers, however, will understand.

They know the damned-if-you-do-and-damned-if-you-don't position of working mothers. Single-parent mothers are accused of spending either too much time with their children at the expense of their jobs or too much time working at the expense of their children. In the eyes of many people, there is no middle ground for mothers. There are lots of ways to lose and very few ways to win.

Life Isn't Fair

Life isn't fair, particularly for working mothers. Emphasizing the unfairness of societal expectations for men and women, television personality Phil Donahue in his book and on his television program tells of his early days as a divorced parent bringing up four sons alone. Wherever he went, he was praised for routine parenting. He was frequently offered help at the laundromat. People (generally women) praised him for doing simple chores like getting the kids off to school and cooking hamburgers. At the same time, hundreds of thousands of working mothers were doing the same thing in addition to supporting the children on far less money than he earned. The difference was that women are expected to perform these tasks. Men aren't.

No U.S. president, although it may in time happen, has called working mothers the backbone of the country. Instead of extending equal respect to working mothers as to working fathers, every societal ill is dumped on them. Let the child of a working mother get into trouble, and she is blamed for neglect. If society's expectations were valid, the children of working mothers and absent fathers would all be delinquent and the children of traditional fathers and nonworking mothers would all be upstanding citizens. "I want to live long enough," says a saleswoman with four young children, "to see a newspaper story that mentions the delinquent child of a 'working' father."

Superwoman

Ellen Goodman, the talented syndicated columnist of the *Boston Globe*, puts her finger on the development of the superwoman. She says the old supermom has turned into the new superwoman. "Supermom," she writes, "was the woman who always made pumpkin-shaped sandwiches with raisin eyes and carrot teeth. Her children's costumes were always homemade. She always had something 'lovin' in the oven.' She was, in short, the woman we carried around in our heads just for the guilt of it."

We have buried supermom and have come up with superwoman, Goodman says. She describes this new dominant American image as a woman who has 2.6 children, feeds them a grade-A nutritional breakfast, makes sure they have lunch money for school, then gets into her Anne Klein suit and goes off to her creative and socially uplifting job.

"Then she comes home after work and spends a real meaningful hour with her children. . . . Following that, she goes into the kitchen and creates a Julia Child, 60-minute recipe . . . discusses the checks and balances of the U.S. Government at a wonderful family dinner. The children then go upstairs to bed, and she and her husband spend another hour in their own meaningful relationship, at which point they go upstairs and she is multi-orgasmic until midnight.

"And tomorrow is another day. . . ."

Goodman says she finds a lot of fear in the image of the superwoman—fear women have of asking their husbands to share the housework. Instead, they try to do it all themselves. "Some of that comes from the old fear of the women's lib divorce thing, which is the fear that if you ask your husband for support, he will run off with his secretary the next day," Goodman says.

Fortunately, time itself generally cures superwoman-ism. After a few years of running on a treadmill, the most determined superwoman runs down. She also discovers that that the treadmill is self-imposed. She either works out a more equitable relationship with her husband or finds divorce a preferable solution to her treadmill.

Calling It Quits a Relief

"When my marriage broke up," says one saleswoman, "it was a tremendous relief. I didn't have a 'grown-up child' to care for anymore. This gave me more time with the real children. My ex-husband's current wife has my sympathy. I'm the one she calls when things aren't going well. She knows I understand."

A West Virginia saleswoman with a grown family is currently going through the superwoman problem. Her family is delighted she's working, but they do little to ease the burdens of her two jobs. She's still expected to keep the house clean, do all the shopping and cooking, and babysit for her grandchildren whenever she's home. No matter how late she gets home, nobody starts dinner without her. "Maybe I'll run away from home," she says, laughing. This year she's kidding. Next year she might not be.

"No matter what people say they want, watch what they do," a psychiatrist advised. "Unless people get something out of what they do, they stop doing it. A woman who allows herself to be overburdened probably needs to feel indispensable because of her low self-esteem." Since working women discover that economic independence increases their self-esteem and relieves their feelings of worthlessness, they stop playing the martyr and start insisting on getting a fair shake.

A man visiting a home where the husband does the laundry observed that unless his own wife continued this chore he would break up their marriage. Replied the husband, removing his white permanent-press shirts from the dryer, "And then who would be doing your laundry?"

Time-Saving

Saleswomen value time. They can't afford to waste it.
Time to them is money, and vice versa. Managing their
time efficiently in their working lives carries over to
their home life. They also learn what's important and
what isn't worth the time it takes to do. For example,
many saleswomen don't send Christmas cards.

"I haven't sent out a Christmas card since the first
year I went to work," says one saleswoman. "I'm down
to basics. That's all I have time for. If I sent out Christmas cards, the time has to come from something that I
consider more important."

Another saleswoman who used to do a lot of home
entertaining has discontinued it. No more big family
Thanksgiving dinners. No more champagne parties
to celebrate somebody's birthday. No more redecora-
ting or shopping just to fill some empty time. Many
businesses are reaping the rewards of such fundamental
life- style changes. Saleswomen eat out more and shop
differently than they did as housewives. They pay less
attention to the cost and more attention to the time involved. All would give a bundle for really good frozen
foods in their particular family's size throwaway pack-
ages. And they'd like a grade-A, all-in-one dinner, perfectly prepared and beautifully decorated, that would
go into a "lovin' microwave oven" and come out good
enough to accompany the finest bottle of wine.

Networking

A new word has been coined to describe a great idea
sweeping the country. It's "networking," which means
that women are helping women. Networking was first
coined in connection with women and their careers;
however, it has been extended to women helping women
in every facet of life.

With the tremendous responsibilities women are carrying, nobody needs or deserves help more than the

hundreds of saleswomen who manage to bring up self-sufficient children while succeeding in demanding jobs.

Men have long had the old-boy network. Women with networking groups across the country are providing the same kind of support for women.

Saleswomen have also discovered a special kind of network with women in the various companies they sell to, particularly women in management who understand the difficulties of sales. Although saleswomen still run into a few "queen bees," their numbers are decreasing almost to the point of extinction. Most working women are supportive of each other.

"In the companies I call on, I find that women in management are particularly eager to talk to other professional women," says a saleswoman whose territory includes several states in the Far West. "It's not like New York City out here," she says. "Career women feel more isolated. The progress of women and the attitudes of people about them is different. We're still far behind the East and the West coasts. Which makes networking all the more valuable."

Another saleswoman in Illinois says the women she has met in her job have been enormously helpful to her. There was one embarrassing occasion, however, that she would rather forget but brings up in order to warn other saleswomen not to make the same mistake. During a sales presentation to several executives of a medium-size company, a woman walked in and sat down. Thinking the woman was probably a secretary since she was holding a note pad, the saleswoman paid little attention to her. Instead she directed most of her remarks to the men. Immediately after the presentation, one of the executives introduced her to "the president of our company." She will never make the same mistake again.

"I felt ridiculous, not because I had done something terribly wrong, but because I had done to another woman what I detest happening to me. I assumed the woman was less important than the men."

Another saleswoman whose previous job involved enforcement of EEO laws is constantly giving advice to women she runs into in her travels. "The companies might think this is to their disadvantage," she says. "But actually it has turned out to be the other way." Using her suggested step-by-step negotiations, several women she advised got results without going to court.

Many men are also being helpful to women in their networking efforts. While they aren't joining groups, they are available for advice and emotional support. One executive for a major company occasionally gets calls from career women across the country. One day he got a call from a former associate who had landed a top management job in another state. She seemed particularly tense. "What's wrong?" he asked, sensing that she must have a very serious problem.

The woman had left a board meeting. The meeting was being held up while she made a call to him. It was her second board meeting in her new job and she wanted to double-check her facts and figures on the possible acquisition of a small company which both at one time had worked for. She needed advice and she needed it in a hurry.

11

The Risks and Rewards of a Sales Career

"A SALES CAREER offers greater possibilities for personal growth and financial gain than any other career field I know," says a woman sales account executive with a major industrial company. "I wouldn't trade it for any other profession."

"To preserve my sanity, I need to know where my next month's rent is coming from," says another woman, who turned down a sales job for one paying half as much. "The financial risks in sales would drive me mad."

These two different points of view accurately reflect the feelings of many women. Either they like selling or they hate it. A sales career is not for every woman, no matter how great the opportunities. There are rewards and risks in every field. Sales is no exception. Whether the risks inherent in a sales career are worth the rewards is an individual choice for each woman to make. However, before you make up your mind, consider the assessment made by women in sales. Although these women are comfortable—even enthusiastic—about their choice, they are candid about the pluses and minuses.

From interviews with dozens of saleswomen, here are their answers to what they like best and least about their chosen profession. Whether the rewards outweigh the risks is a decision only you can make.

The Negative Side of Sales

• *Self-discipline.* In a nine-to-five job, discipline is built into your career choice. You're required to show up for work on time and perform satisfactorily. At quitting time, you can go home or out on the town or sleep for fifteen straight hours. You can forget your job. A lot of people need this kind of structure.

In sales, you provide your own discipline. For those first few years, while you are building your sales skills along with your territory, you generally work longer and harder than in a structured job.

"When it's eleven P.M. and you're still doing paperwork, you feel like changing places with somebody in an eight-hour job you can't bring home," says a saleswoman. "Every salesperson bitches about paperwork. It never ends."

• *Salary uncertainty.* Although salespeople have vast potential, most never know exactly how much money they will earn from month to month and year to year. (This is not true of salaried salespeople.)

"I expect to earn around sixty thousand dollars this year," says one saleswoman. What she means is if she earns in the last half of the year at the rate she earned in the first half, she will end up earning $60,000. Before the end of the year that figure could be up to $75,000 or down to $40,000.

So how do you plan ahead, not knowing your exact earnings? "Very, very carefully," say most saleswomen. They tend to underestimate earnings, rather than end up behind the eight ball by overestimating. Generally, time and experience enhance your ability to figure your total earnings. You can also earn more money when you need it by selling harder for a short period of time, one saleswoman says. Regardless of the pluses, uncertainty is always with you to some extent.

• *Things you can't control.* Suppose you are setting the world on fire selling more farm machinery than anybody ever sold in your territory and there is a sudden and prolonged drought? Your sales will dry up like the farmers' fields. Your earnings depend on whether farmers have enough money to buy your products. You have absolutely no control over this kind of a financial disaster. Sales can be affected by many things outside your control. Salespeople don't like it, but they have to live with it.

• *Goofing off on the job.* Few people who hold down regular jobs continue steady high performance. There are slow periods when they can relax on the job—one of the benefits of a nine-to-five job. Your salary stays the same in slow weeks and slow months. You can goof off in sales, but the results will show up in your paycheck; therefore, the tendency among salespeople is to work harder than ever during slow periods in order to keep their earnings as stable as possible. It may feel good to goof off occasionally in a regular job, but in sales you pay for the privilege. Goof off long enough, and your job will go with you.

• *Always being tactful.* "Just once, I'd like to sound off at somebody without considering the sale," says a saleswoman whose political views clash with those of some of her clients. "I have to listen politely to a lot of hogwash. Instead of being constantly on guard, I'd really like to tell one person, in particular, what I think he's full of. I may be working on an ulcer just by having to listen to him."

As with goofing off, a salesperson may pay dearly for the privilege of behaving like people in other jobs. Effective salespeople stop and think before shooting off their mouths. They wait until they're home or with friends, friends who are neither clients nor prospects. Otherwise it can be expensive.

• *Being pleasant when you feel rotten.* "There are times I feel that my face will crack from smiling," a Utah saleswoman says. No matter how they feel, or if they're coming down with double pneumonia, salespeople must be pleasant. "I go home and yell at the cat," she says. "But when I'm selling, I keep right on smiling."

• *Traveling.* Saleswomen who travel—and not all do—become accustomed to it. Some enjoy traveling as long as they're not on the road constantly. A few rate it a plus in the job. "After being home for twenty years packing for my husband so he could go flying off to exotic places while I changed diapers and cooked hot dogs," says a housewife turned saleswoman, "it's fun to fly off on my own." Another saleswoman's daughter, watching her mother pack, observed that life would be easier for herself when she grew up. "I'll know how to do a lot of things from watching you," she said. Her mother agrees.

• *Rejection.* Strangely enough, almost all saleswomen listed rejection last in what they like least about sales. Many didn't list it at all until asked. They learn early to deal with rejection and discard their former feelings of terror about it. "Rejection is just part of the job," they agree. Unless you become comfortable with rejection, you don't last in sales.

The Benefits of a Sales Career

• *Independence.* Successful saleswomen value their independence highly, claiming that it offsets the risks. All hated the idea of being tied to a desk and a schedule set by somebody else. Most had been through a series of female-type jobs that bored them, or had left professional careers that paid far less. They feel sales is exciting because it offers risks. "You appreciate rewards more when you have risked something to gain them," a saleswoman says. "There's risk in everything. Salaried jobs are not risk-free. The risks are just less obvious. The rewards also are less obvious, particularly on payday," she adds.

• *Earnings.* All are motivated by money and interested in the earnings potential of sales. It's easy to understand why the desire to earn a lot of money is one of the features many companies look for in the women they recruit. Women not motivated by money or who feel uncomfortable about earning money will not select sales. Saleswomen are ahead of most women in dealing with money.

• *Ability to control earnings.* Even though salespeople don't know the exact amount of their earnings from month to month, a few years' experience in sales provides more control over annual earnings than in most other jobs. "You have a better chance of keeping up with inflation in sales than in most-salaried jobs," says a former legal secretary who is now in sales. Many saleswomen mention the "ability to give themselves a raise" as a plus factor. They do this by setting higher sales goals and working extra hard to meet the objective.

• *Interaction with interesting clients.* Saleswomen deal with a variety of clients, from top executives to lower-level managers, on down the line. Generally, the people they see on a day-to-day basis are interesting, intelligent people who add to job satisfaction.

• *New job opportunities.* Sales skills, once learned, are valuable in virtually every job category. Good salespeople are constantly being offered new job opportunities, both in and out of sales. An excellent sales record is a golden ticket in getting new jobs. One company president wanted a sales competitor so much that he hired an expensive recruiter to offer the person a job. He's not the first, nor will he be the last, to do this. The recruiter he hired also works for many other companies. If your sales record is good enough, you need not look for jobs, because they will look for you. In addition, really good salespeople frequently end up in high executive positions. A listing of important executives of large corporations who came up through sales and marketing would fill several books. If you're interested in management, there is no better way to get there.

• *Challenging work.* Salespeople are constantly learning. They learn about their products, their clients, their competitors, and the world in general. The more you know, the better you sell. Selling is a fascinating psychological laboratory with unlimited learning possibilities. No salesperson ever died of boredom.

Sex and the Saleswoman

In discussing the risks and rewards of being female in a sales career, few women see an even-up balance sheet. Instead, they describe a lopsided balance sheet, heavy on the risk side. Dealing successfully with sex in sales requires skill, confidence, courage, and practice. The risks of unwanted and unwelcome sexual attention confront every saleswoman at some time in her career, generally early on, when she's least able to handle it.

The greatest advantage of being female, all agree, is that it helps in getting your foot in the door—an important factor in successful selling. Saleswomen usually have less difficulty setting up that critical first appointment with a client. (This will disappear as the number of women in sales increases.) However, even though an advantage, this is far from a compliment. Instead, it fits into the category of Samuel Johnson's famous sexist remark two centuries ago when he compared a woman preacher to "a dog walking on its hind legs. It is not done well; but you are surprised to find it done at all."

A saleswoman selling expensive medical equipment says she always prepares for a grueling test with each new client. Even though she has a Ph.D. in biochemistry and several years' experience as a top saleswoman for her company, new clients react to her sex. They have difficulty believing that a tall, beautiful blonde would choose to travel over several states selling complex medical products. "Being a woman is difficult enough," she says. "Being female and blonde is worse."

In many situations, once a woman gets inside the door, the advantage can quickly vanish only to be replaced by the age-old male-female, pursuer-pursued, no-win ego-gratification trip. A saleswoman learns early to walk on eggs without cracking shells. Unlike salesmen, they constantly call on the opposite sex. It's a rare occasion when a woman sells to another woman. This sets up in one month more potential sexual situations for a saleswoman than a salesman might encounter in a lifetime. In addition, many of the clients, frequently powerful within their own companies, seem unaccustomed to hearing the word no from the women in their lives.

Sexual Greetings

Many well-meaning men are so conditioned to react sexually to women that it seems natural to treat saleswomen in ways that would be totally inappropriate with salesmen. What sane executive would open a conversation with a salesman he had never seen before by commenting on his appearance, no matter if Robert Redford walked through the door? What marketing vice-president would tell a salesman that he "smells good" or ask him the name of his after-shave lotion? What sales manager would comment on the length of a salesman's legs or the color of his eyes or tell him that he's a "looker," a "comer," or a "lollipop"? And what executive would end a business meeting by expressing surprise that the salesman knew his own product line? What masquerades as compliments for saleswomen would be putdowns of salesmen. Except in rare cases, women patiently endure the putdowns in order to sell the product and figure out innovative ways of handling sex in their jobs.

Handling Sex

Every saleswoman works out her own way of dealing with potentially damaging sexual situations. The possibility lurks in every sale. Enormous creativity goes into putting off an amorous client without putting off the sale. Successfully handling such delicate problems requires great tact and uncanny perception. Luckily for women, these are areas of strength.

"Females have been schooled in handling tight situations since birth," says an industrial saleswoman. "Because of our conditioning, we have it all over men in this area.

"Little girls are taught to smile a lot, listen a lot, and never hurt anybody's feelings by blurting out the truth. They aren't supposed to tell Uncle Ben he's a bore or Aunt Fanny that she has bad breath. A little boy can punch Uncle Ben in the stomach and get away with it as long as he's wearing a football helmet. Because of their social training, women are better equipped to deal with subtle sales situations," she adds.

Using Humor

This saleswoman deals with sexual overtures by turning to humor whenever possible. This requires quick thinking and nondestructive humor. There's a difference between laughing at somebody and laughing *with* him. She is careful to put herself down, not her clients, when somebody is needed to be the butt of the joke.

"I try to keep things moving comfortably," she says. "After all, sex is a natural part of life, and sexual attraction need not be an insult. So why make a big deal over it?" This woman has a quick wit and a natural skill for coming up with a fast and funny rejoinder. One of the lines she uses with a client overstepping the fine line is that she feels sexual only in the back of a Rolls-Royce, something she learned from old Joan Bennett movies. As luck would have it, she said this once to a man who owned a Rolls-Royce. "Sorry," she quickly recovered. "It has to be hot pink."

This woman, among other things, has promised to "call just as soon as the operation heals," and "to consider anything as long as my husband is allowed to watch." She's ready "anytime except Monday nights, when my husband watches football instead of me."

This woman confirmed something she long suspected. That turning the tables on men, if done deftly and without destructive humor, works instantly on men who count on having their offers refused. Instant acceptance is often the best of way of foiling a big talker. Of course, you have to be able to separate the big talkers from the others.

The Dividing Line

A pharmaceutical saleswoman claims she instinctively knows this dividing line. After letting a few innuendos pass, she once stood up in a new client's office and said, "Okay. Let's go. I passed a Holiday Inn about a mile down the road. If we hurry we can finish before lunch." The man was panic-stricken until he discovered she was joking. When men paint themselves into corners, they often expect women to get them out gracefully.

This episode has since provided the basis for a lot of good-natured ribbing where traditional roles are reversed. She often opens up the conversation by asking "if today is going to be the big day." Since both know the "big day" will never occur, sex has become a comfortable subject. The man is the one who thinks up excuses to match her offers: He has a headache. Other women won't leave him alone. His ex-wife's in town. She won't respect him in the morning, etc. One day he greeted her with, "I've got a big order for you today if you promise to leave my body alone. It needs a little wrinkle rest from you aggressive saleswomen."

With many men, this saleswoman feels it is imperative to "put the sexual issue to bed," so to speak. As a result, many men and women are realizing for the first time that male-female friendship is possible. The enforced sexual separation of the past plus the subservient role of women in business served to heighten sexual awareness. Today's business mix makes the old attitudes outdated and impractical.

"After all," remarks one executive not exactly in tune with the times, "if you work in a candy factory, you can't munch chocolates all day. If these high-powered women want to be daytime pals, they're going to have to give up being nighttime princesses." This man may not understand, but a lot of women eagerly accept his offer. Pals are more comfortable than pedestals.

A New Problem

Women who once had little sympathy for a salesman's sexual indiscretions are gaining new understanding about the temptations of the job. They have learned that resistance is easier when there are few temptations. Some saleswomen find certain clients difficult to resist.

"Don't use my name," says one saleswoman, "because there is one special client that I'm having difficulty with myself about. Thank goodness he hasn't the foggiest notion that I'm in danger of falling off my self-imposed perch. No wonder. He probably thinks I can't stand the sight of him, since I race in and out of his office so fast.

"What saves me is that he thinks I am obsessed with succeeding in my career. He keeps telling me that success isn't the only thing on earth. Little does he know how I really feel, and I hope he never finds out."

Friendly, but not too friendly. Close, but not too close. That's the advice of saleswomen who walk the tightrope daily. As long as the saleswoman has no sexual interest, this is easy advice. However, avoiding pleasant situations is harder than the reverse, which often occurs.

"I am more sympathetic to the problems men have

had now that I'm confronted with the same thing,"
another saleswoman admits. "I used to think that
traveling salesmen were some kind of animals. Little did
I realize that the loneliness of the job makes temptation
harder to resist. You constantly have to think beyond
one day at a time or you'll really screw up your private
life. I guess I'm speaking literally," she laughed.

A traveling saleswoman who calls mostly on married men with families is bitter about the protector role
women are expected to assume. Although single, she's
still expected to protect the wife and kiddies by rejecting
the man rather than the reverse. She feels it is grossly
unfair for wives to blame women for being there rather
than their own husbands for their actions. "I've been
through a divorce, and I don't want to be part of
breaking up another family," she says. "But I'd like a
little help from the married men I meet on the road.
Shouldn't their own families be more important to them
than to me?"

Unfair Competition

Although saleswomen know that using sex in selling is
potentially more harmful than beneficial, salesmen
often see a saleswoman's sex as unfair competition to
them. They think of women's sexuality as a powerful
bargaining tool that can be used to gain an unfair competitive edge.

"I've had a couple of heated arguments with the
guys in my office," says an East Coast saleswoman. "I
couldn't make them realize that merely the suggestion is
demeaning. They keep up the hostile jokes, leering and
suggesting they would welcome such 'problems.' I once
called them the 'midnight cowboys' and they loved it.
One of them told me he'd sure use it if he had an edge
like I have.

"I keep wishing they would run into a fat, flabby,
middle-aged cigar-smoking queen-of-the-roost woman
who pesters them for sex in return for her company's

business. Only then will they get the message, and I hope I'm alive long enough to see it happen.''

Other saleswomen say that some salesmen they compete with set up a damned-if-you-do-and-damned-if-you-don't situation, blaming a woman's sex for success or failure. However, most salesmen—and particularly sales managers—care about results, not excuses.

Dress

Successful saleswomen advise beginners to dress very carefully in order to avoid any suggestion of sex. How you look is extremely important in how you are perceived. They try to strike a balance between looking casual and severe. They avoid Brooks Brothers pinstripes as well as frilly, feminine patterns. They prefer plain pumps that are comfortable yet stylish—no open-toed sandals or spike heels. They wear little jewelry and no heavy scents. They use little makeup and never color their eyelids blue. They are neat and clean and well groomed but understated. Their goal is to blend unobtrusively into a business atmosphere. They invest a great deal of money in achieving the desired results, but as several point out, it is an investment that pays off.

"I buy three-hundred-dollar suits, seventy-five-dollar blouses and ninety-dollar shoes," says a California saleswoman, "but I consider it an investment in my career. I believe that looking professional is a part of being successful. The old idea that you have to spend money in order to make it is true."

A beginning saleswoman with little money left to buy clothes after feeding her children and paying the mortgage found a cheap temporary way of looking professional. She buys $200 suits for $25 at a special thrift shop in her city. Other saleswomen buy off-season clothes during sales. However, the investment of time and money in being well groomed helps establish professionalism, which in turn helps avoid sexual suggestions like the following.

A rugged paper-company executive became a nuisance to the company's saleswomen by refusing to take no for an answer and substituting his own wishes based on their dress. "I know women," he would roar. "Any broad who wears a skirt with a slit in it wants a hand up it no matter what she says." It isn't fair, but sewing up the slits is easier than remedial teaching.

Sex Motivation

A midwestern saleswoman, asked to meet a client at a motel to discuss an order, reacted in a special way. She didn't go and she didn't tell him off, but she decided to "get every nickel I could get out of selling to him." She turned her anger into job motivation. Several months later, after immense effort, her motivation paid off. She got a large contract from his company. "I don't think any sale ever gave me as much satisfaction," she says. "I was so angry with the awkward situation created by this man that I decided to get even my own way. Generally I will tell a client if he is overordering. I'd sell that SOB the Brooklyn bridge if I could."

Another woman tells of a strange invitation from the sales manager of a large company after her sales presentation. The man, one of four at the meeting, was hostile during the meeting. "I just couldn't get a handle on what he was angry about," she says. "He kept interrupting and challenging me on minor points. He made insulting remarks about my product and company. He was so rude the other men were embarrassed."

This woman ended the meeting prematurely by suggesting that she come back later with more information. Determined to remain businesslike, she said nothing about the man's rude behavior. Instead, she put out her hand to shake hands with him. "After putting me down publicly," she said, "this man took my hand, held it an uncomfortably long time, and asked me to dinner so I could continue my presentation. I almost burst out laughing. I thought of several brilliant one-liners for his behavior. I wanted to say, 'We sure fooled those other clowns in there. I'll bet they thought you didn't care.' "

This woman felt the sales manager was so uncomfortable dealing with a woman in that type of business that instead of being rude to her, he was trying to control his own anxiety by trying to get into more comfortable surroundings. Regardless of his problems, she didn't go to dinner with him. "I'll go so far to make clients comfortable," she says. "But that was too far."

Entertaining

Saleswomen who entertain report that clients have less difficulty with certain male-female traditions than others. Saleswomen are taking men to lunch and dinner without serious problems. There are a few funny incidents, as could be expected. However, to date, no man has suffered permanent ego dysfunction because a woman picked up a check. Business entertaining for women has become perfectly normal behavior on the East Coast and the West Coast, particularly in large cities. The trouble spots are generally in between, and even they are becoming more the exception than the rule. Some men enjoy the switch. Most pay little attention. "Ten years ago a man would fight for the check and be insulted unless he won," says an East Coast saleswoman. "Now they'll toss it to me."

Even in a Nebraska, a group of men proved that the battle of who pays the restaurant check is over. A saleswoman who went to great lengths not to embarrass a group of clients could have saved herself the effort.

"Not knowing how they might react," she says, "I made arrangements with the restaurant to pay the check later, thinking it would be the main problem. My clients were having a fine time when our waiter revealed his own discomfort. He stood between my chair and the man to my right, holding the wine list and staring at the floor. Instead of taking the wine list, the man said in a loud voice, 'Sonny, the lady at the head of the table gets the wine list. She's paying the bill.' "

Another saleswoman, however, says she still has difficulty with one very good client when they go to lunch. He always pays. She discussed it with him, but when he asked to be allowed to pay as a special favor, she agreed. "I felt it was the easiest way out," she says. "He is an older man, exceedingly courteous and old-fashioned, so I go along. I can't see making a big deal out of it either way."

Traveling

"It has been at least five years since a man sitting beside me on an airplane made a crack about my being a 'traveling saleswoman,' " says a woman who is an architectural representative for a large furniture company. "With almost thirty percent of airline business travel coming from women, an unescorted woman is not considered an oddity anymore."

Airports across the country are filled with women, many of them saleswomen. The atmosphere of travel has dramatically changed, reflecting the discovery of a new market. Enough women are buying tickets, staying in hotels, eating in restaurants, taking vacations, and renting cars to cause some welcome changes. Airline attendants no longer ask "gentlemen" to fasten their seat belts. National Airlines now urges all to fly their planes instead of suggesting, "Fly me, I'm Susie." Eastern still clings to its "Wings of Man"; however, Delta, when asked, will give a set of pilot's wings to a little girl. Young male flight attendants see the world in exchange for a low-paying job—just as young women have always done. Passengers manage quite well with restrooms marked "occupied" and "unoccupied," and once in a great while the captain resembles members of the airlines' rapidly growing market. The captain is a woman.

Safety in Number

The old saying that there's safety in numbers is usually true. But not always. There are some situations in which men, as a group, will behave with less restraint than a man alone would. One saleswoman learned this the hard way early in her career.

This woman, selling a communications service, was asked to give a presentation to a group of doctors who were meeting in a remote motel about fifty miles outside a major city. The saleswoman was young, trusting, and blonde. After her presentation, she accepted an invitation to have a drink at the bar rather than retire immediately to her room, as she later wished she had done. It was shortly before midnight, the time when a group of doctors who might otherwise have been princes turned into frogs.

This saleswoman was surrounded by doctors, each trying to top the other with humor that ran the gamut from juvenile to morgue, all based on her anatomy.

"They swooped down like buzzards," she says. "I finally broke and ran, their suggestions were so bizarre. The whole evening was a nightmare I'll never forget."

It took this woman a long time to recover from this experience, which meant many lonely nights in motel rooms. She finally ventured out when she examined the consequences of her actions. She was punishing the victim—herself. Aside from this, her actions reinforced the prejudice that women should not venture out alone. She began to ask the right questions.

Why shouldn't every individual, male or female, be responsible for his or her own actions? If a decent family man can have a drink at a bar, why should a woman on a barstool signify "open season"? Who made such nutty rules?

By the time this woman came out of exile, she found that many others had done the same. No longer is she the only woman at dinner, sitting alone at an obscure table near the swinging kitchen doors. Women are coming out of motel rooms into the open and into their own.

They are sending a symbolic message to men who think they have a right to stake out a claim on any unattached woman.

It is unfortunate, but true, that women must fight to gain equal access to public places. Public places and public laws go hand in hand. Whether women, because of men, should be banished from bars has been the subject of intense legal wrangling and a host of confining laws since this country began. The United States Supreme Court has spent a disproportionate amount of time deciding whether what's good for the gander should be permitted for the goose. Traditional legislation has limited women's access rather than prohibiting men's behavior. If other laws were based on similar logic, pickpockets would have a field day and those who carry wallets would be jailed.

Don't Be a Victim

A midwestern saleswoman who travels over several states sums up her experience in handling sexual overtures by advising women to trust their own instincts and not become victims.

"I've paid my dues in the past five years," she says. "I've gotten a fair number of bruises, but it happens less and less often. When things cooled down, I first decided men were behaving better. Now I realize that I'm more able to nip problems in the bud. My attitude creates no openings for inappropriate behavior. Men select women for sexual exploitation the way a robber chooses a victim. They sense the vulnerable ones.

"Men size up a saleswoman's victim mentality. Is she young, inexperienced, dependent, apologetic, and willing to blame herself if they get out of line? I get fewer passes because I create a risky climate. I sense it immediately if a new client is up to something. I trust my guts and give myself the benefit of the doubt."

Just as they learn how to sell, saleswomen learn to protect themselves. Aside from attracting sexual abuse, a victim mentality inhibits selling. A good salesperson, by definition, is self-confident, assertive, and independent. In addition to her sales territory, the confident saleswoman stakes out her own personal territory and sets her own boundaries. Her attitude signals that trespassers are not welcome.

12

Six-Figure Saleswomen

ARE THERE REALLY six-figure sales jobs for women, or is this pie-in-the-sky nonsense put out to cover one saleswoman with a good job whose father owns the company?

Most women, scraping bottom each month to hang onto solvency, can't imagine themselves earning $100,000 a year or more. The thought of earning this kind of money is a modern-day fairy tale, and working women—with good cause—don't believe in fairy tales.

A major accomplishment of the feminist movement has been to unite women, ambition, money, and reality. Previously, women behaved as though "his" earnings were an accomplishment, while "hers" carried all the status of a social disease. For centuries, women's financial growth has been nipped in the bud by a Cinderella fixation that a prince would appear and provide (explained accurately by Colette Dowling in *The Cinderella Complex*). Ladies awaiting his highness could get their hands on money only through secondhand transactions

214

—marriage or inheritance. A woman hitched to her own plow was an object of scorn or pity. In being forced to support herself, a woman proved that she was neither a lady nor deserving of a prince. Recognition was acquired through others, not by the fruits of her own labor.

Satisfaction in Accomplishment

Millions of modern-day Cinderellas have awakened to the realization that a woman today, even if she wants to, has about the same chance of capturing a wealthy husband as breaking the bank in Las Vegas. It happens, but the odds are against it.

Currently, married women will work on an average of a quarter of a century to earn their daily bread, almost twice that long if single. One-income families are becoming an endangered species as their numbers decrease by about more than a million a year.

Women, far from disappointed by the news that they're in the labor market for the long haul, are scrambling for dollars and enjoying it. Many married to wealthy husbands, even chief executive officers, are out in the workplace, proving what women should have long suspected from observing the Rockefeller clan—that money is not the only work incentive.

The truth of the matter is that women have discovered what men know—that there is joy in pursuing a life's ambition, a life's work. There is satisfaction in accomplishment. There is increased self-esteem in success, and, last but not least, there is freedom that comes with economic independence.

After centuries of culturally and legally imposed financial dependency, women are realizing that financial independence is both liberating and exhilarating. So much so that it is not unusual for today's new career women at dinner parties to discuss business over brandy in the library while the men go off to rehash the Super Bowl.

Earning a Living Is Not Easy

To suggest, however, that earning a living is easy or that there are lots of $100,000 jobs around today for women would be a gross exaggeration. Not many men, and far fewer women, earn this kind of money. Fewer than 2 percent of tax returns to the IRS are in this classification. But where there once were no women in this classification, now there are a few. And, it's hoped, more will follow. Once the heavy doors of equal opportunity are shoved open, closing them requires out-and-out repression.

Anytime a woman succeeds in a nontraditional job, she makes the field easier for other women to enter. Unfortunately, the reverse is true when women fail.

The following women have exploded every myth about women, because of their sex, being incapable of succeeding in highly paid, competitive jobs, myths handed down through generations, reinforced by discriminatory laws, written into the world's religions, and woven into mass consciousness.

Only a few years ago the successful woman was cast as a villain in movies. The higher up the job ladder she climbed, the harder she fell. And unless she repented her masculine ambitions by pledging eternal nesting, she ended up like the bad guy in westerns—resting in Boot Hill.

Heroines of the Future

The women described in this chapter, unlike those in the formula movies of the past, have proved that success is neither a sex-linked trait nor unpleasant. Financial success has neither ensured nor destroyed their personal happiness.

These women are competitive, make shrewd business decisions, have developed their own individual styles, and have no hang-ups about earning a lot of money. They are comfortable with success, comfortable with men, and comfortable with themselves. All highly recommend selling as a great career for women as well as men. On the personal side, one is a widow, one is divorced but remains friends with her ex-husband, and one is divorced and remarried. None of the three grew up wealthy, yet neither did they grow up poor. One has no children, another is the mother of one son, and the third has five children.

May their success be an inspiration to you, and may their numbers increase.

A Wall Street Woman

"Rosemarie Sena has drive, ambition, and a remarkably analytical mind. She is dedicated, deals easily with people, and exercises exceptional judgment. Even though she is feminine, she doesn't trade on her sexuality. She's independent and treats people the way she wants to be treated—as individuals. Everything she does reflects her concern and dedication to detail. If I had to settle the West, Rosemarie would be driving the wagon."

This description might not be surprising if one of Sena's parents or brother were speaking. Or one of her many close friends. However, a client doesn't describe his broker and money manager with such superlatives every day on Wall Street. Add a competitor who calls Sena one of the nicest people in the financial district, and the profile of a remarkable person begins to emerge.

Sena's delicate appearance has been likened to that of the Bouvier sisters. "Could pass for their sister," wrote one interviewer.

Certainly true. There is a striking resemblance. However, here is where the similarity ends, because Sena, through her own efforts, earns every cent that pays for her life-style.

Sena is a senior vice-president at Shearson, American Express, a Wall Street investment securities firm. Her lucrative line of work includes being a money manager, adviser, and broker. Her success has been nothing short of phenomenal on a turf where only the fittest survive. Whether measured by volume of business, quality of corporate institutional and individual accounts, or compensation, Sena is one of Wall Street's most outstanding performers.

Earnings Match Performance

In a field where earnings are tied directly to performance, Sena's income speaks with authority. Her salary plus commissions currently totals upward of $700,000 a year—quite a bit upward. She also sets a high minimum figure for investments she is willing to handle. In fact, her business has grown so much she recently added a partner, Eric Petersen. Petersen had been chief investment officer at one of her institutional accounts.

"Instead of looking for business, Rosemarie is in the enviable position of being able to choose her clients," says the same client. "She's makes no claims of always buying low and selling high. She lets you know she doesn't carry a crystal ball. But she is tireless in terms of time, research, teamwork, and flexibility. In addition, she has a fantastic memory. No wonder her clients have tremendous confidence and trust in her."

However, to hear Sena explain how she got to Wall Street and into a job earning three times as much as the president of the United States, you'd think it was simple.

"People are incredibly generous," she says of her clients. "They constantly go out of their way to help me. They refer other clients to me all the time. I've never made a cold call in order to get new accounts."

She modestly makes no mention of the well-known fact that clients who lose their shirts by taking the advice of their brokers and money managers do not refer clients. They ask other brokers' clients to refer them. Their "generosity" reflects the quality of her advice.

She also has high praise for her staff, especially her administrative assistant, who's been with her for twelve years. "I wouldn't be where I am today without Mary Ann [Calise]," she says.

Does she feel that men or women envy her success? "No," she says. "Both women and men have been extremely helpful to me."

"Rosemarie Sena is an exceptional human being," says a Wall Street competitor. "She works hard, does a terrific job, and still manages to be one of the nicest people in the financial district. I've never heard anybody say a bad word about her."

Growing Up in New Jersey

When Rosemarie Sena, a Catholic, was growing up in Morristown, New Jersey, she absorbed a large dose of the good old Protestant work ethic. The older of two children, she saw work as something desirable and character-building. Work was good. Idleness was bad.

Sena credits her parents for the home life that helped shape her values. They encouraged self-reliance and individual development. "They are really wonderful parents," she says. "They gave my brother and me the kind of solid foundation that's so vital for healthy emotional development."

She is also very proud of her brother, Dr. John Sena, a Princeton graduate, a Fulbright Scholar, and an Ohio State University English professor. "He is the brilliant one in the family and extremely supportive of me."

Her father, a real estate developer in Morris County, taught her the value of long-term goals and establishing trust with clients. "Never look at monthly figures," he would say. "Look only at comparative yearly figures when you're building a business. When you're building a business, you're building yourself."

Her mother, in addition to running their home, helped in the family business. Both parents gave her the freedom to pursue her own destiny, no matter what that might be. The choice she had was real. She could do anything in the world or she could do nothing. It was all up to her. She went to college.

A Career Begins

After graduating from Michigan State University with a major in landscape architecture, Sena's life took a strange turn. The closest she got to landscape architecture was a potted palm in the local bank where she began her first full-time job. It was a bank where she had held summer jobs.

Nine years on the commercial side of the bank provided her with experience so vital in her job today. She filled in her business education by going to night school, where she studied accounting, finance, and other business-related subjects.

Combining work with specialized business education, she got what she believes every man or woman needs, a thorough knowledge of a basic commodity—money. She learned how to save it, manage it, invest it. Up close, she saw its power and its limitations. She learned its psychological force, its mystique, and its misuse. She learned that ignorance about money is a lifelong handicap. Although men as well as woman are frequently ignorant about money, Sena feels this is a special handicap for women. "Often, when women are divorced or their husbands die, they are lost. The problems such ignorance causes are sad and unnecessary. Everybody should know how to handle money," she says.

Moving Up to Wall Street

Hard work, dedication, and night school paid off for Rosemarie Sena. She became an officer of the bank. During this time a member of a large Wall Street investment firm, impressed with her knowledge of the business, suggested she give Wall Street a try. It took her several years to take the suggestion seriously. The leap from a small-town bank to the financial capital of the world takes a little courage. This is the place where the bravest can bet their careers and lose.

When she finally made the leap, Sena decided not to go with the large investment house her Wall Street friend suggested. Instead she chose Faulkner, Dawkins and Sullivan, a smaller firm where she felt she would have more opportunity to learn and advance.

From the beginning of her Wall Street career thirteen years ago, her success has been phenomenal. Among many awards and citations, she was recognized as one of the five top corporate women by NBC. She rose to officer and director of her firm before it was acquired by her current firm, Shearson, Loeb, Rhoades, which since has merged with American Express, and now is called Shearson, American Express.

On Wall Street, she carved out for herself another unique opportunity. Ordinarily, brokers sell and money managers manage—period. However, she saw no reason these related fields could not be combined, one enhancing the other. After all, she reasoned, if as a money manager she was willing to take her own advice—advice she was selling to others—wouldn't that make her advice more believable? It has worked out exactly as Sena planned. At every turn of her career her judgment, with no pun intended, has been right on the money.

How Sena Sells

Successful salespeople must be dedicated and disciplined, have the highest integrity, and be persistent, Sena believes. Men or women unable or unwilling to put in long hours should stay out of competitive fields. There are no shortcuts.

Sena, taking her own advice, is a stickler for research and detail. No matter how much preparation is required for a client, she never takes shortcuts. Throughout her career, she has been her father's daughter: She always has had long-range goals, constantly pushes forward, and never looks at monthly figures. She has built a business on trust, integrity, and performance—the only kind of business that results in building a base of satisfied clients.

Career Advice for Women

Sena's career advice for women is exactly the same as for men. "Real independence for women is economic independence," says Sena. Her strong feelings are emphasized by a favorite quotation from Somerset Maugham's *Of Human Bondage:* "There is nothing so degrading as the constant anxiety about one's means of livelihood," Maugham wrote. "I have nothing but contempt for people who despise money. They are hypocrites or fools. Money is like a sixth sense without which you cannot make use of the other five. Without an income half the possibilities of life are shut off. The only thing to be careful about is that you do not pay more than a shilling for the shilling you earn."

"For a woman to gain economic independence through a successful career," Sena says, "she must have dedication, self-discipline, and complete knowledge of her field. In a successful sales career, you must combine all these qualities with integrity. Your clients should know that you will never betray their trust."

Although Sena attended a coeducational college, she also supports women's colleges, believing they can provide the basis for higher attainment free from distractions. She chairs the board of trustees of Mary Baldwin College in Virginia, the oldest women's Presbyterian school in the United States. Initially heading the financial committee, she was elected chair of the board of trustees after her first year, the first woman chair in the 138-year history of the college.

Sena feels women today must prepare themselves for greater participation in society. "Society desperately needs all the help it can get," Sena says. "The gender, color of eyes, and pigment of skin are irrelevant. We're going to have huge problems in the coming decade that will affect us all. Everybody must assume a role in society.

"However," she adds, with characteristic optimism, "this is a great opportunity."

How Sena Keeps Her Career Path Clear

A unique person, Sena has made a mark for herself in a field where the stakes are high and the competition keen. She neither minimizes her accomplishments nor enlarges upon them. She enjoys her work and wouldn't trade it for anything; however, she doesn't allow it to consume her life. She devotes time to aiding worthwhile causes, such as medical research, loves horseback riding, and cares for any stray dogs and cats lucky enough to find their way to her door. If she retires as planned someday in the future to a farm in Virginia, the local ASPCA will have an event to celebrate.

Sena's last word of advice is as simple, elegant, and understated as the clothes and furnishings she chooses. Yes, she realizes that in every person's professional life there are those delicate times when push comes to shove and you find your career on the line. For those times she has a small suggestion she believes important in keeping a career path open.

"To meet such interference," Sena says, "you may have to run around, over, and—if necessary—right through the resistance. You have to be quietly but firmly aggressive."

Flying High in Sales

Athley Gamber is the first to admit that she has spent a large part of her life with her head in the clouds—and she loves it.

In her case, keeping her head in the clouds is good

business. She may fly to Europe one week to sign off on a business deal or hop over to South America the following week to begin a new one. She sells planes internationally, at home in the U.S. and in twenty-two other countries, and has built a small aircraft service and sales company into a $10-million-a-year business with no end to its upward course in sight.

A "small" sale to her is a $40,000 Piper Arrow compared with a $300,000 Convair or a $750,000 Beach King-Air turbine. No matter which she's selling, she knows every part that goes into it down to the last bolt and screw, and she can hold her own with the most demanding customer.

She has developed her own unique philosophy about selling, and backs up her advice by a success record that makes disagreement difficult. In selling millions of dollars' worth of planes, she combines old attitudes with new ones and traditional values with some very nontraditional ones. Being original is her style. With comfort, compassion, and good humor, she walks a narrow line. Through a combination of assertiveness when appropriate and motherly understanding the rest of the time, she has prospered in a field totally dominated by men.

"We're a family," she says of her Ft. Lauderdale, Florida, holding company, Cigma, which includes Red Aircraft Services, Red Aircraft Sales, Twin Town Leasing, Holiday Wings, Island Investment Corporation, and Red Aircraft Services International. She has a staff of fifty and meets an impressive yearly payroll.

Although quick to volunteer that she is "no woman's libber," she immediately adds a "but" that separates her from traditional thinkers. Her ideas will be of little comfort to antifeminists. She feels that all women should have careers, believes divorce frequently occurs because housewives have no place to grow, thinks competition is terrific, and wonders who ever started that silly idea that women cannot command others or run corporations.

"Since time began, women have been doing all the things required in running a corporation—a lot of things at the same time," she says. "Women have been running families, taking care of children, and handling the family finances. Whether they know it or not, they are in a corporate structure."

People had better not believe they can flatter Athley Gamber, however, by telling her that she thinks like a man. That gets her dander up in a hurry, and she's not the slightest bit hesitant about explaining why.

"I simply will not be accused of being like a man," she says. "Women should be molding their careers in an entirely new structure instead of following the patterns established by men." She wants to be seen as a woman who enjoys what she is doing and can do it better than anybody else. As a proven success, she finds plenty of people willing to confirm that view. However, it was not always true. There was a time when the business was small that Gamber had to make a crucial decision— whether to remain or go home and putter around the rest of her life as a few well-meaning friends advised her to do.

"If you stay in this business," they told her, "you'll lose it all. A woman can't compete in a man's world. Give it up."

A Woman Takes Over

Born and raised in south Florida, Gamber married her high school sweetheart, whose love of aviation was contagious. At the age of sixteen she learned to fly alongside him. When he started Red Aircraft along with a partner, Gamber was there, too, working as a vicepresident of the tiny company. They made joint decisions on which airplanes to buy and sell, and both took economics and business courses offered by universities and airplane manufacturers.

In 1968, tragedy struck. Clayton Gamber, Sr., disappeared into the Atlantic on a flight to the Bahamas, leaving behind his wife and a son. Gamber was advised to give up the business and go home or risk losing it. She never really considered the possibility that her friends were right.

"Negative thoughts," Gamber says, "just don't bother me. I don't ignore advice, but my idea was that why should I allow the fear of losing the business keep me from doing something I enjoyed? I kept thinking that it's a good business, I enjoy it, why shouldn't I keep it? The only real question I had to ask myself was whether I liked the business for myself or was I there only because I had been placed there? The answer to that question kept me here."

Cigma, the present umbrella corporation, was formed five years ago after Gamber bought out the partnership. If things continue to progress, the next expansion will be into airplane manufacturing. Gamber's son, Clayton Jr., has been through every phase of the business and will someday take over. But not for a while, Gamber says. As the company grows, there's more work that pushes thoughts of retirement into the future. Aside from that, Gamber is having the time of her life. Why should she quit?

Growing into a Selling Career

Athley Gamber has worked since she was six years old and was self-supporting by the time she was fourteen. She enjoys working. She likes the sense of accomplishment that comes from making a sale, building a business. Recently she signed a contract that expires in the year 2005. "When you reach the point in time that you begin to look back a bit rather than ahead, I want to feel that I have left a part me. It gives me a good feeling to know that the base I have developed will extend into the next century because of things I did twenty years before."

Her advice in selling is to "find out if the person you are selling to is buying with his heart or for practical reasons and, with that knowledge, I can sell anything," says Gamber. "I love to fly. I love aviation. And I am convinced that anybody I sell a plane to will be delighted with the purchase. I believe you can sell anything as long as you truly believe in it.''

Success in selling airplanes, like success in selling anything else, Gamber believes, is a simple matter of transmitting to the buyer that he or she will be better off as a result of the purchase.

Gamber has no use for any kind of formal sales training. "I don't want to develop from stage one into stage two," she says. "Selling is a very personal act. There are no two sales alike and no two salespeople alike. It is a one-on-one contact in which psychology plays an important part. Formal sales training is the worst thing you could do."

Gamber adds a vital ingredient to this spontaneous package: meticulous preparation in product knowledge. You should learn every detail about the product you are selling, plus the same amount of knowledge about competitors' products. Fail to answer a single question, be unsure of any feature, and your potential sale is likely to disappear mysteriously. High-pressure tactics are out, in her book. Slow persuasion is in. "We've got a deal going here that we've been working on a year. It may not happen this month or next month, but it'll happen," she says quietly but firmly. "In sales, you can't rush things."

Years ago, when Gamber first entered the aviation business, selling airplanes was relatively simple. Today all that has changed. In order to sell planes today a salesperson needs to understand the customer's business interests, which include depreciation of the plane, financing, investment credit, whether to lease or buy, and the risks of the investment. If she were beginning all over again, Gamber would take more business courses sooner than she did and get a thorough grounding in finance, accounting, and economics—all essential in understanding today's customers and their needs. A salesperson, to be effective, must understand the business world in which he or she sells. Sales are won or lost on knowledge.

Although Gamber disapproves of formal sales training, she thoroughly approves of other kinds of training necessary to keep abreast in a high-technology business. "We've got somebody in school here all the time," she says.

Salespeople constantly update their product knowledge. When a new wrinkle is added to a plane, it is investigated, dissected, and incorporated into sales. When a customer points a finger and asks what that new gadget can do, a Cigma salesperson is ready with an answer.

Adapting to a Sales Environment

When Cigma branched out into international markets, Gamber faced another wave of negativism from her well-meaning advisers, who apparently hadn't learned that "can't" wasn't included in Gamber's vocabulary. Being told that something is impossible to overcome increases her motivation. So when she was told that a woman could never overcome the cultural resistance in selling airplanes internationally, Gamber saw it as another irresistible challenge. Like other barriers, this one also fell.

"When you're the seller, it's up to you to adapt to the customer, not the other way around," she says. "I had to be tolerant of foreign ways of doing business or I would have gotten nowhere. In adapting to their ways, I have learned many things from foreign cultures that I prefer to our own. I find this very exciting.

"For example, the Latins are very relaxed about doing business. They don't get too uptight about anything, and once you're in, you receive unbelievable treatment. With the Europeans, there is a different atmosphere. They're more formal about business, and you have to do things their way.

"In most situations, however, once they find out that you are qualified and know what you're talking about, the barriers fall, and it doesn't matter whether you're a man or a woman.''

Only once in the international sales arena was Gamber unable to overcome a barrier related to being female. This was with a Japanese who had contracted with Cigma for modification work on several airplanes before the planes left the United States.

Knowing the Japanese tradition about women, Gamber stayed in the background during preliminary transactions. Sooner or later, however, they had to learn they were dealing with a woman, since Gamber had to sign the final contract.

During the contract signing, she thought things were going rather well. The final negotiations went smoothly, and finally all the papers were signed. The deal was set. However, in Japanese fashion, a short ceremony followed the contract signing in which the head of the Japanese group brought out some beautifully embroidered jacket emblems to present to the Americans.

''As he went down the line, giving the emblems to our people, he got ready to present mine. He almost handed it to me, but he stopped dead in his tracks. It was more than he could handle, and he didn't care if I was the president. This just couldn't happen in his country.'' Instead of giving her the emblem, the man presented it to a male vice-president of Cigma, who in turn gave it to Gamber.

Instead of being insulted, Gamber understood the man's feelings, which were conditioned through generations. His reaction was not unlike that of American tourists who sample Sushi in a Japanese restaurant and are horrified when they realize they've eaten raw fish. Some things, Gamber points out, take time to change. A shrewd salesperson, Gamber kept her eye on what was important. The barrier she was interested in crossing was back at the contract signing.

The Future of the Family

This remarkable women retains her enthusiasm no matter what she is doing. Whether talking about her pride in a former secretary who's currently breaking sales records at Cigma, her son and her daughter-in-law who work in the business, her grandchildren, flying, competitors, or life in general, Gamber has something positive to say.

A strong believer in marriage and the family, she feels the families of the future will be stronger. She sees evidence that this is happening, despite the gloom and doom projected by others.

"Men and women are finding a true partnership in marriage today," she says, "because both partners are working. A career is just as important for a woman as a man. She needs a sense of identity just as much as a man. Men are wonderful because of the way they are pitching in with the housework and the children."

Gamber believes this will produce happier and longer-lasting marriages because couples will grow together instead of growing apart. She and her husband did this early, but millions of others are following suit today.

"If I had stayed home all these years, look at what I would have missed," she says. "To this day I don't want to miss out on anything. I keep my bags packed."

Athley Gamber feels it is too bad that the older people get, the harder it becomes for them to be what she describes as "childlike"—to retain that wonderful enthusiasm that comes from seeing a sunset for the first time while flying high above the clouds in a plane she loves almost as much as she loves her grandchildren.

She need not worry about herself. Whether she's racing off to a foreign land to chalk up another series of sales for Cigma, flying down to the islands for a vacation, stopping off at a golf course for a quick game, going fishing, or landing at her beloved home in North Carolina, her enthusiasm for life remains childlike. For somebody whose head has been in the clouds a half century, Athley Gamber is not about to come back to earth now.

A Woman Who Sold to Aristotle Onassis

She has sold a ship-cleaning contract to Aristotle Onassis, leisure homes in a Washington suburb, Oriental rugs from a rented ballroom. She has been down and out and she's earned as much as $600,000 in one year. She's got a deal going now that she's convinced will earn millions. Through it all, Betty-Nina Rote keeps right on selling.

"I've been selling all my life," says Rote, "just like all women. We sell when we want our children or husbands to do something. We sold our parents when we were children. Women begin and end their lives selling. Women can sell better than men because powerless people must persuade. Women cannot force anything, so we are forced to sell our ideas."

This philosophy comes from a woman who led a comfortable upper-middle-class existence until a marital separation forced her to fend for herself and her children twenty years ago. With four children to feed, she found herself financially at the survival point. The food and rent depended upon her wits. With a bare cupboard and the mortgage coming due, Betty-Nina Rote had to think on her feet.

Applying for a job in a real estate office nearby, Rote was told that the agency's policy was to hire men only. No woman need apply. "Women," the manager explained, "couldn't stand up to this kind of selling."

Instead of meekly looking elsewhere, Rote decided to start selling the manager on the idea of breaking his male-only rule. To her, rules like these were made to be broken.

Tired of being pestered day after day, the real estate manager allowed Rote to take the aptitude test given to men before they were hired into the agency. He wanted to get rid of her by proving that she couldn't even pass the aptitude test. Instead, she racked up the highest score ever recorded in that office.

Still reluctant, the manager was finally "sold" on giving her a try. During the next twelve months she sold more real estate than the thirty-two salesmen on the staff combined. By this time, she had proved her point to even the most hardheaded manager. She could sell.

Success in Selling

"Men are pattern people," says Rote. "The salesmen at the agency sold when it was convenient for them. They took regular lunch hours and went out for cocktails after work. I did none of those things. Instead, I followed the customers' patterns. Anytime I could sell, I sold.

"In addition, the salesmen constantly prejudged people by their appearance. Often they wouldn't bother trying to sell to a person who wasn't dressed the way the salesmen thought they should be dressed. For example, they wouldn't bother with people who were wearing blue jeans and dirty sneakers. I didn't prejudge people. I knew that people with money don't have to look rich. Frequently they are the ones who look the worst. Once I sold two vacation homes to an admiral who was dressed like a beach bum."

A reconciliation with her husband ended Rote's budding real estate career, but a few years later—now with a fifth child—a divorce made it necessary once again for her to find a way to support herself and her children. With necessity knocking at her door, she again turned to selling.

Oriental Rugs

In this sales adventure, Rote found a product with which it was possible to cut out all the middle men and be on her own from the manufacturer to the buyer. She began buying and selling Oriental rugs from Iran. Rote would travel to Iran and buy rugs for shipment to the United States. When the rugs arrived, she would pick them up in a rented van and personally deliver them to a rented ballroom, a place where she sold the rugs directly to the public.

In order to sell the rugs, Rote did her own public relations. In addition to putting ads in newspapers, she would call up every friend and acquaintance she had and ask them to pass the word about her ballroom full of Oriental rugs, at prices her competitors didn't like. She also instituted some innovative sales incentives. She would allow prospective customers to take the rugs home and try them out with no obligation to buy. Just bring back the rug if they didn't think it fitted in with their furnishings. Few of her competitors would think of allowing an expensive rug out of the store unless they had sold it. Her first week in the Oriental rug business, she had racked up more than $20,000 in sales. With her profit, she paid her bills and had enough money left over to buy another ticket back to Iran.

A New Business

In the meantime, Rote's brother had developed a secret chemical-cleaning formula that Rote applied to cleaning Oriental rugs. Interested in an entrepreneurial opportunity, Rote borrowed $100,000 and went into the chemical-cleaning business. She saw other opportunities for the cleaning formula.

Rote salvaged an old dairy, turned it into a plant to produce her new product. She used the dairy tanks to mix up her chemical formula. With no paid help, she mixed the formula, bottled it, demonstrated the product, sold it, and made deliveries. She did have four unpaid workers—all her kids except her two-year-old.

Thinking beyond rug cleaning for her new product, Rote made an important discovery. She learned that

NuClear Industrial Cleaner not only cleaned rugs, but that it was terrific for other applications. She discovered that the compound would clean ships' tanks without etching the surface, something other cleaners wouldn't do. From her sales calls, she began to get contracts from some of the country's largest marine industries.

In 1970, she gave a personal demonstration of her product to Aristotle Onassis, using one of his ships docked in Bayonne, New Jersey. Onassis was impressed with the personal demonstration. Rote got a contract to clean his ships. In addition, Onassis was helpful in getting other clients for her. Although the meeting with Onassis had been arranged by Rote's father, a scientist-philosopher who was a friend of Onassis, Rote made the sale.

Rote now sells cleaning contracts as well as the chemical compound itself. She has two distributing companies in this country and plans to establish others soon in Germany, Saudi Arabia, and Brazil. Living in New York City, she is now married to Kyle Rote, one of America's all-time-great athletes who was a member of the championship New York Giants football team of the 1950s.

An Empire

Not content to coast along with her cleaning and chemical companies, Betty-Nina Rote has embarked upon another entrepreneurial venture. She has the worldwide distribution rights for Willard Water, a "Catalyst Altered Water" patented by its founder, Dr. John W. Willard, Sr., who is professor emeritus of South Dakota School of Mines and Technology in Rapid City, South Dakota.

Willard Water, originally made in the Black Hills of South Dakota, has testimonials from satisfied users in the West who claim it will cure everything from clogged drains to cancer in livestock. Discussed on two separate programs on CBS's "60 Minutes," Willard's Water is off and selling, although nobody yet knows exactly why. Its extravagant claims are made by the users—a nun who swears it will produce the biggest crop of zucchini she ever saw, a man who credits it with his unscarred recovery from serious leg burns, and rugged cattlemen who spray it on newly branded calves in order to prevent infections. And, as usual, Betty-Nina Rote is a firm believer in her product. She's launching a marketing program that she believes will make WillGrow and Bio-Water, both Willard Water products, household words and their distributor a new fortune. Thinking ahead to the vast agricultural applications for her new product, Rote has contracted NASA to arrange soil analysis from the U.S. space satellite. If one-tenth of the claims turn out to be true, Betty-Nina Rote has hit the jackpot.

The idea that the elaborate claims by users won't hold up in the long run or that her marketing program could be a failure is something Rote isn't wasting time considering. She believes in her product and she's ready to sell it. Watch out, world, WillGrow and Bio-Water are here.

"This time," Rote says, as if her past accomplishments were insignificant, "I'm not fooling around anymore. I'm building an empire."

13

Where the Jobs Are— and How to Find Them

AT THE TELESESSION CORPORATION, headquartered on Manhattan's Fifth Avenue, Loren F. Zesch sits in her plush swivel chair in front of an elaborate instrument panel. She's in a custom-designed, soundproof control room, talking to people thousands of miles away. She might be talking to a half dozen doctors in as many states one evening and a group of farmers from Kansas to California the next. Regardless of the group, Zesch is doing the same thing: she's selling in a newly designed marketing system that extends the word-of-mouth concept. The TeleSessions enable satisfied buyers to discuss the benefits of various products with potential customers. This unique idea is a way for companies to multiply an individual salesperson's effectiveness. The new concept works particularly well in selling complex, highly technical products such as pharmaceuticals. For example, a doctor in Philadelphia who has used a new medicine successfully is able to talk about his or her

236

experiences to a physician in Dallas who might otherwise reject it.

This new selling idea, like all new ideas, creates selling jobs. Zesch has an excellent job. She's the president. She also has a marketing department that hires sales representatives to sell the new idea of using TeleSessions across the country.

In Chicago, Marjorie Leopold is supervising her staff and wondering how far over the million-dollar mark her company will go this year. Things weren't always so good. Back when she and Pat Keeton started Keeton/ Leopold Associates, the young film producers hit the pavement selling what they had gone deeply into debt producing: EEO films. Passage of Title VII of the Civil Rights Act of 1964 had inadvertently created a new market. Whenever a new market is created, selling opportunities are also created. Companies, in complying with the new legislation, bought *Boomerang*, the training film on which Keeton and Leopold had staked their new company's future. They were producing a product that, as women, they knew something about firsthand: how discrimination denies women and minorities equal job opportunities and what companies can do to eliminate discrimination. The superb film, depicting realistic problems and solutions, worked for companies across the country.

Leopold, who bought out Keeton, is now producing another series of *Boomerang* films. As owner of the company, she hires her own sales representatives and has a marketing organization.

Out in Minneapolis, Jodie Peter might be packing her bags to fly off to North Dakota one week, Nebraska the next, and back to Minnesota the third. As a sales representative for Xerox Learning systems, her territory includes these three states.

Before going into sales, she was director of a unique federal nontraditional-jobs program for women. In administering the successful pilot program, which has since been replicated in other locations, she discovered the confused ideas many women have about selling jobs. Some women with excellent backgrounds for sales were so fearful of selling they felt they could never learn. Others wouldn't consider sales, to the extent of taking the lowest-paying jobs over sales.

Peter's educational background and experience are excellent for making a successful transfer to sales. She has an undergraduate degree in political science, a graduate degree in international politics, plus experience in teaching, politics, and management, all utilized in selling. Peter is delighted she made the switch to sales, even though it might not be as glamorous as her first job out of college, political organizer for John F. Kennedy. Kennedy hired her on the spot after he learned who organized her college for his campaign visit there. Of course, says Peter, there are other benefits to her present job. For one thing, it pays a lot better than political organizing.

Leah L. Tracy, a former IBM saleswoman, has moved up into management through a series of job changes, but she's still selling. She left IBM to become branch manager of a small California- and New York–based high-technology company, selling the services of data-processing professionals. She moved again to her current position as director of marketing for The Tarrytown (New York) Executive Conference Center, internationally known for its unique seminars, business conferences, and film weekends.

Early in her career, Tracy began moving up through a series of new opportunities, accepting the risks in leaving the known for the unknown. Fresh out of college with a master's degree in music, she went to work as a legal secretary when she found she couldn't earn a living in music. As a secretary she earned $250 a month, which prompted her first move.

She became an investment analyst and did much better. However, at this point in her life she did something people often say they want to do, but few actually do.

She went to Vail, Colorado, for a skiing vacation and stayed, later becoming a ski instructor. She also found new opportunities when she began to do some part-time bookkeeping for a local hotel and ended up running it.

On the ski slopes in 1970 she met an interesting businessman who later brought a group of his company's executives to her hotel. He wasn't the only one impressed with her efficiency. Tracy turned down his offer of a job in New York, but later accepted another offer in San Francisco with the same company—IBM. Her guest had been Tom Watson, chairman of the board of IBM and son of the founder of the company.

After a successful eighteen-month training program, Tracy found she loved selling data-processing equipment for IBM. However, after selling for IBM for several years she wanted to move into a smaller business offering an entrepreneurial opportunity. Her first-rate technical training, combined with a successful sales record, enabled her to choose from a wide variety of career opportunities. Tracy enjoys new and different ideas that reach into the future, which is what attracted her to her present job. The Tarrytown Conference Center's stock in trade is the velocity of change and trying to keep up with it. Acclaimed as the "granddaddy of all conference centers," it began as a brainchild of the center's chairman, Robert L. Schwartz, who provided a meeting place for people who want to change the world. For seventeen years the world's most famous scientists, futurists, entrepreneurs, philosophers, business leaders, theorists, and thinkers have assembled there.

New ideas bring change, which creates new and exciting selling opportunities. Every large corporation today began in somebody's entrepreneurial mind. IBM began as a small card-punch business. Xerox began in a Rochester, New York, garage. From new ideas come thousands of new sales jobs. Because of risk takers like Tracy, always pushing into the future, thousands of people will be selling new products and services tomorrow.

Industrial/Professional Sales

The previous women are examples of thousands of industrial/professional saleswomen across this country in small towns and large cities. From small entrepreneurial ventures to selling for large corporations, sales offers a great opportunity for women who like the challenge of competition, and the risk of betting on themselves. Regardless of these facts, however, mention selling to women and, like a programmed computer, retail sales and door-to-door soliciting leap into their heads. Women know all too well the dreary world of sales behind so many store counters, jobs where you put in long, backbreaking hours for peon wages; jobs where your earnings stay the same no matter how much profit you bring in for the company.

Door-to-door and direct sales are even worse, with a few remarkable exceptions who, because of their personal drive, energy, and determination, really are driving pink Cadillacs and taking Hawaiian vacations. However, let nobody be dazzled by these exceptions in the door-to-door selling game. Check the average earnings for these "pin money" jobs and you'll discover that whoever named them knew them. According to a 1977 Louis Harris survey, median earnings for door-to-door selling produce less than $27 a week. Only one door-to-door salesperson in ten earns more than $100 a week, and one in five earns less than $10 a week. A description of the "typical salesperson" is even more revealing: a female high school graduate under the age of fifty.

"When a man invites me to a Tupperware party or the doorbell rings and it's the Avon man calling, door-to-door sales may become more interesting to me," says an industrial saleswoman who earns $40,000 a year. Interestingly, this woman hit the nail on the head with her flip remark. According to Bureau of Labor statistics, job earnings go up or down depending upon the number of men or women in them. Up for men, down for women. As long as this continues, it's only logical for women to search out jobs where today's males cluster instead of waiting for men, in meaningful numbers, to start typing, filing or selling door-to-door.

So when you think of sales, stop thinking about female-typed, low-paying, dead-end, over-the-counter, door-to-door selling. Be enterprising and check into professional/industrial sales. That's where you'll find the good sales jobs. That's where the opportunity is. It's where the money is, and it's where you ought to be.

Where to Look

Nancy is a nurse who for ten years worked diligently in one of the nation's most prestigious hospitals. She became more and more unhappy with the earnings gap between nurses and doctors. She figured she could stay and fight another quarter century for better wages and conditions or find another way to solve her problems. She didn't cure the problems of her profession, but she solved her own. As a sales representative for a pharmaceutical company, she has tripled her salary. She's now using her nursing education to sell to the medical profession. She has a lot of sympathy for the nurses she left behind and believes many will end up also leaving the profession if the inequities in another female profession are not addressed.

Pat has a master's degree in English literature. She has always loved books. She had her heart set on working as an editor for an important publishing company. She's realized part of her dream. She's a sales representative for an important publisher. Now she's not so sure she can afford her original dream. If her company transferred her to their editorial department as an editor, she'd have to take a pay cut. People who sell books frequently make more money than people who edit books or, for that matter, those who write books.

Helen is a high school graduate under the age of fifty

who got tired of a dull, routine typing-and-filing job
for a trade association. She began talking to a word-
processing salesman who serviced her company. He suggested she apply for a job with his company. Now she's
in a brand-new career selling word-processing equipment. She's earning more money than would ever be
possible in her boring, dead-end job.

Where to Begin

A complete list of selling opportunities could fill this
book and several others. Wherever business is conducted, you'll find sales jobs. Whenever a new idea is
thought up by some enterprising person, other equally
enterprising people sell the idea or it dies on the vine. No
matter how old and established, a business must continue selling to survive. Fortunately for thousands of
women, this means that the very best place to start looking for a sales job is *right where you are—in your own
company.* If you are currently working for a company
in a part of the business that offers little advancement,
begin investigating the possibility of transferring to
sales, either in your company or in another one.

In looking for a job, the very best place to be is inside
a company that has its own sales force. If you like the
company you're now working for, begin your search by
investigating getting into sales right where you are. Your
experience is valuable, no matter if all you've been
doing is typing company reports. You can absorb a lot
of information about a company by typing. Your familiarity with the company and easy access to management
puts you ahead of a stranger who starts from scratch.
Talk to the sales manager. If you haven't the required
background it takes to qualify for sales now, consider
going back to school to get the requirements. The more
persistent you are and the harder you work to get into
sales, the more impressed the sales manager will be. So
sell him or her on your potential. And don't overlook

the possibility of enrolling in school at your company's expense. Ask about tuition reimbursement. Many companies pay part or all of the cost of job-related education.

Inside Looking Outside

The next-best place to look for a job in sales is outside your own company. Looking for a job when you're employed gives you time, flexibility, and bargaining power. Here again, the knowledge you have acquired in your current job should suggest logical transfer areas into sales. The nurse who transferred her skills to selling pharmaceuticals made a logical skills transfer. The English major who is now selling books transferred her knowledge to an area she know something about. The secretary who is selling word-processing machines also found a prime place to use the business knowledge she had accumulated in her job.

If you're with a company that doesn't have a sales force, talk to the salespeople who sell to your company. Like the secretary, the salespeople you meet may be able to suggest sales areas for you. And if you are a woman at home who wants to get into the labor force via sales, talk to your friends. Strange as it may seem, salespeople are the least likely to sell themselves by talking about their profession.

At social gatherings you're likely to go home knowing who are doctors, lawyers, and accountants, but not salespeople. Find the salespeople. If you're at a party and you ask twenty people what they do for a living, chances are you'll find at least one salesperson. Once you've shown an interest in the subject, you'll also discover a lot of fascinating people who will be delighted to talk to you about a fascinating subject.

Matching Up Skills and Job Categories

To give you an idea of how your background and skills may match up with a sales category, check out the following sample list, which mixes and matches possibilities. Don't forget that some of your best skills may have nothing to do with your current job. If you find yourself bored by your job but fascinated by interests outside your work, get out of your boring job by transferring skills developed in these interests to sales. For example, a former full-time housewife sells specialty items to retail gift shops. A clerical worker is selling recreational equipment, and a dental hygienist sells dental equipment.

NURSE
Medical equipment / supplies
Pharmaceuticals
Health care

DENTAL HYGIENIST
Dental equipment / supplies
Medical / dental insurance

ARCHITECT
Architectural services /
    equipment / office space

LIBRARIAN
Publisher's representative
Library supplies / equipment

CHEMIST
Chemistry automation
Chemicals and drugs

SECRETARY
Word processing
    Office supplies / equipment

TEACHER
Word / data processing
    equipment / services

FLIGHT ATTENDANT
Aircraft equipment
Travel services

DIETITIAN
Food services / products /
supplies

CHILD-CARE SPECIALIST
Playground equipment
Hobbies and crafts

Sample Sales Categories

Here's a sample listing of industry sales representative categories you might be interested in matching up with your job skills and interests:

automobile accessories; florist supplies; general hardware; photographic supplies and equipment; stamps or coins; wall coverings; sales promotion; abrasives; aircraft; barber and beauty equipment supplies; boats and marine supplies; chemicals and drugs; church furniture and religious supplies; commercial equipment and supplies; communication equipment; dairy supplies; electronic parts; elevators, escalators, and dumbwaiters; farm and garden equipment and supplies; hotel and restaurant equipment and supplies; industrial lubricants; industrial machinery; jewelry; malt liquors; musical instruments and accessories; novelties; oil-well equipment rentals; oil-well services; paper and paper products; plastic products; radiographic inspection equipment and services; railroad equipment and supplies; sporting goods; textile designs; textile machinery; ultrasonic equipment; veterinarian supplies; videotape; weighing and force-measurement instruments; welding equipment

Growth Areas Mean More Jobs

Ralph Baruch, chief executive officer and chairman of the board of Viacom, a diversified communications and entertainment business, advises women to get into the emerging technologies, where he believes the best opportunities exist. In a special "Careers" section of the *New York Times*, October 11, 1981, the wisdom of Baruch's advice was confirmed by the following:

"Sales and senior service employees in computer manufacturing and service companies are expected to earn $65,000 to $100,000 in 1990," according to an article entitled "The Office of the Future: A New Land of Opportunity?" In addition, an earlier study by the American Electronics Association concluded that the electronics industry alone could hire two hundred thousand college graduates with electronic and computer sciences backgrounds through 1985; however, only about seventy thousand will be available.

In stressing the opportunities emerging in the information field, the article pointed out that "major manufacturers in the information industry, such as the Hewlett-Packard Company, Texas Instruments, Wang

Laboratories, and the International Business Machines Corporation, will account for approximately 15 percent of the nation's total annual output of goods and services this year [1981]," and could account for as much as 30 percent by 1990.

With such massive projected growth, a word to the wise is sufficient to steer them into high-technology, high-growth areas. To keep up with the market trends, a saleswoman's second language in the very near future must be computer fluency.

A Competitive Advantage

If you happen to be working in a business where women type and men sell and there's nothing you can do to change the mind of your management, look for a competitor of your company who has different ideas. In certain difficult areas, the world can pass you by while you wait for attitudes to change. Selling trade secrets or disclosing confidential information is dishonest, but marketing your services to the highest bidder is not. Loyalty is a desirable trait. Displaced loyalty puts you in the position of being your own worst enemy.

Women generally have more difficulty than men selling and negotiating for themselves. In her book *Winning the Salary Game*, Sherry Chastain says that most women have a great deal of difficulty talking about money. She gives an amusing example to illustrate her point. Several years ago a letter was sent to Dear Abby in which a young woman complained about the high cost of birth-control pills. This young woman said she felt her boyfriend should be sharing the cost; however, she added that she didn't feel she knew him well enough to discuss money.

While this is an extreme example, it points out the fact that almost nothing is as difficult for women to talk about as money. Chastain feels this comes from a feeling that financial knowledge conflicts with perceptions of femininity. Feminine women are not supposed to worry about money. Somebody else is supposed to take care of all financial problems. In real life, the reverse is true. Women who worry about money and learn about managing it efficiently are the ones who have the least to worry about. Ten times out of ten, the others have a lot to worry about.

So, anytime you have a chance to better your job by offering your services to a competitor, negotiate the best deal you can. Don't allow your employer to play on your sympathies. Many a woman, wanting to be needed, has been flimflammed by a boss who kept her for half of what she was worth by telling her his business couldn't do without her. If you're that important, it will show in your paycheck. The old saying that the more you're paid, the more you're valued is not just an old saying. It's true. The first step in getting paid what you're worth is to value yourself.

Finding Sales Jobs Through Newspaper Ads

EARN BIG MONEY: $50,000 a year plus. We pay you $500 a week while in training. All benefits plus profit sharing. No experience necessary. Call now. Telephone sales.

FINANCIAL SALES: Last year 10 of our 18 experienced salespersons earned $70,000 plus. Seeking person with drive and ambition; extensive training program. Salary plus commission. College degree preferred.

INDUSTRIAL SALES: $25,000, car, commission. Leading roller-bearing manufacturer seeks reps to call on distributors. College degree & 2 to 5 years experience preferred.

Which ad would you answer?

These are examples of ads that run each day in the *New York Times*, the *Chicago Sun-Times*, the *San*

Francisco Examiner, and newspapers across the country. Sales is usually the largest single category in the classified ads. Some lead to excellent jobs; some lead you down the garden path if you're willing to go.

The first rule to remember in reading ads is that if it sounds too good to be true, it won't be. There is no gold at the end of the rainbow. What you get for nothing is nothing. Skip right over the ads like number one. If anybody can make $50,000 in that job, it will be a relative of the person who placed it.

The second ad is interesting and tempting. Of course, the first question to ask is, What about the earnings of the other eight? This ad, while it could lead to a good sales job, probably won't. Since a phone number was included, it may be worth a call. But you need much more information before you waste time on an office visit. Unless you get more unexpected information for your phone call, this one is also a loser.

Number three is the honest ad. The manufacturer's name, although not included here, was listed, the salary is realistic, and the ad doesn't overpromise. It promises the opportunity to earn a commission. Anytime you see an ad that promises big commissions, the company is promising something only you can deliver. They don't know what kind of commissions you can earn. One person may make big commissions and another may make small ones. If the ad had listed sample commissions of other salespeople, it could have given you an accurate idea of the possibilities. Always ask *average* commissions of salespeople, and make sure the answer you get *is* average, not the commissions of the company's all-time star performer.

Sales want ads are filled with extravagant claims in an attempt to hook the gullible. If you can be talked into bad selling jobs, you'll find yourself recruited into the army of the working poor, repeating one bad experience after the other. Many classified ads read as if they were written by a team of con artists and science-fiction writers. Pass them by.

However, among the bad ones are terrific, honest ads that lead to good jobs. You can't afford to ignore classified ads in your job search, since the best companies use them. A few weeks of carefully reading the ads will reveal the dishonest ones. Blind ads often are come-ons, but not always. Many companies advertise, listing only a box number for replies in order not to be flooded with phone calls and walk-ins. In most areas, the Sunday newspapers carry more ads than the daily paper; however, don't ignore the other six days a week. Also, don't be impressed by the size of the ad. Many terrific jobs come from two-liners.

Applying Directly to Companies

Most companies of any size have special personnel offices where you can apply for jobs, ask questions about the company, and get free literature. It's a good place to start if you know nothing about a company, but if you are really serious about joining a company's sales force, the person you need to talk to is the sales manager. Often it's a good idea to bypass the personnel department and phone the sales manager. If he or she reroutes you through personnel, then you'll have to apply through personnel. Large corporations in particular often have slow, bureaucratic personnel departments. For some strange reason, many personnel departments seem to discourage applicants with petty rules, long waits, and ambiguous answers to reasonable questions. Head of departments inside corporations often go to great lengths to avoid their own personnel departments. Therefore, you may discover a kindred soul in a sales manager you contact directly. Try it. You'll discover that people in sales are direct and seldom waste your time.

Seminars

There are seminars that bring together people looking for sales jobs with prospective employers. There are also seminars that cost a lot and give you little beyond a day of generalities about sales jobs or selling. Learning to separate the two saves you time and money. People who write books about sales often give seminars, which is fine if they give you more information than you can get by reading their books. Otherwise, read the book and skip the seminar.

Seminars that feature salespeople or sales managers who are looking for applicants can be very helpful. But a hall filled with five hundred people is generally not the place to learn the specific information you are looking for in order to find a sales job.

Special Classes

Schools, like the rest of the free-enterprise system, are in business to make money. If they aren't, they'll be out of business before long. It's good to consider their problems before you sign up for special courses. There are good, mediocre, and bad courses. You'll also find terrific teachers, along with others who can't teach. Most colleges and universities now have adult-education classes taught by professionals instead of teachers. A good example of this is the New School for Social Research in New York City, where you can find courses on virtually every subject, taught by professionals who currently do for a living what they teach. These classes give you the straight goods on what to expect in the real world. Many of these courses are worth their weight in gold, but before you sign up, make sure you have a winner. Talk to a few people in previous classes. Word gets around quickly. Fifteen minutes on the telephone can save you from a boring series of dull lectures.

Employment Agencies

Corporations use many methods to recruit salespeople, including employment agencies. Some agencies specialize in various fields. There are a few agencies devoted exclusively to sales. Find out if you pay a fee or if the employer foots the bill. If you wish, you can specify that you're interested only in fee-paid jobs. The right employment agency can save you time and trouble and cost you nothing if the employer has contracted with the agency to find salespeople, but a bad one can send you out on wild goose chases, try to influence you to take jobs you shouldn't take, and waste time you could utilize better by contacting companies directly. Unless your job needs are general, it generally works better to apply directly.

Counseling Centers for Women

Down a cramped corridor on the seventh floor of a tall building on New York City's East Sixtieth Street, you'll find Sharon Berman bouncing back and forth behind a desk piled high with papers or eating a BLT—her dinner at 9:00 P.M. The floor and filing cabinets also are piled high with papers. If you sit down, you must first remove the papers. Neatness is not one of Berman's virtues. Neither is promoting her business, called simply Counseling Women.

Helping women, however, *is* one of Berman's virtues. Filed somewhere in a desk drawer—give her a week and she'll find it—are impressive lists of women who are now happily employed as a result of Berman's counseling center. Many are employed in sales. Off the top of her head Berman will give you twenty names, and she's just begun to remember.

• A former medical social worker is selling data-processing equipment for a large multinational company.

• A former teacher is now a sales representative for a television and radio station.
• A former day-care-center teacher is selling for a large New York investment firm.
• A housewife, who was terrified of getting a first job, is selling space for a magazine.

Berman, a psychologist, is busy explaining a special professional sales seminar to a newcomer. The fees for the courses are modest: $15 for a single session, $30 for a series of three. The center barely manages to stay in the black, while other centers offering women far less prosper. In the meantime, Berman earns $500 a day consulting for private industry, the money used to subsidize the center. Why does't she close up the center and concentrate on earning $500 a day? Because Berman is in business to help women, not to earn money. She could probably do both, but she probably won't.

In the meantime, her idea works for women. Her sales seminars are taught by sales professionals. Like Berman, they teach because they want to help women, not for the small fees they are paid. Typical courses on career opportunities in professional sales might cover the following:

• an overview of employment opportunities and career paths in sales and sales management
• a pragmatic discussion of working conditions, salaries, benefits, and training programs for different industries
• an introduction to relevant terminology and concepts
• a lengthy question-and-answer period

Even more impressive are the credentials of the professionals who conduct the seminars. Examples are the following:

• account manager, *Seventeen* magazine
• account executive, Software Design Associates

- marketing director, American Express Company
- marketing director, Pay Television United Artists Corporation
- sales development manager, WNBC Radio
- marketing manager, IBM Corporation
- general manager, New York Life Insurance Company
- sales manager, Merrill Lynch
- personnel manager, Pfizer, Inc.
- marketing manager, Wang Laboratories
- planning manager, Union Carbide

Since the women's movement began, a network of counseling centers has sprung up to help women with their special problems in education, in jobs, and in their personal lives. It's a small town these days that has no place for women to find help. Choosing the effective ones is more of a problem than finding one. Colleges and universities often have special career help for women. Women helping other women has been an important part of the women's movement. As usual, there are well-intentioned centers but, unlike Berman's and others, they are ineffective. Unfortunately, there are so many centers with constantly changing personnel that it's not possible to separate and rate them for you. It is important that you do this, however, for yourself.

If your area has a center similar to Counseling Women—where saleswomen really level about their jobs and sales managers sign you up on the spot for job appointments—it can change your life. If there aren't any, perhaps somebody interested in helping women may be encouraged to start one.

But watch out for the centers that charge premium prices for little more information than you could get by spending an hour in the local library. It is possible to help women *and* run a financially successful counseling center—the very best kind. If you find one, your money will be well spent. Quality and cost in counseling, however, don't always go together. Frequently you're asked to spend the most for what benefits you the least.

(For a national listing of counseling centers, see page 230, but investigate the ones in your area.)

The National Association for Professional Saleswomen

Barbara Pletcher, founder and executive director of the National Association for Professional Saleswomen (NAPS), spends about a third of her time criss-crossing the country to tend her growing organization. The philosophy behind NAPS is another networking idea in which saleswomen (men are also welcome to join) support each other. All activities and programs are designed to improve job performance and increase productivity and earnings. NAPS benefits include information, group discounts on certain items such as books, supplemental insurance coverage, and a NAPS award for individual performance.

Sales managers and trainees are welcome members of NAPS—both male and female and associate memberships are available to people interested in sales. As a nonprofit organization, NAPS was founded to promote women in sales and marketing careers by providing:

- useful career information
- contact with others in sales
- increased public awareness of salespeople

Pletcher, a former marketing teacher and a Ph.D. in business administration, says she sees one major difference in men and women in business: Men are far more likely to spend money on themselves for career advancement than are women. When Pletcher first became aware of this tendency, she began carrying a money clip and recommends the same for other saleswomen. Now nobody can grab a bill and pay it while she fumbles into a purse inside another purse for money.

Earn More

Pletcher advises women to think of earning more money instead of concentrating so much on saving money. She suggests you keep in mind the old saying that it takes money to earn money, and invest wisely in your own career.

Established in the fall of 1980, NAPS expects to have more than fifty chapters by the end of 1982. For more information, write: National Association for Professional Saleswomen, 2088 Morley Way, Sacramento, CA, 95825. Also check to see if your own location has a chapter. If it doesn't and you're interested in starting one, Pletcher would be glad to hear from you.

According to a 1977 national survey by Louis Harris and Associates measuring the prestige of occupations, "salesman" ranked last on the list. "Scientist" ranked highest, with "doctor" in second place. It's obvious Pletcher has her work cut out for her.

Business and Trade Publications

Expanding your knowledge and keeping up with business in general will greatly enhance your sales ability. You will discover a whole new world in business publications. There are big ones and small ones. The best-known of them, the *Wall Street Journal*, is a first-rate national newspaper filled each day with interestingly written business news. Virtually every executive in the country reads it, and so should you. A salesperson in certain areas who never read the *Wall Street Journal* would have little to talk about at lunch with prospective clients. The same is true of publications like *Business Week*, *Dun's Review*, *Fortune*, and *Forbes*.

As in any other area, the more you know about business in general and your competitors in particular, the better you will sell. Check the library for a listing of trade papers in your sales area. These are smaller publications you can subscribe to directly. They are filled with product announcements and new business developments in specific areas. They may be dull reading for outsiders but fascinating stuff for the salesperson. These trade papers can give you new leads and ideas when your own creativity needs a little help. For example, if you're selling to or for the banking industry, there's *Banker's Life* and a dozen other trade publications; for the computer industry, *Datamation, Electronic News*, and many more; in the aerospace industry, *Aviation Week & Space Tech, FAA, Aviation News*, and others.

No matter what your area, you'll find a specific trade publication covering it: science, insurance, marine industry, transportation, securities, printing, education, medicine, journalism, construction, etc. You can even find special trade publications for selling itself— *Marketing Times, Meetings and Conventions, Sales and Marketing Management*, and others.

Smaller, general-subscription local business newspapers are also helpful to saleswomen. They can keep you informed about business in your sales area and often provide excellent sales leads while keeping you up to date on competitors.

In addition, read business publications in your territory for sales jobs. You'll be surprised at the number you'll uncover by reading not only the ads but the editorial pages as well. If your job prospecting is unproductive, you're not really trying. Sales jobs are all around you. Other sales opportunities are waiting to be created.

How to Choose a Company

The following checklist may help you in choosing the kind of company you won't be sorry you went to work for ten years later. Since so much of your life is spent at work, a little care in choosing the right company is warranted. Find out the answers to the following:

Does the company
- give women an equal opportunity?
- promote from within on the basis of ability?
- have at least some women in management positions?
- provide first-rate sales training?
- supply back-up help critical to success?
- provide good benefits?
- have a reputation for honesty and integrity?
- pay for job-related continuing education?

Is the company
- in a growth industry?
- well managed?
- a leader in its field?
- attracting other bright, intelligent people?

Last but not least, is the company one you'd be proud to represent? If you can answer yes to all these questions, you've found the place to begin. Now that you've found the right company, all that's left for you to do is to sell your way to the top of it. You can do it. Good luck, and during your journey, don't forget to lend a helping hand to other women.

Resources: Educational and Job Counseling Centers

*Catalyst National Network
of Career Resource Centers*

The following is a listing of all the Catalyst National
Network of Career Resource Centers except those in
colleges and universities. The network is made up of a
wide variety of profit and nonprofit groups providing
career and educational guidance to women. If a group is
located in your area, ask if they sponsor workshops or
special programs for women interested in sales careers.
Also check other counseling centers in your area, plus
special college and university programs related to sales
careers.

Catalyst is a nonprofit organization founded in 1962
to expand career options for women.

Code:
1-Education counseling
2-Career counseling
3-Personal counseling

4-Employment services
5-Workshops and courses
6-Fees

California

Crossroads Institute for
Career Development
2288 Fulton St.
Berkeley, CA 94704
415-848-0698
1-2-6

Susan W. Miller
360 North Bedford Dr.,
Ste. 312
Beverly Hills, CA 90210
213-837-7768
1-2-5-6

Institute for Family and
Work Relationships
1020 Prospect St., Ste. 400
La Jolla, CA 92037
714-459-0155
1-2-3-6

Patty DeDominic
Industrial Relations/
Personnel Services
5900 Wilshire Blvd., Ste. 450
Los Angeles, CA 90036
213-930-2120
Referrals only
2-5

Anita J. Goldfarb
19434 Londelius St.
Northridge, CA 91324
213-885-7653
1-2-5-6

Resource Center for Women
445 Sherman Ave.
Palo Alto, CA 94306
415-324-1710
1-2-4-5

Job Resource Center
2015 J St., Ste. 23
Sacramento, CA 95814
916-441-2850
2-4-5

Foster, Forsythe & Company
225 Broadway, Ste. 1600
San Diego, CA 92101
714-232-7593
2-4-5-6

Advocates for Women
414 Mason St., 4th Fl.
San Francisco, CA 94102
415-391-4870
2-4-5

New Ways to Work
149 Ninth St.
San Francisco, CA 94103
415-552-1000
2-4

Caroline K. Voorsanger
2000 Broadway, #1108
San Francisco, CA 94115
415-567-0890
1-2-5-6

Woman's Way
710 C St., Ste. 1
San Rafael, CA 94901
415-453-4490
1-2-4-5-6

Colorado

Women's Resource Agency
25 North Spruce St., Ste. 309
Colorado Springs, CO 80905
303-471-3170
1-2-4-5

Denver Women's Career
Center
1650 Washington St.
Denver, CO 80203
303-861-7254
1-2-5-6

Connecticut

YWCA of Greater
Bridgeport
1862 East Main St.
Bridgeport, CT 06610
203-334-6154
2-3-5-6

Barbara Holt Associates
Gay Bowers Rd.
Fairfield, CT 06430
203-259-0199
2-3-4-5-6

Albertus Magnus College
Life Career Development
Center
700 Prospect St.
New Haven, CT 06511
203-777-3363
1-2-3-4-5-6

Connecticut

Career Directions for
Women
3113 Yale Station,
301 Crown St.
New Haven, CT 06520
203-436-8242
2-5-6

Career/Life Alternatives
100 Whitney Ave.
New Haven, CT 06510
203-865-7377
1-2-5-6

VOCA: Vocational and Academic Counseling for Adults
115 Berrian Rd.
Stamford, CT 06905
203-329-1955
1-2-6

YWCA of Stamford
Career & Educational
Counseling Center
422 Summer St.
Stamford, CT 06901
203-348-7727
1-2-3-4-5-6

Florida

Face Learning Center
Career/Community
Development
12945 Seminole Blvd.
Bldg. 2, Ste. 8
Largo, FL 33540
813-586-1110 or 585-8155
1-2-3-4-5-6

Georgia

Deeley-Fenton & Associates
1365 Peachtree St.,
N.E., Ste. 110
Atlanta, GA 30309
404-872-1874
2-3-5-6

Illinois

Flexible Careers
37 South Wabash Ave.,
Ste. 703
Chicago, IL 60603
312-236-6028
2-6

Applied Potential
P.O. Box 19
Highland Park, IL 60035
312-432-0620
1-2-3-5-6

Indiana

YWCA
Woman Alive!
229 Ogden St.,
P.O. Box 1121
Hammond, IN 46325
219-933-7168
1-2-5-6

YWCA
Women's Career Center
802 North Lafayette Blvd.
South Bend, IN 46601
219-233-9491
1-2-3-5-6

Kansas

Work Options for Women
1358 North Waco
Wichita, KS 67203
316-264-6604
2-4-5-6

Maryland

Baltimore New Directions
for Women
   Administrative Offices
   2517 North Charles St.
   Baltimore, MD 21218
   301-366-8570

   Career Counseling Center
   2511 North Charles St.
   Baltimore, MD 21218
   301-235-8800
   1-2-4-5-6

Center for Displaced
Homemakers
2435 Maryland Avenue
Baltimore, MD 21218
301-243-5000
1-2-3-5

Statewide Displaced
Homemakers Project
2517 North Charles St.
Baltimore, MD 21218
For Displaced
Homemaker Centers
throughout the state,
call: 301-366-3717 or 8570

Catonsville Center
4 Winters Ln.
Catonsville, MD 21228
301-744-8308
1-2-4-5-6

Frederick New Directions
for Women
23 West 3rd St.
Frederick, MD 21701
301-694-6322
1-2-4-5-6

Middle River Center
1515 Martin Blvd.
Middle River, MD 21220
301-574-7878
1-2-4-5-6

Binder, Elster, Mendelson &
Wheeler
4948 St. Elmo Ave., Ste. 202
Bethesda, MD 20014
301-657-1898 or 652-4983
1-2-5-6

Womanscope
Harriet Tubman Center
8045 Rt. #32
Columbia, MD 21044
301-997-2916
1-2-4-5-6

Massachusetts

Career & Voluntary
Advisory Service
Project Re-Entry
14 Beacon St.
Boston, MA 02108
617-227-1762
1-2-4-5-6

Wider Opportunities for
Women—Boston
413 Commonwealth Ave.
Boston, MA 02215
617-437-1040
1-2-5-6

Women's Educational &
Industrial Union
356 Boylston Street
Boston, MA 02116
617-536-5651
2-4-5-6

The Next Step Career
Guidance Center
P.O. Box 423
Mansfield, MA 02048
617-339-9910
1-2-3-6

Continuum
785 Centre St.
Newton, MA 02158
617-964-3322
1-2-4-5-6

Massachusetts

YWCA
Why Not? Program
1 Salem Sq.
Worcester, MA 01608
617-791-3181
1-2-5-6

Michigan

Women's Resource Center
226 Bostwick, N.E.
Grand Rapids, MI 49503
616-456-8571
1-2-3-4-5-6

A Better Way
4000 Town Center, Ste. 1030
Southfield, MI 48075
313-352-4320
2-4-5-6

Women's Resource Center
for the Grand Traverse Area
918 West Front Street
Traverse City, MI 49684
616-941-1210
2-3-4-5

Minnesota

Chart
123 East Grant St., Ste. 1210
Minneapolis, MN 55403
612-871-9100
1-2-3-4-5-6

Working Opportunities for
Women
2344 Nicollet, Ste. 240
Minneapolis, MN 55404
612-874-6636
1-2-4-6

Working Opportunities for
Women
2233 University Ave.,
Ste. 340
St. Paul, MN 55114
612-647-9961
1-2-4-6

Missouri

Career Management Center
912 East 63rd St.
Kansas City, MO 64110
816-363-1500
1-2-3-5-6

New Hampshire

Nashua Adult Learning
Center
Project PLACE (People
Learning
About Careers & Entry)
27 Burke St.
Nashua, NH 03060
603-882-9080
1-2-5

New Jersey

Reach
Box 33
Convent Station, NJ 07961
201-267-2530
1-2-4-5-6

Jewish Vocational Service
111 Prospect St.
East Orange, NJ 07017
201-674-6330
1-2-4-6

Eileen Wolkstein
87 Cedar St.
Millburn, NJ 07041
201-467-8097
1-2-4-5-6

College Counseling &
Education Center
369 Forest Ave.
Paramus, NJ 07652
201-265-7729
1-2-3-4-5-6

The Professional Roster
171 Broadmead
Princeton, NJ 08540
609-921-9561
1-2-4-5-6

County College of Morris
Women's Programs
Rt. 10 and Center Grove Rd.
Randolph, NJ 07801
201-361-5000
September–June
1-2-5-6

New York

Career Research Institute
455 West 44th St.
New York, NY 10036
212-247-5351
1-2-3-5-6

Council for Career Planning
310 Madison Ave.
New York, NY 10017
212-687-9490
2-4-5-6

Counseling Women
14 East 60th St., Rm. 702
New York, NY 10022
212-486-9755
1-2-3-5-6

Hilda Lee Dail
140 East 56th St., Ste. 10F
New York, NY 10022
212-838-7714
1-2-3-5-6

Federation Employment &
Guidance Service
215 Park Ave. South
New York, NY 10003
212-777-4900
1-2-4-5-6

Rhoda Frindell Green & Co.
392 Central Park West
New York, NY 10025
212-222-3445
Evenings only
1-2-3-6

Barbara Holt Associates
527 Madison Ave.
New York, NY 10022
212-758-2906
2-3-4-5-6

Janice LaRouche Associates
Workshop for Women
333 Central Park West
New York, NY 10025
212-663-0970
2-5-6

More for Women
1435 Lexington Ave.
New York, NY 10028
212-534-0852
1-2-3-5-6

New Options
11 E. 80th St.
New York, NY 10021
212-535-1444
1-2-3-5-6

New School for Social
Research
Human Relations Center
66 West 12th St.
New York, NY 10011
212-741-5684 or 5685 or 5686
1-2-5-6

New York

Personnel Sciences Center
341 Madison Ave.
New York, NY 10017
212-661-1870
1-2-6

Ruth Shapiro Associates
200 East 30th St.
New York, NY 10016
212-889-4284
2-3-4-5-6

Vera Sullivan
114 East 91st St.
New York, NY 10028
212-427-5717
2-5-6

Women's Career Center
121 North Fitzhugh St.
Rochester, NY 14614
716-325-2274
1-2-4-5-6

Academic Advisory Center
for Adults
Turf Ave.
Rye, NY 10580
914-967-1653
1-2-4-5-6

Regional Learning Service of
Central New York
405 Oak St.
Syracuse, NY 13202
315-425-5252
1-2-5-6

YWCA
Vistas for Women
515 North St.
White Plains, NY 10605
914-949-6227
1-2-3-5-6

North Carolina

Fayetteville Family Life
Center
Bordeaux Shopping Center—
Mini Mall
Fayetteville, NC 28304
919-484-0176
1-2-3-5-6

Ohio

Akron Urban League
Labor Education
Advancement Program,
Women's Affairs Program
39 East Market St.
Peoples Federal Bldg.
Akron, OH 44308
216-434-6106

Women's Network
Ste. 502,
Peoples Federal Bldg.
39 East Market St.
Akron, OH 44308
216-376-7852
1-2-3-4-5

Pyramid
1642 Cleveland Ave., NW
Canton, OH 44703
216-453-3767
1-2-4

YWCA
Women's Opportunities
9th and Walnut Sts.
Cincinnati, OH 45202
513-241-7090
2-5-6

Resource: Women, The
Untapped Resource
1258 Euclid Ave., Ste. 204
Cleveland, OH 44115
216-579-1414
2-4-5-6

Options: Adult Career/
Education Services
96 South Grant Ave.,
Rm. 210
Columbus, OH 43215
614-464-2662
1-2-5-6

Cleveland Jewish Vocational
Service
13878 Cedar Rd.
University Heights,
OH 44118
216-321-1381
1-2-4-6

Pennsylvania

Lifeplan
40 East Broad St.
Bethlehem, PA 18018
215-866-8888
2-3-5-6

Community Resource Center
Carson Valley School
1419 Bethlehem Pike
Flourtown, PA 19031
215-233-1960
Tuesday and Wednesday
only
1-2-5

Dauphin County Library
Probe
101 Walnut St.
Harrisburg, PA 17101
717-232-4768
1-2-3-4-5

Creative Alternatives
for Women
431 Old York Rd.
Jenkintown, PA 19046
215-576-5533
2-5-6

CLEO (Compact for
Lifelong Educational
Opportunity)
37 South 16th St.
Philadelphia, PA 19102
215-425-2536
1-2-5

Options for Women
8419 Germantown Ave.
Philadelphia, PA 19118
215-242-4955
1-2-5-6

YM-YWHA
Institute of Awareness
401 South Broad St.
Philadelphia, PA 19147
215-545-4400
5-6

Tennessee

YWCA of Nashville
Career/Life Planning Center
1608 Woodmont Blvd.
Nashville, TN 37215
615-385-3952
2-4-5-6

Texas

VGS Resource Center
2525 San Jacinto
Houston, TX 77002
713-659-1800
1-2-3-4-5-6

Utah

The Phoenix Institute
383 South 600 East
Salt Lake City, UT 84102
801-532-5080
1-2-3-4-5-6

Virginia

Educational Opportunity
Center
Virginia Tidewater
Consortium for Continuing
Higher Education
3830 Virginia Beach Blvd.
Virginia Beach, VA 23452
804-463-4810
1-2-5

Washington

Focus
509 Tenth Ave. East
Seattle, WA 98102
206-329-7918
2-4-5-6

Individual Development
Center
(ID Center)
Career and Life Planning
1020 East John St.
Seattle, WA 98102
206-329-0600
1-2-3-4-5-6

The National Association
for Professional Saleswomen (NAPS)

The rapidly growing National Association for Professional Saleswomen was founded less than two years ago
by Barbara Pletcher to link women in sales across the
country. In the first survey of their members, NAPS
learned that most of the saleswomen questioned earned
between $15,000-$20,000 during their first year in sales,
however 16 percent expect to earn more than $50,000 in
1982. Many more chapters will be established during
1982 to join the thirty-one now in a dozen locations,
listed below. If one is not listed in your area, call NAPS
for current information about new chapters.

ALABAMA
Birmingham

CALIFORNIA
Bakersfield
Fresno
Los Angeles
Modesto
Peninsula
Sacramento
San Francisco
San Jose
Stockton
San Diego

COLORADO
Denver

FLORIDA
Gainesville
Tampa

GEORGIA
Atlanta

ILLINOIS
Chicago

KANSAS
Kansas City

MONTANA
Great Falls

NEW YORK
New York City
Buffalo

OHIO
Columbus
Cincinnati

PENNSYLVANIA
Harrisburg
Lancaster

RHODE ISLAND
(call for location)

TEXAS
Houston
Dallas
San Antonio

WASHINGTON
Seattle

WASHINGTON, D.C.

For more information write to:

NATIONAL ASSOCIATION FOR PROFESSIONAL
SALESWOMEN
2088 Morley Way
Sacramento, California 95825
Phone: Sacramento (916) 484-1234 if you are closer to
California than New York City.

If closer to New York, phone (212) 772-0196. You will
be charged only for a call to New York City although
your call will reach NAPS in California (call forwarding
at the expense of NAPS). In this respect, don't forget
the time difference which can save you money—i.e., at
5:01 P.M. in New York—when phone rates go down—it
is three hours earlier in California.

Also, more NAPS chapters are forming all the time;
therefore if none are listed in your state or city, a chapter may have been started since this listing.

Glossary: The Special Language of Sales

EACH PROFESSION has its own special language. Words and shades of meanings develop, terms that might mean one thing on the outside and another on the inside. The following is not an all-inclusive list, but enough to give you some idea about your new language.

Knowing the various pay-combination possibilities and how to negotiate the best deal for yourself is important. Few things are non-negotiable as long as you're selling something the buyer wants. The same holds true in negotiating with a company to sell their products or services. The more a company wants you, the greater your bargaining power. Therefore, familiarity with the following terms will be helpful:

- **Action plan.** A plan that will help you reach the objectives and goals in your marketing plan. It is generally designed by you and discussed frequently with your management.

• **Bluebird**. The easiest sale you'll ever make—one, in fact, that has been so effortless it seems to fly out of nowhere and into your welcome order book.

• **Calls per week**. Calls you should be able to make in a given period of time. Varies tremendously from several calls per day to one or two calls a week depending upon what you sell.

• **Call reports**. Information you write up about each call you make. Although all salespeople complain about making up call reports, this is invaluable information. Without it, salespeople would mix and match names and information, producing mass confusion rather than sales. Nobody has an accurate enough memory to avoid this task.

• **Co-call**. A joint call. If your sales manager or another experienced salesperson accompanies you on a call, it is called co-calling. This is an effective way to hone your sales skills, since you have an experienced salesperson with you to help analyze the call with you later.

• **COMMISSION/SALARY ARRANGEMENTS**

• **Base salary**. A guaranteed amount of money that you will be paid, regardless of how much or how little you sell.

• **Draw against future sales**. The guarantee of a certain salary, which will be deducted from future earnings. Allows a salesperson time to develop a territory. Later, when sales increase, the amount is slowly deducted from higher earnings until the draw is repaid.

• **Partial commission**. A smaller salary than a straight salary and a smaller commission than a straight commission. Varies from as much as 5 percent salary and a 95 percent commission to the reverse. Generally, somewhere in between. A small base salary can save your sanity by providing a worry-free financial floor. For example, many saleswomen prefer a 15 to 20 percent salary and an 80 to 85 percent commission. The salary provides enough money coming in each month to pay the rent or mortgage and a few other bills while building motivation to earn high commissions.

- **Straight salary.** There are sales jobs in which you receive a salary just as in any other regular job. However, many commissioned salespeople don't include this type of job in their definition of a "real" sales job.

The better the salesperson, the worse this deal is, although it may seem risk-free. There is risk, however. Unless you sell in any sales job, your management won't keep you around just for the privilege of paying you a salary. With a straight salary, no matter how much you sell, you'll have to wait for management to raise your pay. Management, being management, may wait longer than you like.

- **Total commission.** Self-explanatory. You can make a million dollars or nothing. It takes a confident soul to survive the ups and downs of a straight commission job; however, those who succeed on straight commission keep more of their earnings than in any other arrangement.

Many salespeople who sell big-ticket items, the kind where one sale might be $500,000, get a percentage of the sale, perhaps 1 percent or a fraction of 1 percent. There are many ways to cut total commissions, but no matter how it's cut, those who sell the most earn the most.

- **Expense budget.** A salesperson is usually assigned a certain amount of money for expenses on a yearly or quarterly basis and given some margin of freedom as to how the money is spent, although documentation is required. The budget is generally adequate but seldom lavish.
- **Forecasting.** A look ahead. An educated guess into the future. Your anticipation of your volume of sales for a projected period of time and where you think the sales will come from. Your manager might ask where you think you will be four months down the road, what you expect your sales to be by that time.
- **Lead.** Information leading to a prospective customer.
- **Lead system.** The system devised by your company to get information to you about prospective customers.

For example, many people interested in buying products or services phone the company, or mail in responses to advertising, indicating an interest in its products or services. Almost all companies have a system whereby such inquiries are relayed to the salesperson in the territory.

• **Marketing plan.** A plan of action a salesperson (sometimes the sales manager does this) is expected to draw up for selling in his or her territory. Usually set up on a yearly basis.

• **Order taker.** What no good salesperson wants to become. A person with no selling skills; an order taker, not a salesperson.

• **Prospect.** A prospective customer who is not yet a client.

• **PROSPECTING.** Finding new business. How well you and your company "prospect" is critical to both you and your company's success. There are dozens of ways to prospect. It's an area where a creative person can really stand out. Here are some of the ways salespeople locate new business:

   • **Advertising/public relations.** When companies advertise or promote their products and services in any way, it results in inquiries from potential customers. Most companies set up systems to get these leads to their salespeople, e.g., a card system or direct referral system.
   • **Cold calling.** Calls you make out of the clear blue, either by phone or in person, in hopes that it will lead to a sale. Most beginning salespeople are terrified of cold calling. Experienced salespeople, while they will do it, prefer other, more productive ways of developing business.
   • **Contact lists.** Lists of people within companies who are the appropriate ones to contact for appointments. For example, in some companies your list might include the vice-president of marketing or operations; in others, a particular purchasing manager; in smaller companies, perhaps the president. Identifying the appropriate person or persons to sell to saves time and also keeps you from looking like an amateur. A good salesperson makes

it his or her business not to waste time trying to sell to the wrong people.

- **Lead letters.** Instead of phoning prospective customers, many salespeople send out a mailing, explaining in the letter that they will follow up on the letter with a personal phone call.
- **Referrals.** Contacting anybody who might know of a prospective client. Salespeople often get the best referrals from customers who are enthusiastic about services or products.
- **Telephoning.** Just what it says. For example, with no idea of where the calls might lead, you might pick out twenty company names from the phone book and telephone them, hoping to connect with somebody who might be interested in whatever you are selling. If you make one sale in twenty this way, it is considered well worth your while.

- **Qualifying a client.** Sizing up a potential client's intentions. A salesperson can't afford to waste time on a call that should have been "qualified" as not worth the effort. Qualifying potential clients becomes even more important as selling costs, such as travel, rise. One consultant recently estimated the cost of a single industrial sales call at $140.

There are tactful ways of qualifying a client without turning off a prospective sale, deftly learning about a client's needs, interests, budge authority, etc. An efficient qualifier sets the stage for success. An inefficient one can produce a lasting disaster.

- **Quarterly reports.** Progress information. How well you are doing by each quarter as measured against your quota and what you had forecast for that quarter.
- **Quota.** The amount, generally a dollar volume for a year, set by the company, that you are expected to sell. For example, it is possible to sell more than 100 percent of quota. It doesn't mean you stop selling when you reach your quota. Far from it. For example, many women interviewed for this book are selling at 110 to 150 percent of their quotas. When you do this, you can expect your quota to go up the following year since

management isn't stupid and will adjust expectations to fit performance. However, earnings generally go up as well.

Your quota could also be in terms of units sold, i.e., 1,000 television sets; 2,000 units of yarn, etc.

• **Selling cycle.** The average period of time it takes to complete a sale from the first contact to the final sale. Some products are sold in a single call. Others take multiple calls over a period of months. In a few industries an average sales cycle might be one to two years.

• **SIC codes.** Government classifications for various industries, broken down into categories. For example, there are SIC codes for manufacturing companies, management training companies, automotive companies, etc. Vertical territories are often identified from SIC codes.

• **TERRITORIES**

• **Geographic territory.** Your assigned sales area. It can be as small as one city building or as large as the country.

• **Name accounts.** A list of specific companies and their divisions or subsidiaries which, regardless of their location, make up your territory.

• **Vertical territory.** Territory where you are assigned to call on companies in the same industry. For example, your vertical territory might be exclusively insurance companies or aero-space companies etc.

• **Tire kicker.** The kind of prospect a qualifier is trying to identify and avoid: a person who's just looking around and will listen as long as you'll talk but has no intention of buying. Undoubtedly coined by an automobile salesperson somewhere between Henry Ford and today.

• **Upside.** A sales forecast for a projected period of time that takes into consideration the best possible circumstances. You may forecast $25,000 in sales for next month, but with luck, $5,000 more may come in. The $5,000 is your upside.

In different sections of the country, there may be variations of meanings for these special words and phrases. There will undoubtedly be many others for you to add to your vocabulary that will have special meaning in certain locations and in different companies.

When you choose sales as your career, may you never become an order taker and may your bleakest days be brightened with bluebirds.

Bibliography

Bender, Marilyn. "The Changing Rules of Office Romances." *Esquire*, April 24, 1979.

Burek, Charles G. "A Group Profile of the Fortune 500 Chief Executives." *Fortune*, May 1970.

Chastain, Sherry. *Winning The Salary Game*. New York: John Wiley & Sons, 1980.

Donahue, Phil. *Donahue: My Own Story*. New York: Simon & Schuster, 1979.

Dowling, Colette. *The Cinderella Complex*. New York: Summit Books, 1980.

Dullea, Georgia. "Vast Changes in Society Traced to the Rise of Working Women." *The New York Times*, November 29, 1977.

Flanagan, William. "High Salaries Now Open to Women in Top Management Posts." *Vogue*, August 1979.

Fowler, Elizabeth M. "Women's Expanding Sales Roles." *The New York Times*, May 21, 1980.

Friedman, Milton. *Capitalism & Freedom*. Chicago: The University of Chicago Press, 1972.

Friedman, Milton and Rose. *Free to Choose*. New York: Harcourt Brace Jovanovich, 1980.

Gilder, George. *Wealth and Poverty*. New York: Basic Books, 1981.

Goodman, Ellen. Excerpts from presentation at the annual meeting of the Association of National Advertisers. Scottsdale, Arizona, November 25-29, 1978.

Gupta, Udayan. "A New Breed of Sales Reps." *Venture*, March 1981.

"Hotels Are Making Changes for the Female Business Traveler." *The New York Times*, January 12, 1980.

Howard, Niles. "Sales Jobs Open Up for Women." *Dun's Review*, March 1978.

"The Industrial Salesman Becomes a Salesperson." *Business Week*, February 19, 1979.

Janeway, Elliot. "Reviewing the Economy." *Working Woman*, July 1980.

Jerdee, Thomas and Rosen, Benson. "Sex Stereotyping in the Executive Suite." *The Harvard Business Review*, March-April 1974.

Jobin, Judith. "Big-Money Jobs for Women." *Women's Day*, February 2, 1981.

Johnston, John D., Jr., and Knapp, Charles L. (professors at law at New York University). "Sex Discrimination by Law: A Study in Judicial Perspective." *New York University Law Review* 46: 675.

Kanter, Rosabeth and Stein, Barry A. "Birth of a Saleswoman." *Across the Board*, June 1979.

Kinkead, Gwen. "On a Fast Track to the Good Life." *Fortune*, April 7, 1980.

Ladd, Everett Carll. "Work Ethic." *Public Opinion Magazine*, Aug.-Sept. 1981.

Lerner, Gerda. *The Female Experience: An American Documentary*. New York: Bobbs Merrill Educational Publishing, 1977.

Linden, Fabian. "Women Who Work." *The Conference Board*, November 1972.

Lowy, Joan. "Male Jobs Looked to by Women." *The Washington Post*, October 5, 1980.

Malabre, Alfred L., Jr. "The Future Revisited." *The Wall Street Journal*, March 15, 1975.

The National Academy of Sciences, Committee on Occupational Classification and Analysis of Behavorial and

Social Sciences of the Research Council. *Women, Work and Wages: Equal Pay for Jobs of Equal Value*. Edited by Donald J. Treiman and Heidi I. Hartmann. Washington, D.C.: National Academy Press, 1981.

"The New Corporate Wife Goes to Work." *Business Week*, April 9, 1979.

"No. 1's Awesome Strategy: How IBM Will Get Bigger and Stronger in the 1980's." *Business Week* (cover story), June 8, 1981.

Overton, Elizabeth. "What Makes an Executive Woman?" *Working Woman*, January 1980.

Pifer, Alan. "Women Working: Toward a New Society." Annual Report, Carnegie Corporation of New York, 1976.

Pletcher, Barbara A. *Saleswoman: A Guide To Career Success*. New York: Dow Jones-Irwin, 1978.

Reinhold, Robert. "The Trend Toward Sexual Equality: Depth of Transformation Uncertain." *The New York Times*, November 30, 1977.

Rockman, Jane. "Door-to-Door Dollars." *Working Woman*, July 1980.

Salamon, Julie. "Few Women Get Top Business Jobs Despite Progress of Past Decade." *The Wall Street Journal*, July 25, 1980.

Serrin, William, et al. "Careers: The Reagan Effect." *The New York Times*, October 11, 1981.

Seuling, Barbara. *You Can't Eat Peanuts in Church and Other Little-Known Laws*. New York: Doubleday & Company, 1976.

"Sexual Tension." *The Wall Street Journal*, April 14, 1981.

Sheils, Merrill, et al. "Women and the Executive Suite." *Newsweek*, September 14, 1981.

Shorter, Edward. *The Making of the Modern Family*. New York: Basic Books, 1975.

Sochen, June. *Movers and Shakers*. New York: Quadrangle/ The New York Times Book Co., 1973.

Thurow, Lester C. *The Zero-Sum Society*. New York: Penguin Books, 1981.

Toffler, Alvin. *The Third Wave*. New York: William Morrow, 1980.

United Commission on Civil Rights. "Statement on the Equal Rights Amendment." December 1978.

"What Next for U.S. Women." *Time*, December 5, 1977.

"Why Have So Few Women Made It to the Top?" *Business Week*, June 5, 1978.

"Women at Work." *The Wall Street Journal*, 8-part series, August 28–September 19, 1978.

"Women Rise as Entrepreneurs." *Business Week*, February 25, 1980.

About the Author

GONNIE McCLUNG SIEGEL is the author of
How to Advertise and Promote Your Small Business and the co-author of *Woman's Work Book*
and *How to Beat the High Cost of Learning*. She
lives in Bedford, New York.

Index

WOMEN'S
BUSINESS BOOKS